ETHICS IN
PUBLIC RELATIONS
RESPONSIBLE ADVOCACY

ETHICS IN
PUBLIC RELATIONS
RESPONSIBLE ADVOCACY

Editors

Kathy Fitzpatrick ▪ Carolyn Bronstein

SAGE Publications
Thousand Oaks ▪ London ▪ New Delhi

For information:

Sage Publications, Inc.
2455 Teller Road
Thousand Oaks, California 91320
E-mail: order@sagepub.com

Sage Publications Ltd.
1 Oliver's Yard
55 City Road
London EC1Y 1SP
United Kingdom

Sage Publications India Pvt. Ltd.
B-42, Panchsheel Enclave
Post Box 4109
New Delhi 110 017 India

Printed in the United States of America.

Library of Congress Cataloging-in-Publication Data

Ethics in public relations : responsible advocacy / edited by Kathy Fitzpatrick and Carolyn Bronstein.
    p. cm.
Includes bibliographical references and index.
ISBN 1-4129-1797-2 (cloth)—ISBN 1-4129-1798-0 (pbk.)
   1. Public relations—Moral and ethical aspects. I. Fitzpatrick, Kathy.
II. Bronstein, Carolyn.
HM1221.E89 2006
174′.96592—dc22

                        2005033909

This book is printed on acid-free paper.

06 07 08 09 10 10 9 8 7 6 5 4 3 2 1

Acquiring Editors:	Margaret H. Seawell and Todd R. Armstrong
Editorial Assistant:	Sarah K. Quesenberry
Project Editors:	Lynnette Pennings and Astrid Virding
Typesetter:	C&M Digitals (P) Ltd.
Indexer:	Will Ragsdale
Cover Designer:	Edgar Abarca

Contents

Acknowledgments   vii

Introduction: Toward a Definitional Framework
         for Responsible Advocacy   ix
Kathy Fitzpatrick and Carolyn Bronstein

Chapter 1. Baselines for Ethical Advocacy in the "Marketplace
         of Ideas"   1
Kathy Fitzpatrick

Chapter 2. Responsibility and Accountability   19
Thomas H. Bivins

Chapter 3. The Ethics of Communicating With and About
         Difference in a Changing Society   39
Larissa A. Grunig and Elizabeth L. Toth

Chapter 4. Negotiating Relationships With Activist Publics   53
Linda Hon

Chapter 5. Responsible Advocacy for Nonprofit Organizations   71
Carolyn Bronstein

Chapter 6. Truth and Transparency   89
Karla K. Gower

Chapter 7. Responsible Online Communication   107
Kirk Hallahan

Chapter 8. Responsible Advocacy Through Strategic Risk
         Communication   131
Michael J. Palenchar and Robert L. Heath

Chapter 9. The Ethics of Public Diplomacy   155
Philip Seib

Chapter 10. Advocacy Across Borders   171
        Donald K. Wright

Chapter Notes   191

Index   227

About the Contributors   237

Acknowledgments

W e would like to thank our colleagues in the academy and the profession who have contributed to this work. The chapter authors provided thoughtful essays that make this collection a significant addition to the public relations literature. We thank them for their respective contributions and for their willingness to tackle complex issues that break new ground. The following reviewers provided helpful feedback that improved the manuscript: Jian Wang, Purdue University; Ken Day, University of the Pacific; Carol Ann Hackley, University of the Pacific; Mike Ryan, University of Houston; and Lois Boynton, University of North Carolina – Chapel Hill. We are grateful for their insights and content suggestions. We also want to thank our editors, Margaret Seawell and Todd Armstrong, for shepherding this project through the publication process and making this work available to scholars, students, and professionals.

—Kathy Fitzpatrick and Carolyn Bronstein
Chicago, Illinois

Introduction: Toward a Definitional Framework for Responsible Advocacy

Kathy Fitzpatrick and Carolyn Bronstein

As advocates and counselors, public relations professionals serve diverse special interests of businesses, nonprofits, and governments. As professionals, they also are bound to serve the public interest. These dual obligations, which sometimes require careful balancing of competing interests, have sparked considerable debate among scholars and practitioners over the core function and fundamental values of public relations. Indeed, the profession's inability to define its purpose has been described as "one of the most perplexing and persistent dilemmas of public relations."[1]

Although some have shied away from the term *advocate* in referring to the work of public relations professionals—preferring *consensus builder* as a better descriptor of the role of public relations in contemporary society[2]— the majority of practitioners seem to have embraced advocacy as a primary function.[3] Yet, even those who view advocacy as a key aspect of public relations have different opinions as to what advocacy means and whose interests should be represented. For example, the public relations scholar Glen Cameron has suggested that although practitioners typically advocate a position or course of action for clients and employers, "advocacy may be directed toward management as well as toward other publics."[4]

In 2000, the leading professional association in public relations responded to the controversy over public relations' advocacy role. In its new code of ethics, the Public Relations Society of America (PRSA) acknowledged *advocacy* for the first time as one of the core values of public relations. According to the code, public relations professionals best serve the public interest by serving the special interests of the clients and employers whom they represent. The code states that public relations provides organizations with "a voice in the marketplace of ideas, facts, and viewpoints to aid informed public debate."

At the same time, the authors of the PRSA code recognized a need to address the potential impact of such voices on internal and external publics.[5] The special ethical obligation of public relations professionals to balance a primary loyalty to clients and employers with a concomitant duty to multiple stakeholders was acknowledged in a code requirement that public relations professionals be "*responsible* advocates for those we represent [emphasis added]." The code did not, however, define the theoretic or practical aspects of "responsible advocacy."

Ethics in Public Relations: Responsible Advocacy lays the foundation for a new dialogue about the ethical dimensions of public relations' advocacy role. This collection of essays provides the views of leading scholars of public relations on the meaning of responsible advocacy and implications for public relations theory and practice.

The authors' fresh perspectives demonstrate the need for ethical standards to evolve as quickly as public relations practice requirements in the dynamic global environment. The work shows, for example, that efforts to build ethical and effective relationships with multiple stakeholders has become more complicated in a world of increasingly diverse and more active publics who are empowered by and connected through the Internet. Ethical standards that were designed to address public relations practices dealing with "old media," such as newspapers and television, are not sufficiently developed for more sophisticated "new media" and the increasingly important world of online communication. Organizations face intensified communication opportunities and challenges, spurring the need for public relations professionals trained to navigate complex ethical questions.

The specific topics addressed were chosen to illustrate the range and depth of theoretic and practical concerns related to responsible advocacy. Readers will encounter concepts and domains familiar to the public relations literature, such as "marketplace of ideas" and relationship management, as well as growing practice areas that require heightened ethical scrutiny. For example, in a post-9/11 world characterized by terror, both the practical and moral dimensions of risk communication must be explicated. Likewise, the desire to promote global understanding of American foreign policy through ethical public diplomacy has become a pressing political matter, raising questions about the requirements for responsible public relations advocacy on behalf of governments.

Although no one collection of essays can adequately define a term as broad as responsible advocacy, the interconnected themes that emerge from this work go a long way toward establishing a definitional framework.

Ethical guideposts for responsible advocacy in public relations in the twenty-first century will include individual accountability, informed decision making, multicultural understanding, relationship building, open communication, dialogue, truth and transparency, and integrity.

In addition to laying the groundwork for the theoretic aspects of responsible advocacy, the book also illustrates the direct link between *ethical* public relations and *effective* public relations. In other words, the work provides considerable support for the axiom that "good ethics is good business." Responsible advocacy based on open and honest communication helps businesses, governments, and nonprofits alike meet the ethical expectations of strategic constituents and build the relationships needed to accomplish organizational goals. In this respect, responsible advocacy in public relations might be viewed as *strategic* advocacy designed to align the special interests of organizations with the special interests of stakeholders.

At the same time, the collective work suggests that a self-interested approach to responsible advocacy in public relations falls short of the professional mandate to serve the public interest. As advocates in the marketplace of ideas, public relations professionals should strive to further the ideals of democratic institutions. Whether in business or government or nonprofit practice, the common good is served only when the "voices" of special interests present their views in ways that advance informed decision making and contribute to the well-being of the greater society.

Ethics in Public Relations: Responsible Advocacy was written for public relations scholars, students, professionals, and others interested in the practice of public relations and issues related to professional advocacy. This collection provides a starting point for future discussions of responsible advocacy and illuminates the importance of ethical performance in the twenty-first century. The book emphasizes the affirmative aspects of responsible advocacy in public relations, but also alerts readers to the implications of unethical practices. The very nature of a call for responsible advocacy suggests that its converse—*ir*responsible advocacy—is also at work. The need for self-regulation in public relations, guided by the kind of introspective and analytic work featured in this collection, has never been greater. When public relations professionals fall short of the ideals of responsible advocacy, they threaten practitioner autonomy and may pave the way for heightened legal regulation of public relations work.

Overview of Chapters

In chapter 1, Kathy Fitzpatrick addresses responsible advocacy in public relations from a legal perspective. She analyzes core concepts of the "marketplace of ideas" as defined in free speech jurisprudence and proposes four legal principles—access, process, truth, and disclosure—that could serve as baselines for responsible advocacy in public relations. The chapter explores the convergence of legal and ethical standards in public relations and the importance of responsible advocacy in sustaining First Amendment protection for public relations expression.

Chapter 2 examines the concepts of *responsibility* and *accountability* from a moral perspective. Thomas Bivins distinguishes functional and moral responsibility, examining such variables as role and function, degree of autonomy, organizational structure, client-professional obligations, and ethical frameworks—all of which affect the ways in which concepts of accountability are interpreted. He also explores "moral buck passing," illustrating the differences between legitimate excuses that mitigate accountability and justifications that do not pass ethical muster. The author makes the case that responsible advocacy will require public relations professionals to be *individually* accountable for their decisions and actions.

The need to communicate ethically with diverse publics is a historical challenge with present-day relevance. In an age of globalization, public relations professionals face the challenge of building relationships and communicating with internal and external audiences who are increasingly different from themselves. In chapter 3, Larissa Grunig and Elizabeth Toth examine the need for collaborative advocacy when communicating with difference and explore the ethical issues that emerge when a White female majority of practitioners communicate with increasingly diverse global publics. The authors discuss feminist and organizational values, the relationship between diversity and effectiveness, and philosophical approaches to diversity and public relations. The authors question organizational values that would oppress either female practitioners or publics and recommend a deontological, principles-based approach as the best means of achieving responsible advocacy. This chapter explains how valuing diversity internally contributes to organizational effectiveness in communicating ethically with diverse publics.

In chapter 4, Linda Hon considers how relationships between organizations and activist groups can be managed ethically. The chapter offers a theoretical framework to explain why responsible advocacy with activist groups is important and discusses communication strategies that allow organizations to negotiate conflict, build quality relationships, and achieve mutually beneficial goals. Hon proposes proactive relationship maintenance strategies based on open communication and empowerment of key publics as a key mechanism in the practice of responsible advocacy.

Carolyn Bronstein analyzes the ethical challenges faced by public relations professionals working for nonprofit organizations. In chapter 5, she takes the position that the advent of electronic communication and the economic decline of American journalism have created significant opportunities and challenges for practitioners who wish to operate as responsible advocates in the nonprofit sphere. These professionals are enjoying greater influence with the news media than ever before, but responsible advocacy imposes certain constraints; practitioners must avoid the temptation to use unethical tactics to garner publicity for issues or causes. Bronstein notes a lack of public role models for responsible advocacy among mission-driven organizations, and discusses cases in which both government and nonprofit groups used unethical tactics to accomplish their goals. This chapter points out how such missteps might be avoided with public relations programs based on relationship management, resource sharing, and dialogic communication.

Chapter 6 examines ethical issues that must be addressed when responding to legal and other crises. Karla Gower considers the negative impacts of corporate scandals—such as Enron, WorldCom, and Tyco–on business, including diminished public trust in corporate leaders, and increased regulatory constraints. She explores the need for public relations professionals to serve as true advocates for the companies they serve, providing objective counsel during periods of crisis and advising clients and employers to practice full disclosure so that stakeholders can make truly informed decisions. Gower maintains that communication policies built on the principles of truth and transparency are at the heart of responsible advocacy. This type of public relations practice can help institutions regain—and sustain—the confidence of important constituents.

In chapter 7, Kirk Hallahan addresses questions of ethics related to online communication. The chapter reviews the limited efforts that have been made to establish ethical guidelines for public relations practitioners operating in cyberspace and explores initiatives to define best practices outside the field. Hallahan identifies eight core ethical concerns for public relations practitioners that must be considered as part of responsible advocacy: access and choice, accuracy of content, deceptive practices, dependability, interactivity and involvement, personalization and customization, privacy and security, and usefulness and usability.

In chapter 8, Michael Palenchar and Robert Heath offer a rhetorical rationale for responsible advocacy in risk communication and propose guidelines for ethical risk communication practices. They emphasize the need to address the people's "right to know" and to involve key publics in risk assessment and decision-making processing. This chapter contends that risk communication professionals should serve as "internal voices for external interests," helping organizations interpret publics' perceptions of risk and fostering trust through open communication and dialogue.

Chapter 9 explores another area of public relations practice that has become increasingly significant in the wake of the terrorist attacks of September 11, 2001: public diplomacy. In this chapter, Philip Seib examines the ethical dimensions of U.S. public diplomacy, or the governmental public relations function responsible for establishing supportive relationships with the people of other countries. Seib addresses the need for advocates of a government's special interests to establish their client as a credible source of news and information in their efforts to win the trust of citizens of other nations. The chapter explores the distinctions between propaganda and public diplomacy and considers how far public diplomacy can stray from objectivity before it becomes dishonest. Seib contends that if practitioners of public diplomacy are to be responsible advocates, they must regard themselves as the collective conscience of the foreign policy process.

As national borders become more porous, the need to define ethical standards for worldwide practice becomes more urgent. Chapter 10 considers public relations ethics from an international perspective. Donald Wright emphasizes the importance of cultural considerations in global ethics and addresses the ethical responsibilities of individual practitioners. He examines international public relations standards and guidelines, noting the shortcomings of codes of ethics, and argues that more scholarly attention to international concerns is needed to aid public relations professionals in serving as responsible advocates in the global arena.

1

Baselines for Ethical Advocacy in the "Marketplace of Ideas"

Kathy Fitzpatrick

"[Public relations professionals] serve the public interest by serving as responsible advocates for those we represent."

"We provide a voice in the marketplace of ideas, facts, and viewpoints to aid informed public debate."

"Protecting and advancing the free flow of accurate and truthful information is essential to serving the public interest and contributing to informed decision making in a democratic society."

Public Relations Society of America Member Code of Ethics 2000

These core concepts of advocacy in the Public Relations Society of America's (PRSA) Code of Ethics reflect democratic ideals grounded in First Amendment legal theory. The "marketplace of ideas" concept was introduced in law by U.S. Supreme Court Justice Oliver Wendell Holmes in his dissent to a 1918 case in which the U.S. Supreme Court ruled that a prohibition on criticism of American symbols and ideals did not violate the free speech provision of the First Amendment. Holmes's argument that the "ultimate good" was better reached by "the free trade in ideas" resonated and, for almost a century, has been the dominant philosophy of freedom of expression law in the United States.[1] The concepts of "protecting and advancing the free flow of accurate and truthful information," and "informed decision making" have long, too, been recognized as democratic principles important in both lawmaking and judicial decision making in the United States.

It may seem odd that legal principles form the basis of the PRSA code since most people believe the law falls short of providing acceptable principles on which to base ethical conduct. Indeed, ethics scholars and educators (including the author of this chapter), as well as professional ethics advisors, routinely counsel students, organizational leaders, and others to look beyond laws and regulations for aids to ethical decision making.[2] Law is about what people *must* do, while ethics is about what people *should* do, they advise. Ethics begins where the law ends. Law is about compliance with set rules and procedures, while ethics involves more discretionary decision making. Legal violations can send perpetrators to the jailhouse and/or the poorhouse, while ethical violations typically result in slapped hands and (sometimes) feelings of remorse. For these and other reasons, law is not an appropriate guide for determining parameters of ethical behavior.

Such advice is technically valid. Yet, there is a fine line between law and ethics. Societal norms inform the laws and regulations by which democratic societies function. Certainly, moral principles are inherent in American jurisprudence. And, as the PRSA code illustrates, the reverse is also true: legal principles inform ethics. In many respects, legal standards define minimal expectations for ethical performance. As Don Welch observed in *Law and Morality,* "legal obligations are essentially subsets of moral questions . . . the nature of law makes a perceived legal obligation a very powerful ingredient in the mix that we consider as we decide upon a responsible course of action."[3]

Thus, there is much to be gained by exploring the application of legal principles to questions of ethics. In examining the legal concept of responsibility, for example, Peter Cane pointed out,

> Because law is underwritten by the coercive power of the state, courts cannot leave disputes about responsibility (for instance) unresolved. . . . Morality can afford to be vague and indeterminate to an extent that law cannot. It is for this reason that law can make a contribution to thinking and judgement about responsibility outside the law as well as within it.[4]

By studying the symbiotic relationship between law and ethics, Cane argued, "we may appeal to the law as providing a pointer to sound thinking in the moral sphere."[5]

Just as the law provides a mechanism for resolving complex questions concerning rights and freedoms in courts, it provides a model for managing the careful balancing of competing values and interests required in the practice of public relations. This chapter examines the core concepts of the "marketplace of ideas" in an effort to identify legal principles that might be useful in both better understanding and defining the parameters of ethical advocacy in public relations. Following a brief introduction to marketplace theory, the chapter reviews how marketplace concepts are applied in the legal regulation of political and commercial advocacy in the United States. The work identifies four marketplace principles that have shaped First Amendment jurisprudence and that have particular application for the ethical practice of public relations: access, process, truth, and disclosure. The chapter concludes with a look at the convergence of legal and ethical standards for regulating communication and the importance of responsible advocacy in sustaining First Amendment protection for public relations expression.

In addition to increasing understanding of the philosophical underpinnings of political and commercial speech regulation in the United States, this discussion of marketplace theory also provides insight into the primary concept relied on by public relations scholars and professionals to justify public relations' social role. As public relations scholar Scott Cutlip stated,

> The social justification for public relations in a free society is to ethically and effectively plead the cause of a client or organization in the free-wheeling forum of public debate. It is a basic democratic right that every idea, individual, and institution shall have a full and fair hearing in the public forum—and that their merit ultimately must be determined by their ability to be accepted in the marketplace.[6]

Rhetorical scholar Robert Heath made a similar argument, noting that public relations is essential to the free exchange of, and fair competition among, ideas in society.[7]

If, as the PRSA Code of Ethics suggests, the "marketplace of ideas" is to also provide the philosophical foundation for the development of professional ethics standards in public relations, then an examination of how marketplace theory is applied in law should be instructive in establishing ethical baselines for public relations advocacy.

The Marketplace of Ideas and the First Amendment

The concept of a marketplace of ideas in democratic societies governed by the people reflects a deep and sustained belief that self-government is made possible by properly informed citizens who engage in informed decision making. The public interest is best served when the voices of diverse special interests are heard. Marketplace theory rests on the premise that "truth" will emerge from robust public debate and be determined by the people who evaluate competing ideas and messages. The works of English poet John Milton, who introduced the marketplace concept in *Areopagitica* in 1644, and British philosopher John Stuart Mill, who two centuries later wrote the influential essay *On Liberty,* provided the framework for the familiar words later institutionalized in American jurisprudence by Justice Holmes: "the best test of truth is the power of the thought to get itself accepted in the competition of the market."[8]

Marketplace theory is predicated, first, on the existence of an objective "truth" that will emerge from a cacophony of voices promoting various interests; second, on a marketplace in which all citizens have the right—and perhaps the means—to be both heard and informed; and, third, on the rational ability of people to discern "truth." Notwithstanding considerable debate regarding the logic of such assumptions,[9] marketplace theory has endured as the most "deeply entrenched [metaphor] in the language of First Amendment jurisprudence" and the philosophical model for resolving free speech cases.[10] In fact, one recent study that evaluated the use of the marketplace metaphor in U.S. Supreme Court decisions found that its use rose dramatically in the 1970s and "continues to increase."[11]

Regulating Political Advocacy

In resolving First Amendment cases in which government restrictions on speech are challenged, the Supreme Court has consistently ruled that although the protection for free speech is not absolute, ideological, or *political,* speech that makes a "direct contribution to the interchange of ideas"[12] . . . "occupies the 'highest rung of the hierarchy of First Amendment values,' and is entitled to special protection."[13] The fundamental purpose of the First Amendment, according to the Court, is "to preserve an uninhibited marketplace of ideas in which truth will ultimately prevail."[14]

Toward this end, in addition to safeguarding the people's right to speak, the Supreme Court has also recognized the people's right to hear by emphasizing the listener's right to receive information that is indispensable to decision making in a democracy. In 1965, Justice William Brennan observed,

"The dissemination of ideas can accomplish nothing if otherwise willing addressees are not free to receive and consider them. It would be a barren marketplace of ideas that had only sellers and no buyers."[15] The Court later said that because the "people in our democracy are entrusted with the responsibility for judging and evaluating the relative merits of conflicting arguments," they are entitled to receive information needed to "evaluate the arguments to which they are being subjected."[16]

In so ruling, the Court has recognized that both individuals and organizations enjoy First Amendment protection to participate in public discussion and debate on matters of public interest and concern. Thus, corporate political speech is not subjected to greater regulation simply because of the commercial nature of the enterprise. In a 1978 case in which the government argued that those with more resources could be restrained in order to enhance the political voice of those with fewer resources, the Court said,

> The concept that government may restrict the speech of some elements of our society in order to enhance the relative voice of others is wholly foreign to the First Amendment which was designed to secure the widest possible dissemination of information from diverse and antagonistic sources and to assure unfettered exchange of ideas for the bringing about of political and societal changes desired by the people.[17]

As Justice Powell observed, First Amendment protection is determined by "the inherent worth of the speech in terms of its capacity for informing the public."[18]

At the same time, the Court has recognized the need to protect the sanctity of the marketplace in situations where speech "threatened imminently to undermine democratic processes."[19] Thus, the Court has allowed certain speech restrictions intended to safeguard the efficient functioning of government. While laws restricting particular viewpoints are presumptively unconstitutional, narrowly drawn regulations designed to prevent undue influences in the marketplace and/or unfair advantage to certain speakers have been upheld. The most significant exceptions have occurred in cases involving corporate speech related to election campaigns and financial matters, where the Court has recognized a need to ensure just elections and protect fair investment markets. For example, in a case involving corporate participation in political activities, the Court found that corporations should not be allowed to gain an unfair advantage in the political marketplace because of their ability to amass substantial wealth in the economic marketplace.[20]

In determining the constitutionality of a particular regulation on individual or corporate speech, the Supreme Court applies a balancing approach, weighing the right to free speech against a government's interest in protecting other important rights or in preventing particular harms. The process recognizes both the inherent worth of avoiding the "chilling" of speech created by burdensome regulation and the need to protect the sanctity of the marketplace. In order for a restriction to be upheld, the government must demonstrate a compelling interest that is directly advanced by the regulation. For example, such an interest might be the need to prevent corruption, or the appearance of corruption, in political processes.[21]

The perceived value of free speech in a democratic society is reflected in the Supreme Court's recognition that even *false* political speech "must be protected if the freedoms of expression are to have the 'breathing space' needed to survive."[22] Although the Court has found that "false statements of fact are particularly valueless" because "they interfere with the truth-seeking function of the marketplace of ideas,"[23] the Court has consistently emphasized the need for some tolerance of falsehoods to prevent the chilling effect of strict liability for false statements. Because "some erroneous statement is inevitable in free debate,"[24] abuses of speech freedoms are dealt with after the fact, for example, in suits based on claims of defamation or other violations of private rights.[25]

In addressing potential harms caused by certain types of speech, the Court has demonstrated a clear preference for disclosure requirements over prior restraints on the core content of communication. For example, in a case in which the Court struck down a prohibition on promotional advertising by electric utilities, Justice Powell wrote in the majority opinion: "If the marketplace of ideas is to remain free and open, governments must not be allowed to choose 'which issues are worth discussing or debating.'"[26]

Disclosure requirements are less burdensome means for addressing potentially deceptive communication practices, according to the Court, because they "do not prevent anyone from speaking."[27]

This brief review of the regulation of political advocacy in the United States demonstrates that public relations professionals have substantial freedom to communicate on behalf of clients and employers in the political marketplace. The Court has provided both the access required and the "breathing space" needed for organizations—and their public relations representatives—to fully participate in the marketplace of ideas. Indeed, one recent study of U.S. Supreme Court cases in which the term "public relations" or one of its many synonyms was used concluded that "even when the justices pointed out publicity practices they deemed unethical, they still emphasized the fact that constitutionally, such practices are protected alongside other contentious exchanges in the marketplace of ideas."[28]

At the same time, a look at the regulation of political communication alone provides an incomplete picture of the legal restrictions placed on public relations communication. Public relations professionals working on behalf of corporate clients and employers also must consider the stricter legal constraints on *commercial* communication. While companies have a First Amendment right to participate in the commercial marketplace, the Supreme Court has ruled that nonideological, or commercial, speech should be afforded only limited constitutional protection.[29]

Regulating Commercial Advocacy

Although the marketplace of ideas concept is most often applied in the context of political communication involving matters of public interest and concern, the U.S. Supreme Court has extended marketplace principles to the commercial arena. Recognizing an informational value in commercial speech—alternatively defined by the Court as "speech which does no more than propose a commercial transaction" or "expression related solely to the economic interests of the speaker and its audience"—the Court has observed that "the relationship of speech to the marketplace of products or services does not make it valueless in the marketplace of ideas."[30]

Yet, commercial speech occupies a lower rung on the Supreme Court's hierarchy of First Amendment values and, therefore, is subjected to a higher degree of regulation, requiring the government to show only that a substantial interest is advanced by a particular restriction. Because commercial speech is "the offspring of economic self-interest," it is less likely to be chilled by regulation, according to the Court.[31] This second-class status is also warranted, the Court said, because commercial speech is more easily verified since it deals with matters about which the speaker has knowledge and control.[32]

Indeed, the Court has made clear that commercial speech that is "false, deceptive, or misleading" is entitled to *no* First Amendment protection and the states and federal government are free to prevent its dissemination.[33] The purpose of regulation, according to the Court, is "to ensure that commercial communication flows cleanly as well as freely."[34]

The Federal Trade Commission (FTC) and state governments are primarily responsible for regulating commercial advocacy in the United States. Institutions found to have engaged in deceptive or misleading communication practices, as defined by the FTC and the states, are held legally liable for their actions and subjected to the penalties outlined in the respective rules and laws. For example, under FTC guidelines, deception is defined as a material representation, omission, or practice that is likely to mislead a reasonable consumer.[35] Falsehoods may be express or implied, meaning that deceptive information may be either technically false *or* may simply mislead listeners because it is incomplete or in some other way creates a false impression.[36] Sanctions for violations range from cease-and-desist orders to corrective advertising. The intent is to prevent injury to individuals who rely on deceptive information in the commercial marketplace.

All fifty states have enacted legislation aimed at preventing unfair or deceptive commercial "advertising" practices, adopting language similar to FTC rules for both defining deceptive communication practices and in determining appropriate sanctions. For example, New York's statute explains that "in determining whether any advertising is misleading, there shall be taken into account (among other things) not only representations made by statement, word, design, device, sound or any combination thereof, but also the extent to which the advertising fails to reveal facts material in the light of such representations . . ."[37]

Importantly, under FTC guidelines, participants in the commercial marketplace must be able to verify the truthfulness of their claims. Additionally, the intentions of a speaker are irrelevant in judicial determinations regarding the deceptive nature of particular communications. Liability is determined on the basis of whether an omission or representation is *likely* to mislead a *reasonable* consumer. Deception is determined by the overall impression of a particular communication. In other words, there is little room for error. The only "breathing space" in the commercial marketplace is that a misrepresentation or omission must be *material*, or important to a consumer's decision to purchase a product or service.

When this strict standard of liability in the commercial marketplace is compared to the broad freedom to communicate in the political marketplace, the significance of distinguishing commercial and political advocacy— at least for regulatory purposes—is clear. Communication practices in the marketplace of ideas are subjected to different legal standards depending on their classification as either political or commercial speech. Thus, the threshold issue in determining the *legal* requirements for public relations advocacy in the United States is whether a particular message is categorized as political speech or commercial speech.

As noted above, public relations communication historically has been viewed as *political* expression broadly protected under the First Amendment. However, the potential for at least some public relations expression to be categorized as *commercial* speech and regulated accordingly is quite real.[38] For example, a recent California Supreme Court decision found that public relations messages disseminated by Nike, Inc., about the company's labor practices were commercial speech subject to the state's strict requirements for truth and accuracy in "advertising" practices.[39]

Baselines for Responsible Advocacy in Public Relations

This discussion demonstrates the complexity of legal regulation of political and commercial advocacy in the United States. The two-pronged approach adopted by Congress and the courts has created a complicated scheme that privileges political communication over commercial communication, providing broad freedom to deceive in the political marketplace and strict liability for deception in the commercial marketplace. In essence, there is not *a* marketplace of ideas but two marketplaces of ideas in which public relations professionals practice and two regulatory schemes under which public relations advocacy might be judged.[40]

At the same time, a common philosophy and shared values and interests are evident in the law's application of marketplace concepts in both the political and commercial arenas. This section discusses four principles fundamental to the application of marketplace theory in law that may be useful in establishing ethical baselines for responsible advocacy in public relations: access, process, truth, and disclosure.

Access

Two interests are dominant in free speech jurisprudence in the United States: the speaker's right to free expression and the listener's right to receive information important to informed decision making. The speaker's access to the market and a listener's access to information are of paramount importance to the proper functioning of the marketplace. If certain voices are stifled or listeners do not receive information needed to make informed decisions, then the marketplace fails to operate properly. Just as the U.S. Supreme Court has recognized the need for certain legal limitations to ensure that these important interests are protected, public relations professionals must consider the ethical requirements needed to ensure responsible participation in both political and commercial contexts.

Determining whether public relations advocacy helps equalize access to the marketplace or, rather, creates an imbalance of power in the marketplace is an important issue in determining the limits of responsible advocacy. Actions intended to monopolize the marketplace freeze out other voices and violate fundamental democratic principles. Public relations practitioners must ask how their work contributes to—rather than interferes with—the efficient functioning of the marketplace. At the same time, they also must ask whether every special interest deserves a voice. For example, are public relations professionals obligated to "open channels of communication to the traditionally underrepresented?"[41] Is it morally sound to serve as professional "hired guns" whose services are available only to clients and employers with deep pockets? Is it "ethically permissible to accept those clients advancing views/agenda with which the practitioner has serious ethical/moral reservations?"[42]

Answers to such questions are not provided by industry guidelines. In fact, the PRSA Code of Ethics is virtually silent on the issue of representation, requiring only that PRSA members "decline representation of clients and organizations that urge or require actions contrary to this Code." Thus, practitioners and firms must wrestle with the moral issues associated with the representation of various causes and interests.

In addressing such matters, ethics scholar David Martinson has argued that it is incumbent on all communication professionals to "guard against a form of censorship where unpopular ideas are denied a hearing not because of formal governmental legal restrictions, but because of the informal—and oftentimes much more insidious—restrictions that are so often responsible for restricting *genuine* access to the marketplace of ideas."[43] Martinson maintains that public relations practitioners have a special responsibility to open the marketplace of ideas to a "broad variety" of viewpoints.[44]

Process

The marketplace of ideas requires a properly functioning forum of public dialogue and debate. For this reason, the U.S. Supreme Court has upheld limited regulations intended to prevent corruption of—or undue influences on—political processes. While competition is a sign of a healthy marketplace, unfair competition that privileges a particular special interest over others fails to serve the common good. As John Warburton observed about democratic societies, "there is no one public interest, only numerous competing versions, which evolve as a function of the complex process of national discourse."[45] For that reason, "it is the *process* of deciding policy that is important, not the policy itself."[46]

Public relations professionals must consider whether their advocacy contributes to or interferes with marketplace processes. They must question whether their advocacy promotes—or stifles—public dialogue and debate. In a properly functioning marketplace of ideas, truthful information flows to and from marketplace participants. In that regard, both public relations professionals and the news media play critical roles. News consumers rely on a range of media sources for objective reporting on issues of public interest and concern. The news media rely heavily on public relations sources for much of the information reported.

To maintain marketplace equilibrium, public relations professionals must provide honest and accurate information to the media, and the media must present a neutral and balanced view of stories covered. Given the symbiotic relationship among journalists and public relations sources, it is particularly important that any relationships that could create real or perceived conflicts of interest be disclosed. A recent PRSA "Professional Standards Advisory" addressed such issues in response to reports of a media commentator being paid by a public relations firm to promote the viewpoint of the firm's client in news broadcasts:

> One of the foundations of a system of free expression is the presumed fairness and independence of reportage, analysis and commentary in the news media. In this system, a diversity of viewpoints and opinions needs to be heard, but must compete on the merits of argument and fact. When a point of view, organization or product is given an unfair advantage as a result of financial payments, it undermines the integrity of the system itself.[47]

While abuses of communication processes are damaging in all areas of public relations practice, interference with processes of government are particularly egregious. Indeed, "whenever and however public relations professionals are involved in the processes of government, they assume ethical responsibilities commensurate with importance of safeguarding democratic institutions."[48] Whether campaigning on behalf of a candidate for office, lobbying for legislative change on behalf of a client or employer, or representing an institution involved in litigation or other government actions, public relations professionals should not interfere with the integrity of political and judicial systems.

Truth

Under First Amendment doctrine, the value of communication is judged by whether it makes a *meaningful* contribution to the marketplace of ideas. In making such determinations, the Court has emphasized the importance of truthful information and recognized possible harms resulting from the communication of false statements of fact in the political marketplace and deceptive omissions or false representations of material information in the commercial marketplace. While the Court has relied primarily on the self-righting process of the marketplace and postspeech remedies to expose falsehoods in the political forum, it has identified a need for closer scrutiny and stricter standards in commercial communication.

Undeniably, "truth" is an elusive term in both law and public relations. Yet, it is the singular most important element in the efficient operation of the marketplace of ideas in American society. Indeed, the marketplace concept rests on the fundamental premise that "truth" will emerge from ideas and messages competing in a public forum. Thus, any effort to achieve an alternative end (i.e., to create "false truths") interferes with the basic intent of the marketplace. To the extent that communication deceives or misinforms, it interferes with informed decision making and violates the listener's right to receive accurate and truthful information.

Media ethics scholars Ralph Barney and Jay Black address this issue in arguing that the "persuasive ethic" of public relations "is defensible and laudable in a participatory democracy."[49] Likening public relations professionals to attorneys operating in an adversarial society, they contend that public relations advocates may advance their clients' interests by distributing "selectively favorable information" and they may "rightfully assume that others will accept the social role of generating counterbalancing messages."[50] The authors go on to note, however, that while the advocate's role relieves the public relations professional of any obligation to tell "objective" truth, it "leaves unanswered the question of outer limits of ethical behavior."[51]

In defining "truth," public relations professionals might begin with the strict legal standards applied to deceptive commercial communication. As a baseline for legal conduct, FTC guidelines provide a high bar. But, as noted early in this chapter, ethical guidelines should go beyond legal requirements. For example, while the moral motivation of a commercial speaker might be irrelevant for regulatory purposes, it is an important consideration in ethical decision making. Thus, while such laws provide starting points for ethical decision making, they seldom address the full expectations of institutional stakeholders for ethical performance.

Public relations professionals should acknowledge and respect the informational needs and interests of those with whom they are communicating. They should consider the potential harms that could result from their communication. They should counsel clients and employers to "tell the truth" in their public communications, helping them to ethically balance constituent interests with the interests of the institution. They should acknowledge and abide by the duty to inquire about the truthfulness of information they disseminate and be able to *verify* the truthfulness of their communications. They should ensure that the truth is advanced by the full disclosure of information needed to fully inform their audiences. Quite simply, when operating in the marketplace of ideas, *responsible* public relations professionals should be "advocates of truth."

Disclosure

A theme running through political and commercial speech regulation is the need for citizens, consumers, and policy makers to have the information needed to make informed decisions. In the commercial marketplace, where full disclosure of material information is required, this theme is particularly evident. In the political marketplace, where speakers historically have been afforded considerable discretion to decide how much and what information to provide, there is some evidence of an increased willingness by Congress and the courts to compel responsible behavior through stricter disclosure requirements requiring greater transparency.

For example, legal mandates such as the Sarbanes-Oxley legislation passed in the wake of the Enron scandal recognize the importance of investors having access to information needed in order to make informed judgments. In financial and other areas, however, legal requirements may stop short of requiring "full" disclosure of information. Practitioners must ask what information would be sufficient to enable the reasonable person to make an informed choice. As one example, Martinson recommends a policy of "substantial completeness" based on "what needs to be communicated to achieve genuine understanding."[52]

According to the PRSA Code of Ethics, a policy of "open communication" is intended "to build trust with the public by revealing all information needed for responsible decision making." The code states that lying by omission is "improper." Omissions might include *not* revealing the true sponsor of an advocacy campaign, *not* releasing financial information that could be relevant to an investor's view of a corporation's performance, or *not* revealing that third parties have been paid to speak on behalf of a client or employer.

Disclosure of timely, relevant, and complete information is particularly important in times of crisis when information voids can be particularly harmful. In many respects, crisis public relations is an "ethical testing ground for public relations professionals,"[53] who must perform the dual role of organizational spokesperson and counselor. In both instances, stakeholders' informational needs and interests must be considered. "No comment" is not an option. Ethical public relations professionals are forthright and honest and counsel clients and employers to adopt responsible communication policies built on principles of openness and transparency.

Principles in Practice

These fundamental marketplace principles—access, process, truth, and disclosure—provide a template for evaluating the ethical validity of public relations practices. For example, one commonly used advocacy technique that has been widely criticized as unethical is the use of "front groups," or artificial third-party coalitions designed to deceive citizens and/or lawmakers about election or policy matters.

Here's how front groups work: an organization with a special interest in the outcome of a referendum or policy debate forms a "citizens" group to advocate on its behalf. The group is typically named on behalf of the citizens it purports to represent, such as "Citizens for a Free Kuwait" or "Citizens for Energy Relief." Such groups serve as the "voices" of institutions (e.g., nations or corporations) that want to hide their participation in the marketplace of ideas. The thinking is that citizens and policymakers who believe that a particular policy or position has broad-based public support are more likely to support that view themselves. The problem is that, despite their names, front groups have few, or sometimes no, citizen members.[54] The "false front" is created to deceive policymakers into believing that citizens support the view of the sponsoring organization.

It is clear that such practices violate marketplace principles. First, well-funded front group practices tend to monopolize the marketplace and diminish other voices, limiting access to the marketplace of ideas and interfering with citizens' and/or policymakers' *access* to information needed to help them reach informed decisions about issues or policies of public interest and concern. Second, front groups corrupt communication *processes* by deceiving marketplace participants about both the source of communication and the true level of support for particular perspectives. Third, front groups create false truths—rather than contribute to the achievement of "objective" *truth*—by misleading marketplace participants about either the potential impact of proposed policies or genuine citizen support for them. Finally, the lack of transparency regarding the true sources of communication violates the marketplace principle of *disclosure,* which requires that information needed to aid informed decision making be revealed.

In addition to helping gauge the ethical legitimacy of specific public relations practices, marketplace principles also might be useful in helping identify unethical public relations activities likely to invite government scrutiny. For example, while front group practices have continued unabated—and essentially unregulated—for more than half a century,[55] Congress and the courts recently recognized the potential damage caused by such practices to American institutions. For example, in 2003, Congress enacted sweeping changes in campaign finance rules that acknowledged the value of listeners being able to "consider the source" of information disseminated in the political marketplace of ideas.

The new legislation, which imposed strict new disclosure requirements on sponsors of political advocacy, included a provision requiring that sponsors of "electioneering communication" be identified in broadcast messages. The impact of this new rule was evident in the 2004 presidential election, in which presidential candidates routinely announced their endorsements in campaign advertisements—"I'm John Kerry and I approved this message."

When the new disclosure regulations were challenged as unconstitutional, the U.S. Supreme Court upheld the restrictions, finding in part that organizations engaging in front group practices could be required to disclose their participation in such efforts.[56] The new disclosure law was needed, the Court said in McConnell v. FCC, because of the significant interest in assuring that voters received "relevant information."[57] The Court chastised those who had challenged the new rules for wanting to preserve the ability to run election ads "while hiding behind dubious and misleading names like: 'The Coalition-Americans Working for Real Change' (backed by business organizations opposed to organized labor), 'Citizens for Better Medicare' (funded by the pharmaceutical industry), 'Republicans for Clean Air' (funded by brothers Charles and Sam Wyly)."[58] According to the Court, such efforts do "not reinforce the precious First Amendment interests of individual citizens seeking to make informed choices in the political marketplace."[59]

Notwithstanding the fact that these new standards were applied in the election context, an area in which both Congress and the courts historically have been most vigilant in their efforts to protect fair government processes, the McConnell decision offers important insights for public relations ethics. For example, the Supreme Court obviously believes there is some value in allowing citizens and policymakers to consider the sources of communication when weighing the merits of information. Although the Court has recognized the need to allow some anonymity to protect individuals from fears of reprisal based on their views,[60] it carved out an exception in situations involving potential distortions of election processes. Additionally, the Court seems to have become less tolerant of deceptive communication practices that threaten democratic ideals and political processes. Certainly, the McConnell Court exhibited a willingness to hold organizations legally accountable for communication practices traditionally judged by ethical discretion.

This blurring of lines between law and ethics in First Amendment jurisprudence has significant implications for public relations professionals, as well as the clients and employers they represent. Most important, such decisions could indicate that constitutional protection for public relations expression may be shrinking and that responsible advocacy in the marketplace of ideas may be judged by heightened legal standards as well as ethical norms.

Converging Legal and Ethical Standards

While it might be premature to suggest that cases such as McConnell reflect a trend toward judicial encroachment into ethical decision making in public relations, it is worth noting that a convergence of legal and ethical standards has been noted in other areas of communication as well. For example, in a 1996 study that analyzed "ethical choices" that became "legal problems" for the news media, Laurence Alexander concluded that "the judiciary is crossing the imaginary ethical barrier, thus infringing on the sanctity of policies and decisions previously reserved for editorial executives."[61]

In a 2000 study examining journalists' views toward law and ethics in ethical decision making, Paul Voakes found that over the last thirty-five years, the U.S. Supreme Court has taken "a decidedly 'Social Responsibility' attitude toward freedom of expression."[62] He observed that "each time what is traditionally a moral obligation becomes somehow written into the law, the media (and all speakers and writers) lose another small measure of expressive freedom."[63]

Although the reasons for the legalization of ethical principles in communication are unclear, Voakes suggested that such movement may reflect judicial views regarding the special ethical responsibilities associated with constitutional freedoms. For example, with respect to the news media, he found that, "whenever a matter of journalistic practice ends up in court, the courts consider whether the press has been performing its First Amendment responsibilities and duties (in exchange for the continued protection of its rights). The more responsive the press appears to be, the less urgent the need to invoke correctives."[64]

The same reasoning might be applied to public relations. Of course, public relations professionals do not enjoy the special status of the "Fourth Estate." Indeed, as representatives of *special* interests—as compared to the *public* interest—they and their clients and employers may have less protection from judicial forays into questions of ethics. Public relations professionals must consider both whether the special obligations associated with the freedom to communicate are being met and whether, in the absence of effective *self*-regulation, the government might step in to hold practitioners accountable for irresponsible behavior.

A recent example makes the point. In early 2005, *USA Today* revealed that conservative commentator Armstrong Williams had been paid $240,000 by the U.S. Department of Education to promote the Bush Administration's No Child Left Behind policy in a deal reportedly brokered by Ketchum, Inc., a leading public relations firm.[65] Williams's relationship with the administration was not publicly disclosed by Ketchum or Williams. After learning that other media "pundits" also had been paid by the administration to influence public opinion on Bush policies, Democratic lawmakers called for new legislation to prohibit such actions. Their argument for heightened regulation was supported by a report issued just months earlier by a Congressional watchdog agency that found the Bush administration in violation of federal law for using taxpayer dollars for purposes of propaganda not approved by Congress. According to the report, the administration—again with the assistance of Ketchum—engaged in "covert propaganda" to promote the president's health care policies by producing and distributing prepackaged video news releases that provided a skewed view of the Medicare reform program and disguised the fact that the government was the source of the information.[66]

These examples, which created considerable controversy regarding the ethics of the government officials, members of the public relations firm, and media representatives involved, illustrate both the importance of adhering to marketplace principles and the potential for heightened legal regulation of communication activities. While the actions were widely condemned in some public relations circles—for example, PRSA called the Williams incident "disturbing" and "harmful," and the editor-in-chief of *PR Week* said it was "an extraordinarily dismal situation" that "reinforces many of the worst perceptions of the [public relations] industry"—the implications are yet to be determined. As one public relations executive said about the so-called pay-for-play deal involving Williams, "I'm worried that if the industry doesn't deal with this ourselves, others will deal with it for us. . . . And that would be a nightmare."[67]

Such examples also demonstrate the fragility of the line between law and ethics and the importance of responsible advocacy in sustaining First Amendment protection for public relations expression. Irresponsible behavior attracts the bright light of public scrutiny and invites increased legal restrictions on public relations work. Indeed, as the distinctions between *legal* public relations and *ethical* public relations narrow, legal standards may become increasingly important gauges of acceptable professional conduct. Although still only baselines for ethical performance, evolving legal requirements provide valuable direction for defining the limits of responsible public relations advocacy in the marketplace of ideas.

Conclusion

This chapter proposes that marketplace principles—as defined by First Amendment jurisprudence—be used to evaluate the ethical soundness of public relations advocacy. The adoption of free speech principles as ethical baselines in public relations acknowledges both the primacy of marketplace philosophy in U.S. society—as reflected in the laws of the land—and the utility of legal reasoning in ethical decision making. The legal principles applied by the courts in balancing the rights and freedoms of various special interests offer a model for addressing the competing values and concerns of an institution's strategic constituents. The fundamental marketplace principles of access, process, truth, and disclosure provide an ethical floor on which public relations practice standards can be built.

2

Responsibility and Accountability

Thomas H. Bivins

"The Buck Stops Here"

Sign on President Harry S. Truman's desk

Human beings seek accountability. People want to know who is responsible for certain actions and who is accountable for the consequences of those actions. Harry Truman referred to his famous desk sign on more than one occasion to point out that responsibility, in the end, must be taken by someone—some identifiable person must be held to account. Truman was willing to accept that accountability. Increasingly today, people are more likely to ask, "Where exactly does the buck stop, or does it ever stop?" In the wake of a multitude of recent corporate scandals, commentary has been rife with questions of responsibility and accountability; however, much of that discussion has been carried on without clear knowledge of the definitional differences between the two terms and the significance of those differences. Of public relations in particular it might be asked, "Why weren't you standing guard?" which is a simplified way of asking, "What is public relations responsible for, and for what is it accountable?" Unfortunately, there is no common perception—at least among business leaders, public relations professionals, and scholars—as to exactly what constitutes both responsibility and accountability, and therein lies the rub.

Responsibility versus Accountability

The roles taken on by public relations practitioners imply a responsibility to perform certain functions associated with those roles. Business historian Vincent E. Barry has defined the term *responsibility,* when used in business affairs, as referring to "a sphere of duty or obligation assigned to a person by the nature of that person's position, function, or work."[1] Responsibility could thus be viewed as a bundle of obligations associated with a job or function. Narrowly defined, *role* refers to a job description, which, in turn, encompasses, but is not limited to, *function.* For instance, a practitioner's role may be that of media relations. Function would refer to the specifics of the job, including press release writing and dissemination, as well as the maintenance of good media relations. In this sense, responsibility refers to more than just the primary function of a role; it refers to the multiple facets of that function—both processes and outcomes (and the consequences of the acts performed as part of that bundle of obligations). A responsible actor may be seen as one whose job involves a predetermined set of obligations that must be met in order for the job to be accomplished. For example, the primary functional obligation of someone involved in media relations is the same as cited in the foregoing sentence: to maintain a good working relationship with the media in order to respond to queries and to successfully work with them to "get out the message." In many cases, simply discharging this primary obligation (the function associated with the role) may be sufficient unto itself; however, responsibility can also include *moral obligations* that are in addition and usually related to the functional obligations of the role. Thus, responsibility assumes that the actor becomes also a moral agent possessed of a certain level of moral maturity and an ability to reason. It is important to note that as early as Aristotle, moral responsibility was viewed as originating with the moral agent (decision maker), and grew out of an ability to reason (an awareness of action and consequences) and a willingness to act free from external compulsion. For Aristotle, a decision is a particular kind of desire resulting from deliberation, one that expresses the agent's conception of what is good. As Australian ethicist Will Barret points out,

> Moral responsibility assumes a capacity for making rational decisions, which in turn justifies holding moral agents accountable for their actions. Given that moral agency entails responsibility, in that autonomous rational agents are in principle capable of responding to moral reasons, accountability is a necessary feature of morality.[2]

For example, the moral obligations of the role of a media relations specialist might include such admonitions as "don't lie to the media" and "use language responsibly, free from intentional obfuscation." These moral obligations are naturally joined to the parallel functional obligations associated with the role. Responsibility, then, is composed of a duty to discharge not only the *functional* obligations of role, but also the *moral* obligations.

In addition, teleological (consequential) considerations tend to demand a level of accountability commensurate with the level of responsibility. In other words, if it is the job of a media relations specialist to carry out the primary functions outlined above, shouldn't that person be held accountable for mismanaged information, bad publicity, lack of credibility, or other troubles associated with the functional obligations? If responsibility is defined as a bundle of obligations, functional and moral, associated with a role, then accountability might be defined as "blaming or crediting someone for an action"—normally an action associated with a recognized responsibility.[3] A problem arises, however, in that while responsibility and accountability are often conflated, and admittedly importantly linked, they are not identical by definition or moral implication.

According to ethics activist Geoff Hunt, accountability

> is the readiness or preparedness to give an explanation or justification to relevant others (stakeholders) for one's judgments, intentions, acts and omissions when appropriately called upon to do so.

> It is [also] a readiness to have one's actions judged by others and, where appropriate, accept responsibility for errors, misjudgments and negligence and recognition for competence, conscientiousness, excellence and wisdom. It is a preparedness to change in the light of improved understanding gained from others.[4]

The simplest formula is that a person can be held accountable if (1) the person is functionally and/or morally responsible for an action, (2) some harm occurred due to that action, and (3) the responsible person had no legitimate excuse for the action. Ideally, the assumption would then be to hold a person who is responsible for an action also accountable for the results of that action. That, however, may not always be the case.

This position assumes that the responsible person is relatively autonomous, or free to make decisions associated with his or her job without outside pressure or influence. And, under normal circumstances, one would hope that public relations practitioners would have that autonomy. However, the nature of autonomy often changes with the environment in which a public relations person works, and is certainly affected by the role and the functions associated with that role.

Responsibility and Autonomy

Most professions stress autonomy among their members. Being able to perform work free from interference (especially from those with less expertise) is vital to being a successful professional. After all, most professionals are hired exactly because their expertise is needed. As philosopher John Christman notes, to be autonomous, by most accounts, is to be oneself,

> to be directed by considerations, desires, conditions, and characteristics that are not simply imposed externally upon one, but are part of what can somehow be considered one's authentic self. Autonomy in this sense seems an irrefutable value, especially since its opposite—being guided by forces external to the self and which one cannot authentically embrace—seems to mark the height of oppression.[5]

There are several ways to look at autonomy as it relates to responsibility and accountability. Philosopher and ethicist Mitchell Haney suggests that the moral community is composed of two kinds of actors: responsible actors and accountable actors. Responsibility is viewed within this model as having a higher level of autonomy by nature in that it implies the actor is able to "self-oversee, self-regulate, and self-motivate responsive adjustments to maintain adherence with appropriate moral standards of action."[6]

"Responsible actors need not depend on external or mediated motivational pressure for responsive adjustment. [They are] expected to be motivated to correct harms and reduce future risk of harms without external or mediated pressure to do so."[7]

Under this formulation, the actor (moral agent) has the capacity to impose moral law on herself, thus achieving a level of "moral autonomy" we would hope to associate normally with professional status. This somewhat Kantian model supposes that we understand ourselves as free, reasoning individuals—invoking a mandate of both self-respect and respect for others (but not control by others).

Freedom means lacking barriers to our action that are in any way external to our will, though it also requires that we use a law to guide our decisions, a law that can come to us only by an act of our own will. This self-imposition of the moral law is autonomy.[8]

According to business ethicist Norman Bowie, if a person is a responsible, autonomous adult, that person can be viewed as a moral agent, directly accountable for his or her actions. "A responsible being is a being who can make choices according to his or her own insights. He or she is not under the control of others."[9]

On the other hand, the *accountable* actor is "held to external oversight, regulation, and mechanisms of punishment aimed to externally motivate responsive adjustment in order to maintain adherence with appropriate moral standards of action."[10] This responsible-/accountable-actor model assumes a dichotomy in which responsible actors, because of moral maturity, are capable of self-motivation in their responsive adjustments for actions they have performed, while accountable actors must rely on external pressure (blame or credit) for this adjustment. This is similar to the "consequentialist" versus "merit" positions on moral responsibility. The consequentialist view holds that the actions of moral agents can be influenced by outward expressions of praise or blame in order to affect certain behaviors (accountable actors), while the merit view assumes moral agents can and do recognize their choices and make their own decisions (responsible actors).[11]

The theory of the accountable actor uses what might be termed a behaviorist approach, which seems to suggest that people are motivated and shaped by forces external to themselves. Certainly people are motivated, at least in part, by rewards and punishments; however, even those considered accountable rather than responsible actors generally have a developed moral sense and a fair idea of social conventions and moral principles. The problem arises when people are affected by forces beyond their control, forces that may even affect the level at which they reason. As philosopher and ethicist Kevin Gibson points out, "Indeed, in the presence of some external factors, individuals may not actively reason at all, but work according to habit or obedience without a thought."[12]

So, in addition to responsible actors being imbued with the ability and the freedom to make self-regulating decisions, they are also able to motivate (free of outside pressure) their own responsive adjustments to situations in which their decisions have had an impact. This is what separates them from accountable actors, who must rely on external oversight for motivation to respond and adjust. However, while this scenario may be appealing in theory, the ability to respond based entirely on self-motivation (or autonomy) is also limited by role and environment.

Environment, Role, and Autonomy

Responsibility can be, and often is, determined by role; however, the environment in which the public relations professional works and the degree of autonomy allowed by that environment have a great deal to do with accountability. Chief among the commonly recognized environments in which public relations practitioners work are agencies (or firms), or they might be employed as full-time staff within an organization or corporation, or as independent counselors. Most public relations practitioners, and many researchers, agree that the independent public relations counsel enjoys the greatest degree of autonomy.[13] Of all the roles in public relations, this is the only one not subsumed within a larger, bureaucratic system—either corporate or agency. Clients hiring such "independent" counselors usually do so out of need for autonomous, professional advice, and by so doing accept the professional recommendations of that person as, at the very least, sound opinion. Independent public relations counsel might be said to be the most autonomous of the roles within the practice, if for no other reason than the lack of bureaucratic entanglements. Because of the level of autonomy normally associated with this role, it may also be the most professional of the roles within public relations. And, as Hunt points out,

> Accountability in the professional context is about answering to clients, professional colleagues and other relevant professionals. The demand to give an account of one's judgments, acts and omissions arises from the nature of the professional-client and the professional-professional relationships.[14]

However, public relations is not just a counseling profession; it can also be said to be an advocacy-oriented practice. To advocate is to take up the cause of another and to work on that other's behalf to promote that cause. One of the key differences between the roles of advocate and counselor is the degree of autonomy allowed to each by the nature of the role. Remember, the general assumption is that autonomy is a highly valued component of professionalism; however, for the advocate, autonomy is not particularly valued or desired. In fact, for the advocate, a more desirable trait might be loyalty.

Most businesspeople would argue that loyalty is indeed one of the chief duties of an employee, and, in fact, being a "team player" is highly regarded in the business world. As a team player, the public relations practitioner is generally expected to follow the directions of the team leader without argument. Thus, advocates are expected to be subjective—that is the nature of advocacy. Subjectivity brings with it an implicit understanding that one's first allegiance is to the client, or employer. To advocates fall the job of bringing skills of persuasion to bear through methods and on issues often predetermined by management. Since they had no hand in arriving at either the focus or the nature of their advocacy, can they be expected to consider the broader implications of their actions? And, to what degree are they accountable for unjust or immoral acts in which they may have been used as instruments?

Part of the assumption of advocacy is that the advocate takes up the client's cause fully, without any value judgment toward the client himself. Advocates use their expertise to advance a client's cause. Thus, advocacy often fits well into what is known as the "agency" model of the professional-client relationship.[15]

Agency and Advocacy

Under the agency model, a professional acts most often under the direction of the client. Public relations firms, for instance, may put together elaborate campaigns to serve their client's interests; however, the client picks the agency, determines what exactly will be "marketed," and decides whether or not to use the ideas generated by the agency. The agency model most clearly exemplifies what legal scholar W. H. Simon calls the "ideology of advocacy." This ideology assumes two principles of conduct: (1) that a professional is neutral or detached from the client's purposes, and (2) that the professional is an aggressive partisan of the client working to advance the client's ends.[16] The argument is that advocacy is ideologically "blinded" to ethical considerations outside those of the client.[17] Such a construct thus allows professionals to absolve themselves of moral responsibility for the client's ethical shortcomings, thus shifting accountability from the professional to the client. In addition, responsibility under this model is mostly functional and links the professional to the client by an obligation to perform to the best of her or his ability on the client's behalf. To cite a moral responsibility here would generally serve no practical purpose. Attorneys, for example, are bound only to observe the restraints of law as they "zealously" advocate on their client's behalf. Obviously, this ideology would work well for professions such as the law, in which even unpopular causes would sometimes need to be defended. Without such an ideology, these causes might go unrepresented. But what about other professions such as public relations?

There are several reasons why the agency model is not suitable for most professions, including public relations. First, public relations professionals are variously obligated morally. These obligations cannot be discharged properly if all decisions are left to the client. Despite the commonly voiced belief that the primary loyalty of public relations practitioners is to the client, we know that significant moral concerns can arise from ignoring third parties. Second, the agency model seriously decreases professional autonomy. Most professionals would object strenuously to abdicating their decision-making authority. Finally, professionals may accept or reject clients who do not meet their moral standards. According to ethicist Michael Bayles, "Professionals must . . . be ethically free and responsible persons."[18]

The author Dorothy Emmet has described a profession as that which "carries with it the notion of a standard of performance, it is not only a way of making a living, but one in which the practitioners have a fiduciary trust to maintain certain standards." Aside from the expectations that a professional will possess a certain technical ability, "professional competence has to be joined with professional integrity." In other words, "the more professional a job, the greater the responsibilities that go with it."[19]

Again, the definition of a professional has to carry with it the freedom of autonomy. The German ethicist and philosopher Immanuel Kant stated as a categorical imperative that all humans should be treated as ends and never merely as means. Broadly speaking, this can be construed to mean that obligations arising out of agreements between professionals can be assumed to have been the result of negotiations between responsible, autonomous adults.

Bivins argued that public relations practitioners operating as advocates may indeed be "ethically free and responsible persons," and suggested that advocacy may be an ethically responsible activity if practiced from within what Bayles calls the "fiduciary" model of the professional-client relationship.[20] In fact, Bayles suggests that the fiduciary model of service best fits the true role of the professional.[21] In this model, a client's consent and judgment are required and he or she participates in the decision-making process. The key to the model is the nature of the decision-making process in which the client consents to proposals rather than decides. For the process to work, the client must trust the professional to accurately analyze the problem, canvass the feasible alternatives, know as well as one can their likely consequences, fully convey this information to the client, perhaps make a recommendation, and work honestly and loyally for the client to effectuate the chosen alternatives.[22] This model allows clients as much freedom to determine how their lives are affected as is reasonably warranted on the basis of their ability to make decisions. To the degree that the client is incapable of making an informed decision, it is incumbent upon the professional to educate them to a point at which they are capable of decision making on their own behalf. In this sense, the relationship between the professional and the client might be said to be symmetric, requiring both mutual understanding and cooperation. Clearly, this model must be based on a trust relationship, thus further obligating the professional morally as well as functionally.

Under this model, it could be fairly stated that both the functional and moral responsibilities of the public relations professional toward the client are discharged in consort with the client. But what about the functional and moral responsibilities toward affected third parties? Practically all professions recognize third-party obligations, and if advocacy is to be considered a legitimate function of public relations, then there must be a way to recognize those moral responsibilities.

The function of advocacy, as it pertains to public relations, can remain a professional role responsible to client interests, professional interests, and third-party interests only if the professional includes a preliminary stage in the process of accepting a client's issue. Under the fiduciary model described above, the public relations professional as potential advocate may be hired, for example, because of her or his expertise in the field of audience analysis, knowledge of the most efficacious persuasive techniques, and the proper methods of dissemination. It is generally accepted that the first job of public relations professionals is to establish a thorough understanding of the issue that they may be addressing on behalf of the potential client. Without that assessment, no professional should ethically proceed to undertake the role of advocate and the moral responsibility that role implies. Thus, a proper ordering of priorities would place a thorough understanding of the issue at the top of the list preceding any attempt at campaign development or even audience analysis.

The role of autonomous professional assumes a certain level of objectivity in the sense of an ability, in the Kantian implication of the term, to use reason to determine action.

As Australian philosopher Will Barrett points out,

> The sources of moral responsibility—the grounds on which moral responsibilities can be ascribed to agents—include our past actions, our roles, and our developed moral agency. The last of these—being capable of recognising *the force of moral reasons,* and of responding to them—is a pre-requisite for the other two sources of moral responsibility, and so of accountability [emphasis added].[23]

By contrast, the role of advocate assumes a certain amount of subjectivity in the sense of one-sidedness of purpose and lack of consideration for third-party interests. However, objectivity and subjectivity, although often at odds, are not necessarily mutually exclusive, and the public relations professional may, in fact, be both objective and subjective. The key is the order of approach. Objectivity, or the capability and freedom to be objective, is certainly one of the benefits of autonomy, and should be brought to bear in the early stages of counseling the client—the period in which a thorough understanding of the issue is obtained. It is during this stage that the public relations professional will determine the ramifications of the proposed actions and their effect on all parties.

During this stage, the public relations professional may apply any of several applicable ethical theories to the proposed act in order to determine if the act itself (means) and the outcome (ends) are morally responsible. Deontologically (dealing with the means), several standards may be applied, including a determination of the legality of the act (whether it violates existing laws or applicable regulations), company procedures and policies or organizational codes, and any codes or standards existing for the profession—in this case, the Public Relations Society of America's Code of Ethics. Although this procedure will merely provide professionals with guidelines, assuming that all that is legally or professionally permissible may not be ethically permissible, these will at least allow them to advance to succeeding evaluative stages.

Teleologically (dealing with the consequences, or ends), public relations professionals may apply standard cost-benefit analysis to the issue, determining the potential financial consequences of the act to the client and the affected third parties. Beyond these monetary considerations, they may attempt to determine societal effects. If, after such applications, professionals determine that the act itself, the intent of the act, and the potential consequences of the act are morally acceptable, then they may proceed with a clear conscience to the succeeding "subjective" stages of advocacy. From this point on, the objective, professional public relations counselor may become the subjective, professional public relations advocate.

Thus, the requirements of subjective advocacy may be honorably met only after the ethical requirements of objective counseling are met. To insinuate that advocacy may take place without a predetermination of the morality of the issue being decided upon is to subscribe to the ideology of advocacy that W. H. Simon denounces. For the truly professional public relations practitioner, the order of decision making is all-important, because responsibilities differ as roles shift from counseling to advocacy, as does attendant accountability.

Public relations professionals must first work from the framework of a fiduciary model of the client-professional relationship in which autonomy is, more or less, equally divided between the contracted parties (responsibility and accountability are shared). They must then undertake to determine objectively the ethicality of the action being proposed, considering both means and ends. Only when the morality of the action has been determined should the advisor become the advocate, acting subjectively in the client's exclusive interest, but with responsibility and accountability shifting to weigh more heavily on the professional. Even then, considerable attention needs to be given to the morality of the message itself and to the techniques by which it is to be disseminated. This ordering of stages from the objective to the subjective will allow the professional public relations practitioner to perform all the necessary functions ascribed to the roles of the profession without either falling into the trap of ideological advocacy or succumbing to a less autonomous position. Ideally, responsibility and accountability would then coincide.

In-House PR: The Effects of Organizational Structure on Moral Decision Making

Ethicist and theologian Marvin Brown describes two ways of approaching the subject of ethics in organizations—the "individualistic approach" and what might be called the "communal approach."[24] Each approach incorporates a different view of moral responsibility. According to Brown, discussions about ethics in organizations typically reflect only the "individualistic approach" to moral responsibility. "According to this approach, every person in an organization is morally responsible for his or her own behavior, and any efforts to change that behavior should focus on the individual." By contrast, the "communal approach" views individuals not in isolation, but as "members of communities that are partially responsible for the behavior of their members." Herein lies the key to understanding the problems associated with assigning responsibility and accountability within organizations.

Complex organizations tend toward decentralized decision making, which, ideally, would require professionalized decision makers at every level.[25] The ideal would be for both the responsibility and the accountability of decision making to correlate. However, as they become more complex and decentralized, these same organizations also lend themselves too readily to a dilution of accountability in decision making. Moral "buck passing" often becomes the rule rather than the exception. It is too easy to blame others for decisions over which we have had minimal input or control. When the public relations function is subsumed within a large, complex organization, decision making can become attenuated and accountability spread thin. In a very real sense, the structure of large organizations tends to affect the way in which decisions are made. Furthermore, the temptation to pass the buck on decisions of all types, including moral decisions, increases mightily as the organizational hierarchy becomes more complex.[26] In fact, the traditional hierarchical structure of most organizations lends itself naturally to blockages in communication.

Understanding is generally developed within organizations through the realization of effective communication flow. The typical "flow" brings task-related (functional) communication through many levels before it reaches its intended receiver. As messages travel downward through the organizational hierarchy, they have a tendency to become less clear and, in some cases, actually distorted. Research has repeatedly shown that distortions such as those that occur during "serial transmission" damage message integrity.[27] In addition, factors such as personality type and an individual's power, status, and role also greatly affect the integrity of both communication channels and the communication itself.[28] Partly because of the tendency of communication to become distorted as organizational hierarchies increase in complexity, assigning responsibility and accountability likewise becomes more difficult as the organization becomes more complex.

It may be that corporations, like individuals, do not set out to do wrong—they are simply driven by egoism (acting in their own self-interest). But, as professional ethicist Gabriel Moran points out,

> Corporations, like natural persons, have inner divisions and an unconscious (the company design) from which most decisions emanate. Corporations . . . live by habit, by doing what they always do. But there are people in the company—supervisors, managers, administrators, executives—who are paid to be conscious of what the company is doing. Even when a result is not intended, the company is responsible for the effect if it did know of the effect or could have known.[29]

The in-house public relations function is undoubtedly the most problematic for assigning responsibility and accountability. The level of autonomy and the weight of decision making, and thus professionalism, will vary depending on whether the head of the department is a middle-level manager, an upper-level manager, or an executive. Thus, owing to the nature of corporate bureaucracy, the public relations practitioner subsumed within an organization may be nonautonomous or, at best, slightly autonomous. The groundwork is then laid for a decision-making hierarchy that may gradually dilute the authority of public relations practitioners to follow their own personal and professional directives.

In addition, the dilution of decision-making authority is more common in larger organizations, in which practitioners may often serve as employees rather than truly autonomous professionals. However, even this reduction in autonomy does not reduce a public relations practitioner's responsibility to act ethically—it only makes the lines of responsibility less clear. As PR professionals and agency principals Bruce Klatt and Shaun Murphy remind us, accountability is a "statement of personal promise."[30]

Accountability applies only to individuals and is both a personal promise and obligation, to yourself and to others, to deliver specific, defined results.

Being accountable within an organization means you agree to be operationally defined as the sole agent for an outcome, regardless of the often-inadequate level of authority or control that you have been formally assigned by the organization.

Less autonomous practitioners must also determine the ethicality of their actions; even though the major difference between them and their more independent counterparts, the degree of autonomy, may inhibit the extent to which practitioners may object to actions they determine are less than ethical. Obviously, independent counselors may advise, and thereby object, from a much stronger position than their counterparts subsumed either within an organization or an agency.

The primary problem is that the tendency toward moral buck passing will not lessen as long as organizational hierarchy encourages the dilution of responsibility and accountability. This now-too-common dilution of accountability frustrates onlookers who can't determine who is to blame when something goes wrong. The tendency to place blame is entirely normal; however, the degree of accuracy involved in assessing accountability is problematic at best.

Moral Excuses (Passing the Buck)

Unaccountable people are into excuses, blaming others, putting things off, doing the minimum, acting confused, and playing helpless. They pretend ignorance while hiding behind doors, computers, paperwork, jargon, and other people. They say things like "I didn't know," "I wasn't there," "I don't have time," "It's not my job," "That's just the way I am," "Nobody told me," "It isn't really hurting anyone," and "I'm just following orders." Unaccountable people are quick to complain and slow to act. In organizations, unaccountability is a highly contagious disease.[31]

In order to protect ourselves and keep our self-image intact, we often choose to rationalize our decisions. *Rationalize,* in this sense, means "to devise self-satisfying but incorrect reasons for a particular behavior." It is, therefore, crucial that we understand our *reasons* for preferring one action over another and to admit them to ourselves. Unless we understand our real reasons, we will be content to rationalize our actions by using other means— most often adopting moral excuses or assigning the blame to others.[32]

As Aristotle pointed out, people deserve blame for their wrongful conduct. Contemporary philosopher Laurence Stern agrees, noting that "[f]or immoral acts which are not sufficiently serious to warrant inflicting harm [punishment]—as well as for all other immoral acts committed without excuse—one can say that the person *deserves blame*."[33] In fact, it's only when a person has a good excuse that we tend not to hold him accountable, and Stern suggests that a recognition of the moral excuses common in every-day life tends to minimize the overall harm of the act itself.[34] Of course, there are good excuses and there are bad excuses. Among the excuses people tend to identify as *not* legitimate are those most often associated with external factors and the dilution of responsibility, frequently a result of organiza-tional hierarchy. As Gibson points out,

> [I]t is important to consider the types of external factors that may influence our individual choices when we are faced with ethical dilemmas. Simple awareness of their existence and the ways in which they exert influence on our behaviors may be enough to lessen their power.[35]

Gibson further defines an *excuse* as "something that acknowledges that a wrong action occurred but seeks to show that the perpetrator deserves little or no responsibility for the action." Among the most common "pass the buck" excuses are the following.[36]

I was told to do it, or *I was only following orders.* This excuse may be given more often than any other in hierarchically structured organizations such as big corporations and larger institutions like the military. The need to follow orders is obviously important in these hierarchical organizations and institutions. For one thing, it tends to bring consistency to an operation. Obedience to those whom we consider to be experts or who possess supe-rior judgment is usually considered a good thing. The downside is the incli-nation to allow authority figures to make decisions for us. It relieves us of the stress of deciding for ourselves, and of the accountability that comes with autonomy. While the excuse of "just following orders" is more common-place inside larger, corporate-like structures in which individual autonomy is diluted, public relations practitioners who work within the agency model are not immune to its lure. It is often much too easy to blame the client who, after all, is technically giving the orders.

However, the likelihood of this excuse surfacing is much greater in hier-archically structured organizations. The moral standing of the order itself is less likely to be questioned if there is a strong belief in the efficacy of a hier-archical organizational structure and a trust of those in power. The human tendency to obey orders has been empirically tested time and again. Blind obedience to authority, regardless of the moral rightness or wrongness of the orders, almost seems to be the norm. However, even in the most formal hier-archically structured institution, the military, rules have been updated to reflect increased moral accountability. It is now clear, under military law, that "military members can be held accountable for crimes committed under the guise of 'obeying orders,' and there is no requirement to obey orders which are unlawful."[37]

In other words, claiming ignorance of the immorality of the order doesn't excuse us from moral accountability. People are individually responsible regardless of orders. As Gibson notes, "Ultimately we must take personal responsibility for our acts, and cannot shrug them off as inevitable or by saying that we are mere instruments of others' will." The scholars Deni Elliot and Paul Lester agree, pointing out that "as long as you are free to act in a voluntary or autonomous way, moral responsibility for your actions are not transferable to someone else. Your boss can take away your job, but not your moral agency."[38]

It was my job. Professionals commonly justify their actions by appeal to the requirements of their professional roles. In his book *Ethics for Adversaries*, Harvard professor Arthur Applbaum describes an official who was an executioner for the French government. He accepted without question the functional responsibility of his role, and discharged it with great alacrity. However, he never once questioned the moral legitimacy of his role nor the propriety of the executions themselves.[39]

It is not unusual for public relations professionals, for example, to claim that they are acting within legal bounds on behalf of clients on whom they refuse to pass moral judgment (the "ideology of advocacy"). It is, after all, their job to serve the client's wishes competently with all their professional expertise being brought to bear on the issue. As noted earlier, however, blind obedience to another's wishes is not an excuse for unethical action, especially by professionals who have a responsibility to more than just a client. This is also why most professions have a code of ethics: to ensure that members are clear on what the profession expects of them outside client interests.

When less-than-ethical tactics are used to serve a client's purpose, the excuse is often that it is the job of the public relations professional to serve that interest "zealously." The public relations firm of Hill and Knowlton used questionable tactics on behalf of Kuwait during the first Gulf War, a clear example of this category.

Everybody's doing it. This is a formulation of what is called "ethical relativism," which states, among other things, that whatever the group you belong to says is right is probably right. Human beings possess a natural tendency to conform to the group. Just look around and observe what others are wearing. How close in style is it to what you are wearing? At its worst, this tendency to conform can lead to a shirking of individual moral responsibility, or even a lack of recognition that such a thing exists. A poor record on protecting whistle-blowers doesn't help in this area either.

However, conventional wisdom doesn't necessarily equate with being right. As John Stuart Mill noted in the nineteenth century, it may be that the one person who disagrees with a widely held point of view is the only person who is morally correct. Consider also the acts perpetrated against Jews and others by the Nazis prior to and during World War II. Certainly there were those within Germany who disagreed. But it is also certain that there were a great many who agreed because "*everybody* was doing it." However, there is a certain degree of empowerment associated with seeing even one individual disagree with the establishment point of view—an empowerment to trust and act on one's own convictions. Dissenting voices can be powerful tools in determining the right action. They should never be discouraged.

An odd formulation of this excuse is the tendency to follow the industry trend. For example, throughout much of the 1990s into the twenty-first century, there was a sense that simply denying facts was a legitimate approach to public relations. Victor Kiam, the entrepreneur who purchased Remington Razors and part ownership in the New England Patriots, denied he had made a sexist remark about a female reporter wanting access to the Patriots' locker room. Firestone denied any problems with its tires in 1999, even though there were numerous fatalities linked to their failure under high-speed conditions. And both Arthur Andersen and Enron spent a great deal of time denying that anything was wrong while both companies literally self-destructed. While this is certainly poor public relations, when everyone seems to be doing it, the temptation to follow suit is sometimes overwhelming.

My actions won't make any difference. This excuse is often used as a way of explaining the futility many of us feel as part of an organization or institution over which we have very little control. It also leads to the parallel excuse that "if I hadn't done it, they would simply have found someone else who would have." In answer to the "I can't make a difference" argument, just ask the people in the state of Washington how they feel about whether their vote counts or not. In the 2004 gubernatorial election, they selected a new governor by fewer than 150 votes.

The second part of this excuse basically assumes there will always be someone with less scruples than you who will step in to take your place at a moment's notice to do the dirty work. However, this assumption negates the possibility that you might actually counter the moral wrong. If you are working on a public relations campaign for a tobacco account, for example, you may be correct in assuming that someone else will probably eagerly take your place if you refuse to do the work; however, your action may inspire others to do the same, and if you then lend your talents to an antismoking campaign, you have further justified your action.

It's not my problem. The poet John Donne once famously observed that "no man is an island." Individuals are responsible for their actions, or inactions, and their effect on others. Each hand that contributes to a chain of corruption within an organization helps forge a link of that chain. Even if we are not directly in the line of responsibility, there may be times when an issue is important enough to act on a broader moral obligation.

Public relations professionals are also bound by an obligation to third parties, their profession as a whole, and to themselves to preserve their own integrity. Remember, you may be painted with the same broad brush of dishonor as those you work for, even if you weren't directly responsible.

No one else knew. As ethicist Deni Elliot says, "Ethics is a first person activity." You know when you've done something wrong. You know if the people you work for are doing something wrong or are hiding a misdeed. As least you ought to know, especially if you are working in public relations. No matter what your standing within the hierarchy, you have a responsibility to your own integrity, regardless of who else knows.

Moral Excuses (Absolution)

But what if it really wasn't your fault? Most of us recognize a legitimate excuse when we hear one. Gibson suggests that the two most commonly accepted "excusing conditions" that allow a reduction in responsibility are ignorance involving fact and the inability to have done otherwise.[40] In legal theory, there are several explanations of criminal law's "excuse doctrines." Chief among them is "causal theory," which makes two general claims: The first is that the criminal law presumes that some human acts are caused by forces beyond the actor's control. The second is that the criminal law adheres to the "control principle," the moral principle that actors cannot be blamed for conduct caused by forces beyond their control. According to causal theory, these two premises explain a host of the criminal law's excuses—including (for example) the involuntary act doctrine, the irresistible impulse defense, and the duress defense. The law grants these defenses, causal theory says, because (1) it presumes that the excused conduct is caused by forces beyond the actor's control, and (2) such conduct is not blameworthy.[41]

In fact, there are several widely agreed upon excuses that are typically accepted as valid when assessing accountability.

Excusable ignorance of consequences. People tend to forgive in instances in which the outcome of an action could not reasonably have been predicted. Note that this doesn't excuse one from knowing right from wrong.

"Traditional morality and jurisprudence typically excuse persons for ignorance involving fact. Both traditional morality and established law tend not to recognize excuses grounded on ignorance of principle."[42] What this does accept is that it is often difficult to predict the outcome of some actions. Utilitarianism, for instance, directs that outcomes be predicted, but does not insist that they be exhaustively predicted. One can make educated predictions but cannot foretell the future in the sense of owning a crystal ball.

Say, for example, that you own a garden store and you sell twenty-five pounds of fertilizer to a customer you have never seen before. He then uses it to make a bomb with which he blows up a local police station. Are you accountable? Unless there is a reasonable expectation that you could have predicted that particular use of your product, the answer is usually no. We don't expect people to imagine every possible outcome of their everyday actions. No one would ever get anything done out of sheer worry if that were the case. However, we do expect people to make reasonable predictions, especially if they know their actions will affect other people. For example, a public relations campaign has been designed to bring attention to a suburban community in order to attract businesses to the area. As a result, businesses begin to move into the community; however, so does increased traffic (predictable), increased property costs (likewise predictable), and increased crime (maybe not so predictable). Can we say that the public relations firm is responsible for the increase in crime? We might—especially if there is a recognized history of crime being associated with community growth. Urban planners are acutely aware of such statistics. Why shouldn't a PR firm be?

For the most part, people recognize a legitimate excuse when they hear one, and truly unpredictable consequences are usually recognized as such. However, a false claim of ignorance is likewise easily identified. For example, when the British sports gear manufacturer Umbro decided to name its newest running shoe the "Zyklon," they ran into some unsuspected resistance. *Zyklon* literally means "cyclone" in German; however, a number of parties pointed out that during World War II, Zyklon B was the name of the gas used to exterminate millions of Jews in concentration camps. Umbro answered the outrage by expressing ignorance and claiming coincidence.[43]

External constraints. *Constraint* refers to physical imperatives, lack of alternatives, and uncontrollable circumstances. For example, if a person is coerced into doing something that he normally would not do, we tend not to blame him for that action. A bank clerk who is robbed at gunpoint is certainly responsible for the money in his till, but is not accountable for its loss. This is a physical constraint. The same would apply in a situation in which a person is constrained by a lack of alternatives. For instance, a company is ordered to comply with new EPA regulations, but the technology needed to comply hasn't been fully developed yet. The company cannot be held accountable for noncompliance until the technology is ready to go on line (as long as the company is attempting to comply in a timely fashion). Uncontrollable circumstances or, as we usually say, "circumstances beyond our control," is the third area of constraint-as-excuse. For example, if a person fails to make an important meeting because her flight was canceled, others can excuse her—even though they might be put out by the delay.

Remember, however, that causal theory holds people blameless only if their actions were truly beyond their control. If you miss a meeting because you were involved in an accident (your car was hit by someone running a stop sign), you can be held blameless. However, if you are the person who ran the stop sign, you are to blame—both for the accident and for missing the meeting.

Internal compulsion. The law holds, and most people agree, that some actions are caused by inner compulsion. This is actually another version of constraint, except that it is not caused externally. For example, the law recognizes as legitimate such excuses as kleptomania (a compulsion to steal), pyromania (a compulsion to set fires), and some types of addictions (gambling, eating, etc.) not caused physically as are drug or tobacco addiction. While this particular category of excuses may not totally satisfy, people do tend to accept them as valid.

The point is that excuses are defenses against either having to take responsibility for an action or being blamed unjustly for an action. The former defenses are typically referred to as bad excuses, the latter as good excuses. Ultimately, excuses are *reasons* and are based on the rational ability of those in a position to judge to decide on the level of accountability. Excuses mitigate harm, but they do not erase it.

Personal Accountability

Although the various roles of public relations carry with them distinctly different sets of obligations, they have in common the overriding obligation to perform within an accepted moral framework. That framework may be provided by the profession (as a code of professional standards), by the organization for which a practitioner works (as a corporate code or simply by the corporate culture itself), or by personal ethical standards. Each of these plays a part in creating the moral ground from which a true professional makes decisions.

The degree of autonomy changes with the various roles and the environment in which public relations is practiced, greatly affecting accountability.

For example, the role of advocate carries with it a primary responsibility to serve the client's purpose. This, in itself, is not, nor should it be considered, necessarily negative. Loyalty is a much-desired characteristic in employees, and as long as the moral climate of the organization within which the employee operates is conducive to the well-being of most of the parties affected by that organization's actions, that loyalty is not misplaced. However, if responsibility and accountability are not equitably shared and if the process by which they are assigned is not transparent, then problems will arise. Less autonomous actors still have responsibilities associated with their roles; however, those responsibilities will typically be dictated by their clients or employers. This is especially important to understand if the public relations practitioner works within a hierarchically structured environment. The more bureaucratic the structure, the more likely that problems with assigning accountability will occur. We must realize that not every actor is blameworthy, especially if the actor's autonomy is limited by structure, process, or circumstance. Likewise, accountability for actions may be lessened as autonomy is eroded by either role or environment. However, lack of autonomy is not an excuse for avoiding accountability entirely. Only legitimate moral excuses hold actors not accountable, and only then under a fairly narrow range of conditions.

While tracing the lines of responsibility and accountability can be difficult, in the end, if one is responsible in any way for an action, then one must accept some degree of accountability. "Individuals are ultimately the authors and arbiters of their actions, for better or worse, and therefore retain ultimate responsibility for what they do."[44] While it is gratifying to see someone like Harry Truman willing to take ultimate responsibility for actions carried out on his watch, this type of magnanimity doesn't absolve others of their part in the actions that are calling for accountability. It is also difficult in these times to find a Harry Truman among those top executives who are so adept at making excuses and passing the buck. The role of public relations in general, regardless of environment, is not only to provide a professional service, but also to act with attention to the highest ethical standards. While there are certainly legitimate excuses that can be used, public relations professionals should have no need for them if they are doing their jobs properly.

3

The Ethics of Communicating With and About Difference in a Changing Society

Larissa A. Grunig and Elizabeth L. Toth

Human knowledge always is connected to and driven by a set of interests of an emancipatory nature, according to the philosopher Jürgen Habermas (as cited in Jones and Jonasdottir).[1] This chapter is concerned with the empowerment of women and people of color in public relations. It is also concerned with the empowerment of diverse publics vis-à-vis the seemingly powerful organizations with which they are interdependent. As a result, the chapter uses feminism—often considered a philosophy of liberation—as its theoretical framework.[2]

In fact, no applied philosophical discourse—feminist or otherwise—would be adequate without concern for any oppression that has been a part of the foundation of the public relations field and its development over time. In public relations, the philosophers' tools have been applied at least in a preliminary sense to explore the structures that have oppressed diverse practitioners. In her introduction of a positive-relativist philosophy of public relations, Larissa Grunig concentrated on the practice of public relations rather than on issues of race or sex while still acknowledging that minorities and women matter.[3] Her philosophy, unique to public relations but based on the work of the education scholar Morris L. Bigge, is an affirmative one.[4] Growth and learning are key. It further assumes that the relationships between publics and their environment are interactive. The philosophy conceives of internal and external stakeholders as neither totally active, self-determined, and autonomous nor totally reactive, passive recipients of messages. It further holds that their behavior is not determined by prior causes. Instead, it sees their behavior as dependent more on what Bigge called "situational choice." In sum, L. Grunig's philosophy of positive relativism is interactive, affirming, and relational in nature.[5] Thus, this worldview seems ideally suited to public relations—which is, after all, all about relationships between organizations and their diverse publics.

L. Grunig, Elizabeth Toth, and Linda Hon developed the argument that, normatively, public relations is about understanding and valuing the perceptions of publics inside and outside the organization.[6] The goal, as they explained it, is collaborating with the organization's strategic constituencies: employees, labor unions, community members, regulators, suppliers, customers, shareholders, competitors, the media, and activist groups.

When public relations professionals are successful in developing and enhancing relationships with these vital publics, they contribute to organizational effectiveness overall. How? By reducing the threats inherent in hostile elements of the environment and by building on the strengths of supportive stakeholders. As L. Grunig, Toth, and Hon concluded, "In other words, public relations is the organizational function responsible for establishing and maintaining relationships with publics."[7]

James Grunig called this form of public relations "the two-way symmetrical model" and "collaborative advocacy."[8] Two-way symmetrical public relations uses social science research methods to achieve mutual understanding and two-way communication rather than one-way persuasion. J. Grunig argued that two-way symmetry is a public relations orientation that "balanced self-interests with the interests of others in a give-and-take process that can waver between advocacy and collaboration."[9] This chapter considers the issues of collaborative advocacy when communicating with difference: the White female majority of public relations practitioners and the increasingly diverse groups or publics on which organizations depend for support.

Public Relations, Oppression, and Changing Demographics

As early as the 1980s, research was establishing how diverse practitioners, educators, and students have been oppressed by societal, academic, and organizational structures. For example, a special issue of the *Public Relations*

Review, edited by L. Grunig, featured a critique of the monolithic White male perspective found in the typical public relations department, firm, and classroom of that era.[10] The International Association of Business Communicators (IABC) commissioned a two-part series of studies called the "Velvet Ghetto" for women in public relations.[11] A cover story in the *Public Relations Journal* concentrated on the oppressed status of minority practitioners at that same time.[12]

This chapter explores whether selected approaches to public relations represent an ethical (rather than merely politically correct and pragmatic) approach to relationship building between communicators and their myriad publics in this time of growing multiculturalism. Because public relations enacts a boundary-spanning role between the organization and its constituencies, the chapter emphasizes the part that communication managers—in particular—play in relationships. Throughout, and because the majority of public relations practitioners are women, the chapter questions any organizational values that would oppress either those women or the diverse publics with which they communicate.

Public relations becomes increasingly complex as publics become increasingly diverse—a trend seen not only in the United States but also around the world. As a result, the 1990s saw the establishment of "diversity" as an autonomous research domain in the literature of organizations, not just public relations. However, scholars Patrizia Zanoni and Maddy Janssens pointed out that the conceptualization of diversity "lacks rigour, theoretical development and historical specificity."[13]

U.S. citizens of non-White racioethnicity represent one-third of the population, "a mix of primarily black [sic], Hispanic and Asian ethnic groups."[14] According to the U.S. Census Bureau, as cited in a recent demographic study, "non-Hispanic Whites made up 69 percent of the population in 2000, a number that is steadily falling." Because 80% of the U.S. non-Hispanic White population is aged fifty or older, this study projects that the U.S. population of non-Hispanic Whites will fall to 50% by 2050.

Given the increasing diversity of the U.S. population, it is ironic that public relations practitioners who must meet the challenge of building increasingly multicultural relationships are a White female majority not in the more influential managerial public relations positions. The percentage of women in public relations varies from 60% to 70% depending on the categories and samples that are reported. For example, a recent study reported that 71.1% of a 2000 sample of Public Relations Society of America (PRSA) members were female and, for the whole sample of 864 participants, 89.1% were White, European Americans.[15] Public relations scholars Julie Andsager and Stacey Hust reported from a 2002 *PR Week* opinion study that 69% of the practitioners surveyed were female.[16]

The Bureau of Labor Statistics reported that in 2002, 36% of the advertising, marketing, and public relations managers were women. Of the public relations specialists, 67% were women.[17] Donnalyn Pompper used U.S. Bureau of Labor Statistics for 2000 to determine that "African American women hold only 4.5 percent of management and public relations jobs as compared to White women (39%) and White men (48.3%)."[18]

Women in public relations reported being underrepresented in the managerial public relations positions and overrepresented as public relations technicians in the Bureau of Labor Statistics until 2003. Then, the Bureau of Labor Statistics changed its classification of detailed occupational categories. The Bureau deleted the advertising, marketing, and public relations manager category and added an advertising and promotions manager category and a marketing and sales manager category, thus eliminating "public relations" as a managerial occupation. In this new set of occupational categories, women made up approximately 66% of the public relations specialist category.[19] However, the Bureau reported for its public relations specialist category in 2004 that approximately 60% of full-time wage and salary public relations specialists were women.[20] This change suggests the male public relations practitioners previously in the manager category have been shifted to the public relations specialist category.

The loss of the public relations manager category in the Bureau of Labor Statistics reports makes it difficult to assess public relations roles and gender. On the other hand, surveys such as those of PRSA members and of *PR Week* samples may overestimate women's participation because women are more likely than men to participate in surveys about gender issues. However, the weight of the many studies that indicate a White female majority is not in dispute. The debate now centers on why women public relations practitioners are underrepresented in strategic management roles.

Given this shifting balance between the sexes and among racioethnic groups, it is vital to discuss the very meaning of "diversity." Diversity is broader than characteristics such as sex, class, age, sexual orientation, ethnicity, race, physical ability, and appearance. Appearance, also called "lookism," refers to others' tendency to focus more (either positively or negatively) on one's appearance than on one's job performance. Women certainly may be guilty of lookism, but at least one participant in L. Grunig, Toth, and Hon's focus group research considered men's focusing on women's physical attributes the "ultimate power play" to demean women's professionalism.[21]

R. Roosevelt Thomas, Jr., an expert in the management of diversity, considered each employee, each stockholder, and each activist as different.[22] Diversity, according to Thomas, is not a group phenomenon whose category represents an essential difference from others. Similarly, Zanoni and Janssens determined that diversity is a social construction that reflects power differences.[23] The implication for the organizational setting of concern to this chapter is that individual employees, for example, are not undifferentiated members of the group they represent but are accorded subjectivity and differing degrees of agency. Unfortunately, today's dominant stereotypes tend to erase the agency of many diverse employees and members of external publics as well.

Also troubling from an ethical standpoint is that management too often perceives diverse publics—especially employees—as means to an organizational end. As Zanoni and Janssens explained it: "Diverse employees are reduced to compliant, flexible workers perfectly fitting the hegemonic economic discourse. They are positively constructed only in as far as they are a means of reaching specific organizational ends."[24] For example, a public relations firm may hire one minority practitioner to carry out public relations work for minority clients, not considering that that practitioner can help with clients from a broad spectrum of racial and ethnic backgrounds. This practice is called "pigeonholing."

Feminist and Organizational Values

The discussion of ethical, collaborative advocacy needs to begin with a clear understanding of values. Values are deeply held beliefs, perhaps too engrained to be noticeable in organizational communication and decision making. Values direct managers' choices about what is considered right or wrong. For example, why is it right to follow the orders of the more powerful managers in a corporation? What value does this reflect? Hierarchy? Efficiency? Competition? Individualism? This set of values makes up a dominance of beliefs, which the communication scholar Lana Rakow called "the White male model."[25]

Diverse standpoints—be they ones of gender, race, ethnicity, sexual orientation, religion, or combinations of these—reflect values about what is important to uphold. For example, L. Grunig, Toth, and Hon have argued that feminist values include "altruism, commitment, equality, equity, ethics, fairness, forgiveness, integrity, justice, loyalty, morality, nurturance, perfection, quality of life, standards, tolerance, and cherishing children."[26]

Organizations, like those of public relations practitioners and scholars, embrace values that are rarely noticeable unless or until the values come into conflict with individual values. L. Grunig, Toth, and Hon have stated that organizational structures and the values they represent have caused women workers to make disproportionate sacrifices.[27] For example, organizations may value having employees at work from 8:30 a.m. until the work is done, Monday through Friday, with one-size-fits-all policies for absences. These expectations often conflict with those of women who wish to integrate their desire to raise children and to care for elderly relatives. Although some organizations have family-friendly policies permitting flexible hours and work schedules, women continue to carry the stress of trying to integrate their values toward work and family life.

Examples from exploratory focus group research illustrate the different values men and women in public relations may bring to the structural demands of their workplace.[28] The following quotes show how both women and men tend to be "on call" all the time—but the men refer to the office and the women to their homes, in addition to the office. One man said about client work, "You are expected to be accessible at all times." Another man said, "How many of us have cell phones and pagers and check e-mail on Sunday afternoon?" By contrast, a woman said, "They are very understanding about me leaving early, but it's been told to me I'm not going to get a promotion anytime soon." Another woman expressed the importance of valuing family as well as work this way: "We women, we refuse to shut ourselves off; we just can't." Another said, "You've got your job at work, then, you've got your job at home." Women spoke of resisting organizational demands by starting independent companies, changing jobs, or "strategically subverting communication with the employer," as one participant in the focus groups put it.

The feminist scholar Julie O'Neil surveyed female and male corporate public relations practitioners to test whether the organizational context disadvantaged female public relations practitioners. She reported that "being female had a negative effect on their influence on organizational decision-making because of their reduced formal structural power."[29] O'Neill concluded that "female corporate public relations practitioners must deal with the stress of having to present a persona that is compatible with a male-dominated dominant coalition, and most do not have the benefit of having a direct report relationship with either the CEO, president, or chairman."[30]

Organizational values that oppress individual differences also lead to stress and perhaps acquiescence as well. Two scholars of public relations recently surveyed public relations professionals working in male-dominated organizations and in gender-integrated organizations to determine whether an appropriate ratio of diversity among employees helped improve women's experiences in top management positions. They concluded, "A gender balance in powerful positions has positive effects on work performance, career growth, and confidence of female practitioners, as well as indicated a more supportive environment for women."[31]

Female public relations practitioners somehow contend with their own oppression as well as perform the role of collaborative advocate. Members of the PRSA's Committee on Work, Life, and Gender Issues (CWLG) have held professional-development seminars at the annual conference featuring organizations that have developed internal support for diverse employees and the role of public relations in brokering these best places for employees, including public relations employees, to work. Speakers have come from Kodak, Hewlett-Packard, Syracuse University, Chevron Texaco, and the SAS Institute. For example, Kathy Burke, former work-life strategy manager at Hewlett-Packard (HP), stated that at HP, "the core value is respect for the individual because this adds value to the organization by improving productivity, commitment, creativity and customer service."[32] John Dillon Riley, a manager of employee assistance for Chevron, spoke about the company's commitment to work-life programs and practices for 53,000 employees in 180 countries, 65% of whom work in safety-sensitive positions.[33] "Consider how important it is for our hundreds of tanker truck drivers to make safe deliveries," he said. "We want them to have the health and personal support they need to get our products and services to your local gas station successfully."[34] In some cultures, this will mean extending health benefits to second and third wives.

The Relationship between Diversity and Effectiveness

The theme of the 2005 World Public Relations Festival was diversity: "Communicating for Diversity, with Diversity, in Diversity." By this title, organizers of the festival—led by Italian practitioner and educator Toni Muzi Falconi and the Global Alliance for Public Relations—explained their triple concept of diversity as follows. First, diversity is a value that, like any other, must be balanced with and by others (without doing what Muzi Falconi called "exceeding into cultural relativism").[35] Second, different relationship models need to be developed with specific publics or individuals (or both). Third, public relations practitioners should take advantage of the multifaceted tools and channels of communication available to them as they reach out to their myriad publics.

Muzi Falconi urged conference attendees to adopt this framework—based on what he called a "tendentially symmetric relationship model"—for professional practice rather than any approach consisting of "communicating to" publics and based on stereotypes.[36] The resulting ethical framework for communication, then, is characterized as one-with-one or one-with-few. As Muzi Falconi emphasized, "You cannot pretend to effectively communicate with all people all the time, and . . . an inevitable consequence of diversity is that you must focus on communicating with your stakeholder publics without pretending to be . . . effective in communicating with everyone else."[37]

Are these the ways in which organizations traditionally have looked at ethics and social responsibility? Arguably, they are not. Instead, the organizational literature typically depicts the business case for diversity: the economic values of a diverse workforce and the practices that help organizations innovate and solve problems. The dean of the graduate school at UCLA expressed well this pragmatic view that many espouse: "Corporations are learning that it's bad business to ignore women and minorities, both because they wield growing economic clout and because they represent a rich pool of managerial talent."[38] This quote suggests not only the economic rationality but also the means-to-an-end mentality highlighted earlier.

To the human resources and market arguments LaForce mentioned, remember the legal considerations articulated by a distinguished international counselor in public relations: "In the USA particularly the need [for skilled internal relations experts] is accentuated by the epidemic of lawsuits brought by employees who claim they have suffered discrimination in hiring practices or have not had opportunity for promotion."[39]

The legal standard is the minimal standard. Ethics represents a higher standard toward which public relations professionals must strive—both for effectiveness in their role as boundary spanners and for their self-identity as professionals.

Many public relations practitioners seek a professional ethical identity for the public relations field. Professionalism, as discussed in the public relations literature, represents the idea of having a "specialized body of knowledge, an emphasis on public service and social responsibility, a sense of autonomy, and peer-monitoring through agreed-upon norms and prescribed behaviors."[40]

Most public relations societies have norms or codes of ethics that prescribe respect for diversity and cultural difference. For example, the International Association of Business Communicators code of ethics holds in Article Four that "professional communicators are sensitive to cultural values and beliefs."[41] The International Public Relations Association code of ethics states that members shall "pay due regard to, and uphold, human dignity, and . . . recognize the right of each individual to judge for himself/herself."[42] The Global Alliance's Protocol on Public Relations bases its ethical principles "on the fundamental value and dignity of the individual." It also dedicates its membership to "the goals of better communication, understanding, and cooperation among diverse individuals, groups, and institutions of society."[43] PRSA does not address diversity directly in its values or principles, but it does mention fairness to all and respect for all opinions and support for the right of free expression.[44]

Professional identity evolves through the process of group collaboration on the beliefs, expectations, and values found to be important by the group. The international public relations associations, for example, lead in recognizing the importance of diversity and cultural difference—perhaps because their members frequently have crossed cultural borders.

To succeed in a global world, public relations professionals must find ways to learn and communicate about difference. This carries global and local moral obligations. Public relations practitioners must balance what they say and do abroad with home country expectations of business behavior. Communication scholars Juan-Carlos Molleda, Colleen Connolly Ahern, and Candace Quinn found, in a content analysis of news, that a Canadian corporation accused of bribing local officials in the small southern African nation of Lesotho quickly became known throughout Canada. As a consequence, the corporation was disbarred from the World Bank and prohibited from operating in other developing nations, even though it claimed innocence of wrongdoing. The authors illustrated how quickly actions in one culture can become known and interpreted negatively in another culture:

> The transnational firm must somehow prove its innocence or it will risk losing many things—not just the profits from the Lesotho dams and other future business projects, but also its reputation and credibility among its multiple publics in Canada and throughout the world business community.[45]

Members of professional public relations groups such as the Global Alliance are providing ethical norms and standards to follow when communicating across cultures, but public relations professionals have self-identities as well. These include gender identity, which has been described as "one of the earliest, and . . . one of the most basic, components of self-identity."[46]

Bey-Ling Sha, a scholar of gender and public relations, has described self-identity as being composed of avowed and ascribed beliefs, attitudes, values, behaviors, and experiences. Like other scholars, she has argued that avowed identity is asserted by the individual, whereas ascribed identity is externally imposed.[47] Women avow building relationships and having feelings, behaviors that organizations desire in public relations workers. But organizations also devalue women by ascribing to them other values, such as being less assertive or aggressive than men. The result is that women encounter resistance when they seek positions in strategic management.

Sha made the point that organizations may devalue women because of their physical and sexual attractiveness, which are viewed as "professional liabilities. . . . We see the rejection of sexuality as 'protecting' the professional reputation of the field."[48] Women have tried to "dress for success" as a means of not calling attention to themselves. Sha pointed to society's still deeply held belief that women are "powerful sexual temptresses who pose danger to males."[49] She argued that women in public relations should not deny their avowed identity of feminine sexuality, "as if gender differences don't matter, when in fact they often do."[50]

Pompper offered an example of ascribed identity for African American women in public relations, who often felt devalued by their employers. They battled racial stereotypes that were both subtle and overt. Instead of resisting these unfair assessments, the African American women spoke of compensating by "setting the bar very high, working harder, arriving early and leaving late, and offering something more."[51] Because employers or professional societies oppress the self-avowed identities of White and African American women in public relations, they seem unlikely to value other diverse groups with whom they need to have effective relationships.

Just as some people only obviously tolerate differences (the minimum), others value differences (the ideal). To the founding director of the American Institute for Managing Diversity, the distinction is often between unsuccessful and successful management of diversity in and around organizations.[52]

Building successful relationships with important publics often depends on what one author has called "requisite variety."[53] In fact, requisite variety is a defining characteristic of effective organizations. The idea of requisite variety is that, to succeed, organizations must reflect the diversity of their environments. The global research team studying qualities of excellent public relations in what has come to be called the Excellence Project interpreted requisite variety as follows:

> Practitioners from both genders . . . and from different racial, ethnic, and cultural backgrounds are needed in an excellent public relations department—not just for the benefit of these diverse practitioners but because they make the organization more effective.[54]

Does requisite variety guarantee effective public relations? No, but providing opportunities for women and racioethnic minorities does create a hospitable environment for excellence—one conducive to using human resources to their fullest. Empowering minorities and women in public relations has been shown to result in greater satisfaction with the organization and greater support for its goals.[55] Does requisite variety mean that workforces must have a one-on-one match or proportional representation inside the organization with each diverse factor in their environments? No, but being the eyes and ears of the organization outside its boundaries—a typical metaphor for what practitioners do—is accomplished more effectively and with greater impetus when women and people of color are empowered. As a senior manager of an engineering research agency included in the Excellence study explained it, "We don't worry as much about the numbers we have of women, Blacks, and Hispanics. The main thing is in the process of making decisions, that we get the opinions of people and staff with different backgrounds. That way, we come up with better solutions."[56]

Understanding this, the leading public relations association in the United States, the PRSA, has established a Multicultural Communications Section. Early on, when it was elevated from a committee on multicultural affairs to sectional status within the society, its newsletter offered members these benefits: networking opportunities, national conference activities, scholarships, an information clearinghouse, quarterly newsletters, a directory of diverse practitioners, and professional development seminars and workshops.[57] These efforts are designed in part to overcome constraints that face people of color in public relations, as identified in a 1988 study by the Atlanta Inter-Association Council: stereotyping, cultural differences that are not valued or are mismanaged by supervisors, the real or perceived "White male club" that has controlled the field, and unwritten rules for success that minorities may not know.[58] Activities of the Multicultural Communications Section provide for networking, mentoring, role modeling, education, and awareness.

Despite their numbers, women continue to benefit from such strategies designed to help public relations practitioners—whether female or people of color—make the transition from technical roles to managerial roles. Since the late 1990s, women have represented about two-thirds of the workforce in this field in the United States. However, because of factors such as socialization and sexism, they remain underrepresented at the highest levels of organizational decision making. Research has established that women and men are equally successful in top communication roles, but women have a harder time than men gaining the experiences needed for that senior slot.[59]

Equality is a value held dear by many people in Western societies. As Zanoni and Janssens suggested, the feminist "ethics of care" based on relationships may be more relevant to public relations practice than is the "ethics of justice" based on abstract rules.[60] Nevertheless, equal opportunity for women—the majority of today's practitioners in public relations—should mean that the communication function will not be constrained to day-to-day technical tasks such as writing press releases and editing in-house publications but may be elevated to the managerial or even to the executive level.[61]

Why does position within the organization matter? Only by being in the room when critical decisions are being made can the head of the public relations function fully represent the perspectives of the publics on which the organization has consequences—or vice versa. This notion of reciprocal consequences, as J. Grunig initially pointed out, is what makes a public strategic to an organization.[62] In other words, not all groups in the organization's external environment are equally important to it. As public relations managers and the most senior members of their organization make decisions about whom to communicate with, the notion of consequences figures prominently. In fact, to J. Grunig consequences actually create publics. He explained:

> When organizations have consequences on people outside the organization, those consequences create problems for the people affected. Some people *detect* the consequences—recognize a problem. They become members of a public. Thus, consequences create the conditions needed for publics to form. The presence of publics, in turn, creates a public relations problem for the organization.[63]

Philosophical Approaches to Diversity and Public Relations

Thus, as well, consequentialist ethics would seem critical to the practice of public relations. Many philosophers have judged the moral rightness of decisions or actions based on their consequences. This consequentialist theory, also called *teleological,* considers the ratio of good to evil that the action produces. The philosophy is often referred to as "the greatest good for the greatest number." But just who is experiencing that good outcome? If we ourselves are the beneficiaries, then the consequentialist theory is known as *egoism.* Egoism determines the morality of an action based solely on the consequences for ourselves—our own (long-term) best interest.

More useful for public relations as a management function is the *utilitarian* branch of consequentialist ethics. The standard of morality in this approach is the promotion of everyone's best interest. However, since organizations typically experience pressure from numerous constituencies—often with contradictory demands—promoting *every* public's interest is difficult to impossible. So, organizations may hope to satisfy the majority stakeholders. This approach, the greatest good for the greatest number, causes concern for the many and diverse minority interests that may go unheard at the highest level of organizational decision making. It also emphasizes the ends: Possible actions are weighed against the likely outcomes for the majority at stake.

Rather than emphasizing such consequences, the Western philosophy of nonconsequentialism—deontology—emphasizes obligations or rules. Here, the rightness of an action is determined not by its consequences but by whether the action conforms to certain principles. Codes of ethics, such as PRSA's Code of Ethics, result from deontological, or rule-based, theory.

According to the theories of deontologist Immanuel Kant, the ethical person (or organization) does something because of moral duty and not because of self-interest.[64] To Kant, moral duty was a "categorical imperative": an action that applies at all times and in all places and that must be obeyed by all rational people. He believed in the importance of treating people as ends in themselves, rather than as means to an (organizational) end.

Other duties typically associated with deontology include what the author William Ross has described as fidelity, gratitude, justice, beneficence, self-improvement, and nonmaleficence.[65] Public relations scholars have added the obligations of dialogue, disclosure or transparency, and symmetry. Incorporating these rules into public relations practice should result in increasingly high-quality communication relationships.[66] The model of two-way symmetrical or balanced communication is especially important in helping build a participative culture inside organizations.[67] The best relationships between organizations and all their publics, internal and external, are two-way and symmetrical. That, to the Excellence researchers, means "the relationships balance the interests of the organizations with the interests of publics on which the organization has consequences and that have consequences on the organization."[68]

Based on these rules and the importance of consequences of organizational decisions on publics, J. Grunig and L. Grunig proposed an ethical theory for public relations that combines both teleological and deontological perspectives.[69] From the former approach, they reasoned that the ethical practitioner would ask what consequences potential organizational decisions have on publics. Based on the deontological approach, they emphasized the moral obligation to disclose those consequences on the publics that are affected and to engage in dialogue with them about the potential decisions. Later, the public relations scholar Shannon Bowen began to develop a theory of ethical decision making for public relations that was based entirely on deontology.[70]

In this increasingly diverse world, deontology makes more sense than utilitarianism for two main reasons. First, consequentialist ethics favors the majority over the minority; second, the effect of emphasizing consequences is the tendency to treat people as ends, rather than valuing them in and of themselves.

Twenty-first Century Standards for Communicating with and about Difference

Philosophical and feminist thought, taken together, represent a forceful challenge to any field.[71] L. Grunig's fledgling positive-relativist philosophy, with its emphasis on the agency rather than the objectification of diverse publics and on interactive rather than one-way communication, affirms that women and people of color do matter in developing relationships.[72] The feminist ethic to which the authors of this chapter adhere calls for nurturing relationships and caring about others—those inside and those outside the organization. Like positive relativism, it is based more on moral than on economic values.

Fortunately, a large body of literature has established that moral responsibility and profitability can go hand in hand. So, ethical public relations can equate with effective public relations. Valuing the perspectives of publics of diverse racioethnicity, gender, age, class, physical ability, sexual orientation, and even outward appearance leads away from mere assimilation and "correctness" and toward innovative ideas, the potential of a larger market, exploitation of personal strengths, reduction of hostility, job satisfaction, and avoidance of the fallout of legal complaints—in short, competitive advantage.

These are all real payoffs for the organization. They are not merely "politically correct," which suggests that fairness to one comes about through unfairness to another, thus causing divisiveness. Rather than being a fad, the issue of diversity is on its way to becoming what Muzi Falconi called "an operative enhancement of our profession."[73] It represents more than a powerful force for top managers to exploit in relentless pursuit of their goals.

Valuing diversity is also the right thing to do. Organizations adopting a deontological, nonessentialist concept of diversity see their publics as more than means of attaining their ends. They reject the instrumental philosophy. Instead, they seek to minimize the power differences that too often have put women, young people, old people, those from minority races and cultures, the so-called under classes, those who are too plain or too good-looking, and the physically challenged in a one-down position based on their supposed reference group. They expect their public relations managers to maximize the potential of two-way, dialogical, balanced communication with publics that, more and more, may be different from themselves.

4

Negotiating Relationships
With Activist Publics

Linda Hon

R esponsible advocacy with activist groups is both a public relations
challenge and opportunity for most organizations. A body of research
in public relations has developed to guide practitioners' efforts, yet public
relations textbooks offer few examples of where theory matches reality.
Many situations seem to demonstrate how organizations were caught off
guard and ended up reacting to a situation rather than proactively antici-
pating and managing activism for the long-term best interest of the organization and the publics involved.

Examples of negative publicity related to activism abound. To name just
a few high-visibility cases, Wal-Mart has faced protests from store union
organizers dissatisfied with working and pay conditions;[1] numerous communities have targeted the company with accusations that the store undermines local businesses;[2] McDonald's has been the target of lawsuits that
charge the company with selling unhealthy foods that lead to obesity;[3] and
clothing retailer Abercrombie and Fitch has been criticized for racist hiring
practices and offending many Asian Americans with a derogatory picture
and slogan printed on one of the company's T-shirts.[4]

This chapter discusses what activism is and why responsible and effective advocacy with activist publics is crucial for organizations. The chapter

also provides a step-by-step model of how to responsibly and effectively communicate with activist publics. Although this model is meant to be two-way, the chapter takes the perspective of the organization or client facing activist pressure. However, the chapter argues that activist publics should use the same ethical approach for advocacy that is prescribed here. In other words, activist publics should communicate with the organizations they target in the same manner that these activists would prefer to be treated.

Public relations scholar Elizabeth Dougall[5] pointed out that an "organization-centric" approach to understanding activism has been criticized for contributing to a biased body of knowledge that prescribes "organizational 'solutions' to activist 'problems.'"[6] It is not this chapter's intent to mirror this tendency, but rather to explain how organizations can ethically and effectively communicate and build quality relationships with activist publics. In other words, the presence of activism provides an *opportunity* for the public relations function to help organizations be more effective and socially responsible.

The major assumption underlying this chapter is that responsible and effective advocacy is analogous to the strategies prescribed by relationship theory in public relations that underlie a two-way symmetrical model of public relations.[7] In this model, the role of public relations is to help organizations understand and respond to the voices of all their publics.[8] The focus here, of course, is activist publics. The chapter stresses that the ethical practice of public relations is enacted in the day-to-day choices, expressed through communication strategies and tactics, organizations make about how to treat the groups of people upon whom they have consequences (and vice versa). In other words, the value of public relations to society is tied to the choices practitioners and other managers make about public relations at the program, functional, and organizational levels.[9]

Public relations scholar Shannon Bowen, who specializes in researching ethics, argued that a two-way symmetrical model of public relations is congruent with a deontological ethical perspective that is grounded in the "moral duty to do what is right based on universal norms of obligation."[10] To make this point, she cited Ron Pearson's[11] argument that organizations have a moral duty to engage in dialogue and Jim Grunig and Larissa Grunig's assertion that two-way symmetrical communication is a way of satisfying that obligation.[12] As Bowen explained,

> The organization should communicate the considerations it employs in its decision-making process to those involved in the issue as well as use input from those publics. . . . This approach is inherently ethical. Use of this approach should help avert problems for the organization by allowing it to communicate considerations to and from publics in a symmetrical manner.[13]

Public relations scholars such as Juliet Roper have questioned whether two-way symmetrical communication is a realistic ideal.[14] She argued that many public relationships are by nature asymmetrical given that organizations tend to have the upper hand relative to their publics in terms of resources (e.g., money, political influence, access to mass media). This power differential allows organizations to choose a strategy of responding to activist concerns by providing small concessions that deflect criticism. Yet, while doing so, organizations fail to change any of the underlying societal conditions that lead to such marked power imbalances, thereby exacerbating them in the long run.

It is not the point of this chapter to argue that issues raised about institutional constraints on activist publics' ability to engage in two-way symmetrical public relations with organizations and organizations' sincerity about doing so have no merit. Rather, the framework presented here is meant to provide an alternative, normative model that suggests practical communication strategies and examples of tactics for enacting the ethical role of public relations in organizations. The examples provided demonstrate that this model leads to responsible and effective advocacy when communicating with activist publics.

One could contend that many activist publics, such as the internationally visible environmental group Greenpeace, are as powerful and sophisticated in their public relations efforts as the organizations they target. Others have made the point that some activist publics, such as the underground organization Animal Liberation Front, are so extreme and unethical in their tactics (e.g., burning down scientific laboratories) that they should be considered terrorist organizations.[15]

At the same time, new media forms, such as blogs, have the potential to level communication access by providing anyone with an Internet connection and a computer an unfiltered communication forum. For example, blogger Jeff Jarvis has received international publicity for his activist "Dell Hell" posts that detail his problems with a Dell computer.[16] Dell has responded by making significant and voluntary improvements in its customer service department.

The example from Dell illustrates another assumption guiding this chapter—organizations and activist groups are engaged in good faith efforts to negotiate genuine solutions to problems. A fundamental principle guiding the ethical practice of public relations is that organizations have an obligation to communicate with any group upon which they have consequences.[17] Public relations scholar J. Grunig linked this notion of consequences to the branch of ethical theory known as teleology.[18] An organizational value system grounded in teleology would expect public relations to address the consequences the organization has had on publics and address the needs of publics.[19] When the organization violates this value system, the public relations function has a moral duty to counsel the organization to change course. Otherwise, responsible and effective advocacy becomes impossible. At the same time, if an activist public dismisses its ethical obligation to communicate, the organization must consider whether it is possible and desirable to work toward encouraging the activist public to alter its position.

Larry Smith, president of the Institute for Crisis Management, warned organizations that some activist groups may have a hidden agenda: "A lot of activist groups are interested only in making noise and drawing attention to their cause. They don't actually want the problem to go away, because if it did, they wouldn't have justification for existing anymore."[20]

Similarly, activist groups have accused organizations of being disingenuous. Making this point, public relations executive Mary Ann Pires provided practitioners guidance that is at the heart of responsible and effective advocacy for organizations. She recommended that in their outreach to activists, practitioners remember the *Scout Handbook* advice about honesty and warned against the pitfalls of organizational arrogance:

> Activists have their own networks too. Their grapevine sings, too. If you use them, mislead them, patronize them, or in any other way attempt to "cash in" on the relationships, they'll remember when the next issue arises. Conversely, equitable, honest brokering will hold you in good stead.[21]

Defining Activism and Its Link to Public Relations

L. Grunig was one of the first researchers in public relations to empirically link activism to public relations theory and practice. She defined an activist public as "a group of two or more individuals who organize to influence another public or publics through action that may include education, compromise, persuasion, pressure tactics, or force."[22] It is important to note that, in her reference to a public, she did not mean the "general" public. Instead, publics are specific groups of people who form around issues.[23] The key word for understanding why and who becomes part of a public is *consequences*—publics form when organizations and clients have consequences on groups of people.[24] And, when these groups of people engage in communication and direct action targeted at the organization, they can be thought of as activist publics.

Activist publics can vary in size and degree of formality. Some might think of Julia Butterfly Hill as a one-person activist public. Hill lived for 738 days in the canopy of an ancient redwood tree to protest destruction of old-growth forests.[25] An example of a larger group is an international consortium such as the World Conservation Union, whose members represent 140 countries. Some activist publics are loosely aggregated and may disband once their issue has been resolved. An example here is a group of citizens gathering signatures for a petition to be delivered to an elected representative. Other activist publics are well established and have a formal membership base, such as the U.S. civil rights group, the National Association for the Advancement of Colored People. A special type of activist public is the NGO, or nongovernmental organization. These organizations are self-governing, private, and not-for-profit organizations that are geared toward improving quality-of-life issues among disadvantaged people throughout the world.[26]

Organizations and Autonomy

Communicating with activist publics is important for organizations because of the notion of autonomy.[27] Autonomy, in the context of public relations, means that organizations would like to be free to pursue their missions without crises, problems, and interference from groups of people that challenge the organization's goals. The presence of activism in an organization's environment usually means that some group is dissatisfied with some organizational practice and seeks to pressure the organization to change. In other words, the group is trying to constrain the organization's autonomy. And, of course, since organizations in open democracies cannot operate as an island unto themselves, they must respond to this pressure—doing so is the only ethical approach. Responding is also more effective because a "no comment" stance typically does not make the problem go away.

When organizations fail to respond to activism in a responsible and effective way, activist publics tend to take their concerns elsewhere. For example, these publics often turn to the media to air their viewpoints. Often planned with shock value in mind, protests may be staged with the explicit purpose of gaining media attention and public sympathy. As noted earlier, activist publics also have a powerful tool in the Internet, which can be used to publicize their concerns and encourage people to engage in grassroots activism such as donating, volunteering, signing petitions, writing legislators, and boycotting companies. Activist publics also may pursue litigation, which can be time-consuming and expensive for the organization. And, these publics might try to further constrain the organization's autonomy by demanding the government impose sanctions or regulations. Industry regulations, in effect, force the company to comply with the mandates of others, which is a less desirable position for organizations to be in than negotiating solutions themselves. Most important, though, failing to respond responsibly and effectively to activist pressure drains organizational resources and may compromise the organization's most valuable asset, organizational reputation.

Writing for the U.S. industry magazine *PR Week,* Douglas Quenqua described the human and financial costs when organizations wind up on the wrong side of an activist group:

> You can lose customers, public support, market share, employees, government funding, contracts, peace of mind, or even your job. All it takes is a few picket signs outside your front door to make people stop and think about whether they wouldn't feel better giving their business to someone not incurring the wrath of the righteous.[28]

A Model of Responsible and Effective Advocacy with Activist Publics

Fortunately, public relations theory about public relationships provides the lens through which practitioners can understand activism and how their organizations should respond. Before addressing the communication strategies suggested by relationship theory, it is important to note that organizations and activist publics are groups of people in a public relationship. This relationship forms because of the consequences that groups of people have on each other.[29] For example, energy companies are often the targets of activism because these companies have environmental consequences on the communities in which they operate. So, these companies and people in their communities become partners in a public relationship.

Step One—Environmental Scanning

As with any public relations plan, the first step for responsible and effective advocacy with activist publics is conducting research. This first-step research is called environmental scanning, which is a general term for any secondary or primary research that helps organizations figure out "What's going on?" in their internal and external environments that might affect the organization.[30] Environmental scanning can take many forms, such as formal polls and surveys, or it can be more casual, such as monitoring media coverage of industry trends and issues. The goal here is to identify and analyze issues and develop a strategic plan for building relationships with potential activist publics before the management of the issue begins to affect the organization's autonomy.

Step Two—Identifying Publics

An understanding of the issues affecting any organization provides insight into the levels of activism the organization might face in managing these issues. The second step, then, in a model of responsible and effective advocacy becomes identifying publics based on whom the organization has consequences (or vice versa) for the issues suggested by environmental scanning. These publics are the groups of people an organization has a public relationship with or with whom they should be working to develop one.

Before examining public relationships in more detail, an important point needs to be made—not all publics are alike. Public relations scholar J. Grunig has developed a situational theory of publics that tells us who is likely to communicate about an issue involving our organization.[31] The theory implies that the people most likely to become activist publics are those who recognize the organizational issue is a problem (or opportunity), feel personally involved, and believe they can do something about the issue.

Situational theory helps public relations practitioners classify all these groups according to their likely communication behavior.[32] If people are unaffected by organizational consequences, then they are unlikely to communicate with the organization. These people can be classified as non-publics, and no communication strategies and tactics should be directed to them. Latent publics are those groups of people who are affected by organizational consequences yet are not aware. Aware publics, obviously, are attuned to organizational consequences but are not necessarily communicating actively. Finally, members of active publics are those people who are aware and are actively communicating about organizational consequences.

A model of effective and responsible advocacy suggests that it is best to begin developing public relations programs for communicating with latent and aware publics. When publics are in these stages, they are more likely to be receptive to organizational efforts to build a positive relationship. Active publics may be less receptive if they have already formed negative attitudes about the organization in relation to their issue of concern. Unfortunately, too often organizations find themselves facing hostile publics that had already become active by the time the organization began to address the issue the publics formed around. And, at this point, the organization's relationship-building efforts run the risk of being "too little, too late."

Step Three—Effective Relationship Maintenance

This chapter argues that responsible and effective advocacy with activist publics is analogous to public relations strategies for building quality relationships between an organization and groups of people upon whom the organization has consequences. Before these strategies are outlined, it is important to note that effective relationship building requires two-way communication and symmetry.[33] Communication designed to negotiate relationships between an organization and an activist public must be two-way. In other words, both sides are willing to talk with one another. Symmetry means that this communication is balanced in that neither party is trying to dominate the other. The goal is listening, building understanding, and trying to find mutually beneficial solutions for dealing with the issue of concern.

Another point is that the organization and the activist public are coming "to the table" with their own position and interests. In other words, each is advocating for its point of view. It would be naïve to suggest otherwise. And, depending on for whom (the organization or the activist group) practitioners work, their obligation is to represent that side's best interest. The argument being made here, though, is that responsible and effective advocacy recognizes the ethical obligation to communicate with the other party in good faith to negotiate solutions that serve each side's interest but still preserve a positive relationship for the long haul.[34]

What Are Relationship Maintenance Strategies?

To understand how responsible and effective advocacy with activist publics is based on proactive relationship maintenance strategies, it may be useful to think of personal relationships. Any effort that someone puts into the relationship to keep it going (and perhaps make it better) can be thought of as relationship maintenance. And, the approach that people take for solving conflicts is key to relationship maintenance and often determines whether the relationship can continue or whether the relationship becomes so damaged that both sides leave feeling bad about the outcome and the other.

Public relations scholars such as Yi-Hui Huang and Ken D. Plowman have borrowed from researchers studying interpersonal communication and conflict resolution to develop a list of relationship maintenance strategies that they argue are the most effective for building and maintaining quality public relationships.[35] These strategies are explained next.

Positivity is the first relationship maintenance strategy that organizations need to practice. This strategy refers to anything an organization or public does to make the relationship more positive or enjoyable for the other party.[36]

An example of positivity related to activism comes from Texaco, Inc. After corporate executives were caught on audiotape making racist comments, the company found itself the focus of a media firestorm and intense scrutiny from governmental officials and activist publics, including U.S. civil rights leader Jesse Jackson's Rainbow/PUSH Coalition. Within six weeks, Texaco had developed a strategic plan for diversity management including specific policies and programs for improving recruitment, hiring, and workplace environment; expanding business partnering efforts; and improving retail performance in a diverse marketplace.[37] Clearly, these initiatives were designed to indicate the company was taking positive action to address diversity concerns. At the same time, this example shows that, when companies fail to anticipate and respond to emerging activist issues, they then face the greater challenge of repairing damaged public relationships.

Another important relationship maintenance strategy is *disclosure*.[38] In the context of personal relationships, friends are the people who share feelings and reveal secrets to each other. And, over time, as they do this, the relationship develops.

Thinking about the public relations context, activist publics want organizations to be open and disclose information about their mission, goals, and intentions. In other words, publics want to understand the organizations that have consequences on their lives as well as the economy and health of their community. Transparency, a term heard a lot in the business community, is just another way of thinking about disclosure. Certainly, a stance of "no comment" by organizations is neither effective nor responsible advocacy. Failure to disclose breeds suspicion that an organization has something to hide. And an unwillingness to communicate with those upon whom an organization has consequences fails the ethical test mentioned earlier.

Discussing the benefits of organizational disclosure, John Doorley, former head of corporate communications at the drug manufacturer Merck, explained how in the early 1990s he negotiated a friendship between the company and vocal AIDS activists. These protestors had accused companies like Merck of intentionally delaying innovation in AIDS drugs to maximize their profits on drugs already on the market.[39] Doorley recruited key activists to sit on a Merck advisory board and flew them to research plants where they could observe the development process for themselves. And, importantly, Merck also put some of the activists' suggestions into action, thereby avoiding the perception that the company's efforts were window dressing or thinly veiled attempts to co-opt activists.

Related to disclosure is *access*.[40] Any quality relationship is based on the notion that people in the relationship have access to one another. In other words, they make sure they are available to each other.

In a public relationship, the same principle applies. So, organizations that engage in responsible and effective advocacy with activist publics create opportunities for these publics to have access. This access could be something as simple and day-to-day as a commitment to answer e-mail and telephone inquiries promptly and directly (i.e., not filtered through organizational buffers such as secretaries and customer relations personnel, when appropriate). Other types of access may be more structured, such as interactive Web sites, town hall meetings with organizational executives, and open houses and tours of the organization.

An example of organizational access related to activism comes from Bruce Friedrich, director of vegan outreach for the People for the Ethical Treatment of Animals (PETA).[41] According to Friedrich, he formed relationships with clothing companies, including LL Bean and Eddie Bauer, which agreed to not use certain kinds of imported leather. So, when learning of violations at one of the company's retailers, PETA first calls one of its internal contacts at the companies to discuss the problem. Friedrich described what this access means for PETA:

> These are human relationships. Without a doubt, once you've established contact with a corporation and they have made improvements, you have somebody to call in the event they are doing something objectionable. This way, you also have someone to call when they have any questions.[42]

Another relationship maintenance strategy is providing *assurances,* which refers to attempts by parties in the relationship to assure other parties that they and their concerns are legitimate.[43] Assurances also might involve attempts by parties in the relationship to demonstrate their commitment to the relationship.

An example of providing assurances to activist publics is displayed by Monsanto Corporation.[44] The company has been a lightning rod for activist publics' concerns about biotechnology and genetically engineered foods. These publics have accused the organization of encouraging a scientific culture of arrogance that failed to legitimize activists' concerns about health and biodiversity issues related to genetic engineering.

The Monsanto Pledge has been one attempt to respond to these concerns. In the pledge, the company promises dialogue, transparency, and sharing. However, the clearest examples of providing assurances are found in the pledge's promises of *benefits*—"We will deliver high-quality products that are beneficial to our customers and to the environment, with sound and innovative science, and thoughtful and effective stewardship"—and *respect*—"We will respect the religious, cultural and ethical concerns of people throughout the world. The safety of our employees, the communities where we operate, our customers, consumers and the environment will be our highest priority."[45]

The effectiveness of Monsanto's efforts to provide assurances, however, may be questionable, given the industry's slow response to years of activist pressure. As the environmental group Greenpeace noted on its Web site after Monsanto announced it was backing away from further research and market introduction of genetically engineered wheat,

> Consumers and farmers have long lost confidence in the company that also gave us pesticides, PCBs, Agent Orange and GE growth hormones for cattle. It's only a matter of time when Monsanto also loses the backing they have enjoyed in certain government offices and among financial analysts.[46]

The activist group Organic Consumers Association (OCA) also has targeted Monsanto in the OCA's campaign against genetically engineered foods. The group's Web site showcases the following quote from Phil Angel, Monsanto's director of corporate communications: "Monsanto should not have to vouchsafe the safety of its food. Our interest is in selling as much of it as possible. Assuring its safety is the FDA's job."[47] The OCA Web site then goes on to list the names of federal officials, including elected officials and appointed officers at the U.S. Food and Drug Administration, Department of Agriculture, and Department of Health, who either formerly worked for Monsanto or received large campaign donations from the company. The point here is that these apparent conflicts of interest undermine the credibility of Monsanto's safety assurances and seemingly damage the company's relationship with some activist publics.

Sharing of tasks is another relationship maintenance strategy needed for effective and responsible advocacy with activist publics.[48] This strategy implies that people in a relationship share whatever responsibilities have been created by the mutual decisions made in the relationship.

Obviously, activist publics expect organizations to share responsibility for whatever tasks are involved in solving the issue they are concerned about. One example is the coffee giant Starbucks's sharing of tasks with the NGO Global Exchange.[49] At first, the NGO planned dramatic protests outside Starbucks coffee stores worldwide to pressure Starbucks into selling fair-trade coffee. Shortly after the first televised protest, Starbucks executives began meeting with Global Exchange to discuss how they could work together to make fair-trade coffee a reality. Kevin Danaher, a cofounder of Global Exchange, noted how the NGO had to "psychologically shift gears" away from seeing the company as the enemy to saying, "We want to help you."[50] The NGO realized that "railing at capitalism" was a less effective approach than appealing to the company's interest in demonstrating social responsibility.[51]

This sharing of tasks helps NGOs and corporations balance economic goals with humanitarian values. As Macbeth Moshoeshoe, head of the African Institute of Corporate Citizenship explained, "If you are not acceptable in the communities where you operate, your business will fail and shareholders will not be happy."[52]

The validity of Moshoeshoe's claim is apparent by the trend toward more corporate-NGO collaboration. For example, in Norway, Amnesty International helped train employees of Statoil to spot and resolve human rights issues in the oil company's third world operations.[53] In the Canadian province of Alberta, energy companies and NGOs work from the outset of every project to limit environmental damage.[54] This sharing of tasks gives NGOs meaningful input, while the companies gain credibility with regulators.

The last relationship maintenance strategy related to effective and responsible advocacy with activist groups is *networking*.[55] In an interpersonal relationship, networking means spending time with mutual friends in order to gain support and make the relationship enjoyable.

In a public relationship, organizations build networks with the same groups that network with their publics, such as employee unions, community groups, and environmentalists.[56] Organizations' effectiveness at this relationship maintenance strategy is shown through the number and quality of contacts with these groups.[57]

Organizational Web sites offer a unique opportunity for organizations to publicize their networking with groups their publics care about and encourage publics to take direct action such as volunteering or donating. Typically, links to these groups are offered on the Web site. Target Corporation's site, for example, lists the following groups as its national partners and provides their URLs: United Way, American Red Cross, St. Jude's Children's Research Hospital, Elizabeth Glaser Pediatric AIDS Foundation, United Negro College Fund, Hispanic Scholarship Fund, the U.S. Department of Education's No Child Left Behind initiative, and Reach Out and Read.[58]

Step 4—Symmetrical Conflict Resolution

In most relationships, conflict inevitably arises, and how organizations deal with conflict is key to responsible and effective advocacy. As the examples discussed earlier in this chapter suggest, aware and active publics often perceive some conflict between their goals and organizational consequences upon themselves or those whom they are acting on behalf of.

Public relations strategies for conflict resolution fall into three main categories: *integrative, distributive,* and *dual concern*.[59] Responsible and effective advocacy within a two-way symmetrical model of public relations emphasizes integrative and dual concern strategies. However, before these two categories are discussed, a definition of distributive strategies is presented to underscore why these approaches should be rejected.

Distributive strategies are asymmetrical because the goal is winning at the expense of the other party involved. These strategies can be thought of as win-lose. In other words, an organization or an activist group seeks to impose its position on the other without concern for the other's position. Tactics the organization or activist group might use include trying to control the other by dominating, arguing, insisting on one's position, or showing anger.[60] The organization or activist group might also engage in faulting the other, hostile questioning, presumptive attribution (attributing insidious motives to the other rather than giving the benefit of the doubt), and making demands or threats.[61]

It should be rather obvious why these strategies and tactics are not responsible advocacy. As other chapters in this book mention, the list of core values in the PRSA Code of Ethics defines one element of advocacy as providing "a voice in the marketplace of ideas, facts, and viewpoints to aid informed public debate."[62] Conversely, denying that voice to others through distributive communication strategies is unethical and irresponsible public relations. The code also lists "free flow of information" as a core principle that is "essential to serving the public interest and contributing to informed decision making in a democratic society."[63] One can easily see how distributive strategies seek to constrain a free flow of information by stifling the other party, another unethical and irresponsible approach.

John Doorley, the corporate communications director at Merck who was mentioned previously, explained a better way of resolving conflict in the context of dealing with activist publics:

> A main objective in any such endeavor is being calm. Any time you get AIDS activists and pharmaceutical executives in the same room . . . emotions will run high. It's important not to get caught up in the hot-blooded exchanges, but rather to stay cool and seek out the middle ground. I remember getting so mad at a certain point that my hands were shaking because they (the activists) got to be really nasty. We said we would not deal with anyone unless they stopped threatening us.[64]

However, an important point about distributive strategies needs to be made. Certainly, cases can be found where distributive strategies were effective at achieving the goals of the organization or activist group using them. But a two-way symmetrical model of public relations suggests that winning through distributive strategies is not an effective long-term approach because often the relationship between the organization and activist public becomes so damaged that future communication may be impossible. And, to the extent that the organization and activist public continue to have consequences upon one another, as is usually the case, both sides have lost the opportunity to resolve other conflicts through responsible advocacy. Instead, they may find themselves facing an intractable situation in which neither side feels satisfied.

A responsible and potentially more effective approach involves integrative strategies for conflict resolution.[65] These approaches are symmetrical because the organization and activist group are looking for a win-win solution. Here, both sides use open discussion to find common or complementary interests and solve problems together.

Obviously, organizations and activist groups want to advocate for their position. But, to do so responsibly, they must consider how to balance their interests with the interests of the other. Within a two-way, symmetrical model of public relations, this balance is negotiated through dual-concern strategies.[66] Some of these strategies are asymmetrical because they give priority to the organization or activist group's interest over the other and are thus not as effective at building and maintaining a long-term positive relationship.[67] Included here is *contending*, whereby either the organization or the activist public tries to convince the other to accept its position. *Avoiding* is another strategy in which either side walks away from the conflict either physically or psychologically. Organizations and publics also might try *accommodation*, whereby either side yields. This strategy can be disappointing to the accommodating side, however, since it usually means giving up on some of its goals. Finally, the organization and the activist group might *compromise*, or meet each other half way. But, in this case, it may be that neither feels completely satisfied with the outcome.

Other dual-concern strategies are symmetrical and may be the most effective because they value building and maintaining a positive relationship in the long term.[68] Dual-concern strategies include *cooperating, being unconditionally constructive*, and *saying win-win or no deal*. This chapter argues that cooperation is the ideal strategy for responsible advocacy because it meets the highest ethical standard and is the most likely to be effective. Here, the organization and activist group work together to negotiate their interests and reach mutually beneficial solutions within the context of the broader public interest.

A compelling example of cooperation is provided by the World Wildlife Fund's (WWF) success in establishing the Tortugas Marine Reserve at the Florida Keys National Marine Sanctuary, an area with a "long history of divisive and controversial battles over environmental issues."[69] According to its Web site, the WWF (an international conservation organization headquartered in the United States) "collaborated with fishermen, environmentalists, tourism operators, scientists, managers, and othes . . . (to create)

a proposal that met stringent criteria providing a 'win-win' outcome."[70]
The superintendent of the sanctuary agreed that WWF's communication
approach was symmetrical and effective: "We had fishermen working hand
in hand with conservation groups in such a way as to identify special regions
that they would be willing to set aside so the Tortugas could be protected for
future generations."[71]

One of the commercial fishermen involved in the negotiation thought
the approach was a win-win. "The Tortugas Reserve came out really good,"
he said. "It's the best working group I've ever seen. The fishing industry has
never really done this before. In the end, it was unanimous. . . . It's a world
class reserve. Everybody will benefit."[72]

However, in some situations, an organization and activist group may not
be able to find a solution that both feel is beneficial. In this scenario, responsible and effective advocacy would suggest either being unconditionally
constructive or saying win-win or no deal. An organization or activist group
is unconditionally constructive when it realizes that maintaining a positive
relationship is so important that giving up some of its position is worth it,
even if the other side does not reciprocate. No deal means that both parties
agree to disagree. No deal is a symmetrical strategy because it preserves
the relationship while leaving open the opportunity to find a win-win solution at a later date.

In his research on conflict and power in public relations, Plowman cited
an example of the win-win or no deal strategy that was used by a city
government. Plowman quoted the city manager:

> If you and I are working on a project, it has to be win/win or we just say we
> are not going to do it. So, we'll go through whatever mechanisms we need to
> do so that you honestly believe that you have won, and have, in fact, won—
> gotten something that's good for you. So, if we have actually, feel like we've
> won, and we're happy with each other—we're willing to do a deal again in the
> future. Or, we just say, "Look, let's agree to disagree, and we won't do this
> thing."[73]

A final example provides compelling evidence of this chapter's argument
that public relationship maintenance strategies and symmetrical strategies
for conflict resolution provide the framework for responsible and effective
advocacy with activist publics. After years of rising tensions over jurisdictional issues that stem from ambiguity in U.S. federal Indian policies (regarding who has jurisdictional claim over non-Indian populations that reside on
Indian reservations), the Idaho Nez Perce Tribe and a coalition of twenty-
three local non-Indian government groups signed a "Memorandum of

Understanding" that sets out procedures and preferred methods for resolving disputes.[74] Both sides also have established several joint working groups to address specific issues.[75]

These communication initiatives have allowed the two sides to reframe their dispute from compromising to win-win. In other words, after years of each side feeling that the only option was giving up some of its jurisdictional sovereignty, both groups discovered that the memorandum and working groups could be a way to exercise their jurisdictional claims and find win-win solutions.

The two-way symmetrical approach that was taken helped the tribe and the coalition realize their past mistake of relying only on the mass media to communicate: "The polarizing spin that news sources had put on their editorials and articles had played a significant role in building mistrust and resentment over the years."[76]

The intergovernmental groups also allowed both sides to establish personal contact (i.e., disclosure, access) instead of going to court, "an alternative that had consumed tremendous time and money from both sides."[77] As one of the Nez Perce members said,

> One important change resulting from the memorandum is that points of communication between the two sides have been established. Now when someone has a question or concern, they pick up the phone and let the other side know, airing problems before they fester and spill out in the local press.[78]

The mediators who worked with the tribe and coalition provide fitting counsel about responsible and effective advocacy between organizations and activist publics. As they said, "Each side's real purpose was to serve the best interests of their constituents, a goal that could not be accomplished without cooperation."[79]

Conclusion

This chapter suggests that all these relationship maintenance strategies—positivity, disclosure, access, assurances, sharing of tasks, networking, and dual-concern conflict resolution—are the communication strategies organizations should use to build quality relationships with activist publics. The focus on relationship theory as communication strategy is appropriate given that, as J. Grunig stated, "the value of public relations at the societal level is the long-term impact of good relationships identified at the organizational level and cultivated at the program level."[80]

J. Grunig went on to explain that the public relations function should evaluate the ethics and social responsibility of the organization and serve as the ethics counselor. The public relations function evaluates its own role in the ethical management of the organization by answering two questions:

- *The teleological question:* To what extent has the public relations staff helped management address the consequences the organization has had on publics and addressed the needs of publics?

- *The deontological question:* To what extent has the public relations staff carried out its moral obligation to communicate with and disclose the organization's behavior to publics when it has consequences on them or when the public expects consequences from the organization?[81]

The goal of this chapter was to illustrate how the strategic management of public relationships allows the public relations function to answer yes to both questions when communicating with activist publics. In doing so, the public relations function acts as a responsible and ethical advocate for organizations and demonstrates its contribution to society.

5

Responsible Advocacy for Nonprofit Organizations

Carolyn Bronstein

Nonprofit organizations occupy an important place in American society. Commonly referred to as the "third sector," after business and government, nonprofits include charitable organizations, social welfare groups, labor and agricultural unions, business leagues, social and political clubs, and other groups that serve a public interest. There are currently more than 1.5 million nonprofit organizations in the United States, and between 20,000 and 30,000 new nonprofits are started each year.[1] Most engage in public relations activities, although the scope of their programs tends to be smaller than those conducted by business and government organizations.[2]

Most nonprofit groups have fewer economic resources at their disposal than business and government organizations, which can explain their more limited public relations programs. Professional public relations programs can be quite costly, especially if video news releases (VNRs), special events, or other major outreach programs are planned, and corporations and government agencies tend to have the deepest pockets. Nonprofits, on the other hand, generally operate with limited budgets; just 26% of all nonprofits earn more than $25,000 per year.[3] Prior research supports the contention that public relations efficacy is inextricably tied to economic resources, and as a result, well-financed corporate and government elites tend to exercise greater influence over the norms and values established in long-term media discourses.[4]

Historically, a relative lack of economic resources has made it difficult for nonprofit organizations to consistently influence media coverage. Today, however, new forms of technology are giving these groups greater ability to contribute to the marketplace of ideas. The advent of electronic communication has made the global distribution of information instantaneous and inexpensive, and many nonprofit groups are seizing the opportunity to expand their public relations programs. They are using the Internet to bring their social causes and concerns, such as deforestation, gun control, and music education, before the world, and to assert a more forceful presence in the public sphere. This outreach effort has attracted attention not only from members of the general public, but also from journalists responding to two different sets of circumstances. First, journalists rely more heavily on public relations materials today due to financial pressures affecting news organizations. Second, journalists are turning away from traditional corporate sources of information, many of whom they no longer find credible. This environment enables nonprofit organizations that conduct public relations programs to heighten their visibility and to make major contributions to public conversation.

As nonprofit organizations initiate more complex programs reaching larger numbers of individuals, new questions about ethical public relations practices and the interests that practitioners ought to serve must be answered. In a sense, nonprofit practitioners have more leeway when it comes to pushing the boundaries of ethical practice. Members of the public are often willing to forgive nonprofits that violate standards of public relations ethics—falsely claiming a celebrity endorsement or overstating member support in group literature—simply because the group is working for the greater common good, and not for private gain. Ultimately, however, practitioners who use irresponsible tactics weaken the organizations they serve. A nonprofit practitioner who means to function as a responsible advocate must place the well-being of the organization before the social or political cause that the organization represents. Although this can require enormous personal restraint when practitioners hold passionate beliefs about such issues as animal rights or public smoking bans, responsible advocacy demands that practitioners prioritize the organization's reputation and relationships with its publics.

Nonprofit practitioners face both opportunities and challenges in their efforts to serve as responsible advocates. This chapter analyzes the environment in which nonprofit practitioners operate, with attention to the opportunities created by new technology and the economic changes affecting American news organizations. It also examines stumbling blocks to ethical behavior, including the temptation to abandon self-restraint and a lack of role models for ethical public relations practice. The chapter concludes with a discussion of the promise of responsible advocacy among nonprofit organizations, especially among those whose public relations programs feature relationship management, resource sharing, and dialogic communication models.

Leveling the Playing Field

The British public relations practitioner George Pitcher has described the Internet as exerting a "leveling effect," by which he means that electronic communication enables resource-poor community organizations to rival wealthy corporate ones in their ability to reach global audiences.[5] According to Pitcher, the Internet has spawned "a parallel universe of alternative authorities" who hold opinions on every conceivable political and social issue, and whose opinions "tend to prevail" in cyberspace.[6] Nonprofit organizations that conduct online public relations programs can leverage the power of the Internet to make themselves visible to members of the public, and to journalists, who increasingly view noncorporate sources as more trustworthy.[7] In other words, the advent of low-cost, high-impact electronic communication affords nonprofits an unprecedented opportunity to contribute to public discourse.

When nonprofit and advocacy groups make themselves easily available to journalists via the Web, they can secure better representation of their points of view and more in-depth coverage of topics that might otherwise be ignored or dismissed as too marginal to report. According to a 2004 survey conducted by the Pew Research Center for the People and the Press, a majority of journalists view the Internet as a vital source of information and believe that the Internet has improved journalism.[8] The most commonly cited benefits include the speed of the Internet in delivering information, the ease of securing facts, and the broader range of voices and perspectives available to reporters. The opportunity for nonprofit organizations is clear; their presence in cyberspace puts pressure on journalists to be more innovative and responsive in their reporting, and more wide-ranging in their search for stories and sources. One survey respondent described this change by saying that the Internet has essentially "democratized the press."[9]

An increasing number of nonprofits are maintaining their Internet presence through blogs, interactive online journals that allow organizations to post information, commentary, and links to other pages of interest, and that contain forums for readers to post their own comments to create a continuing conversation. This form of electronic communication received a great deal of attention when Howard Dean, the former governor of Vermont, used a blog as a mainstay of his campaign for the 2004 Democratic presidential nomination. Dean's blog included essays from supporters and periodic messages from the candidate, and it generated widespread name recognition and donations.[10] Nonprofit organizations such as Oceana, a global network of individuals committed to restoring and protecting the world's oceans, have discovered that blogs are effective public relations tools that attract potential members and journalists alike.[11] A recent Columbia University study revealed that journalists are turning to blogs in record numbers, with 51% of those surveyed reading blogs regularly and 28% relying on them for day-to-day reporting.[12] In response to these findings, a media executive observed that blogs are changing the landscape of journalism: "The fact that the media are using blogs for reporting and research also demonstrates that blogs have an enormous potential to not only influence the general public, but to influence the influencers—journalists and the media—as well."[13] When nonprofit organizations leverage the power of electronic communication as part of their public relations programs, their ability to compete with powerful corporate voices is greatly enhanced.

Economic Pressures on News Organizations

During the last decade, the U.S. public relations industry has grown exponentially while American journalism has suffered a number of setbacks, including a decline in the number of working journalists and widespread budget cuts for news organizations.[14] As a result, the balance of power between journalists and public relations professionals has shifted, leaving many understaffed and financially strapped newspapers, radio and television stations, and Internet news and entertainment sites dependent on low-cost public relations material. Public relations practitioners are enjoying an unprecedented opportunity to wield significant influence over the news.[15] The challenge of responsible advocacy means that practitioners must uphold the public interest even in the face of market forces that might make it possible to bias the news in favor of a client organization.

U.S. Department of Labor statistics bear out the assertion that the field of public relations is enjoying unprecedented growth at the same time that American journalism is experiencing a downturn. The number of individuals working as public relations specialists in 2002 was estimated at 158,000, compared with just 66,000 news analysts, reporters, and correspondents.[16] Job opportunities in public relations were also predicted to increase "faster than the average for all occupations" in the United States through 2012, whereas employment of news analysts, reporters, and correspondents was expected to grow "more slowly than the average for all occupations" during the same period of time.[17] The Department of Labor cited numerous market factors as causing the stagnant number of journalism jobs, specifically mergers, consolidations, and closures of newspapers, as well as decreased circulation, increased operating expenses, and a decline in advertising profits.[18] Recent communication scholarship predicts little improvement in these economic conditions.[19]

The comparative advantage that public relations practitioners enjoy over journalists may be even greater than current government estimates indicate. The Council of Public Relations Firms, a prominent industry trade association, has contested the Department of Labor's employment figures, arguing that the agency failed to count a large number of individuals who carry out public relations functions such as speech writing and internal communication management, but whose job titles do not specify public relations.[20] The Council maintains that the total number of public relations specialists working in the United States today is closer to 600,000 to 800,000.[21] Other estimates indicate that there may be as many as one million practitioners.[22] No matter which set of figures one accepts, it is clear that the number of public relations professionals is far greater than the number of working journalists, one of several conditions that has made the latter group dependent on the free news and entertainment content generated by the former.

The economic realities of American journalism today mean that a reduced corps of full-time working journalists is producing the news with fewer resources, and news organizations as a whole are under tremendous pressure to meet profit goals.[23] The push for profits has resulted in layoffs, hiring freezes, and editorial cutbacks at many news organizations, ranging from local television stations to prominent national newspaper chains like Knight Ridder.[24] In a 2004 survey conducted by the Pew Research Center for the People and the Press, about half of respondents working at newspapers or magazines reported that the size of their newsroom staff had decreased in the past three years.[25] Sixty-six percent of journalists polled in the Pew survey agreed that financial pressures were changing methods of reporting in 2004, as compared to 40% in a 1995 Pew survey.[26]

The effect of these market conditions is evident when one considers the increasing use of VNRs, which are prerecorded television segments created by public relations professionals. More television news organizations than ever before are willing—even eager—to air VNRs in their entirety, as they eliminate both the production effort and costs that stations incur when they report original stories. Producers can use them to fill airtime without depleting resources.[27] Marion Just and Tom Rosenstiel of the Project for Excellence in Journalism surveyed local television stations and found that the pressure to yield high profit margins was driving news producers to incorporate more of this free, prepackaged content. Just and Rosenstiel analyzed almost 40,000 news segments broadcast during local television news programs and found that from 1998 to 2002, the percentage of "feed" material from third-party sources rose from 14% to 23% of all segments. Meanwhile, the percentage of stories that included a local correspondent fell to 43% from 62%.[28]

Ethical Challenges

For public relations professionals, the financial pressures affecting news organizations constitute a double-edged sword. Journalists need more low-cost, prepackaged fare, which means that practitioners have greater opportunities to contribute to media content, whether through VNRs, news releases made available on an organization Web site, or blogs. At the same time, however, these opportunities can present ethical challenges. For nonprofit practitioners, many of whom are passionate about the causes they represent, the temptation to do or say whatever is necessary to draw attention to an issue can prevail, even if it means overstepping the boundaries of responsible advocacy.

Journalists rely on the free news and entertainment content that public relations practitioners supply. Experts estimate that between 25 and 40% of what appears in the daily newspaper or on the nightly news originates with public relations professionals.[29] Given these odds, practitioners understand that a passive reworking of public relations material will frequently substitute for original reporting, and that even one-sided or incomplete accounts may be printed or broadcast. For example, a VNR that distorts facts or downplays opposition still has a very good chance of making it onto the air, and even if only a portion of the original footage is retained, its inherent viewpoint tends to dominate the final message conveyed to the television audience. Television news producers who are eager to build audience share are especially likely to air shocking or graphic footage, such as a VNR from the British nonprofit organization League Against Cruel Sports, which showed a bloody foxhunt.[30] In many cases, emboldened public relations practitioners overstep the boundaries of ethical practice to publicize their organizations' efforts, yet still achieve positive results because of market conditions that favor low-cost, high-impact public relations materials. In other words, current market forces have created conditions ripe for the abandonment of responsible advocacy.

These conditions are particularly significant for nonprofit practitioners, who typically are considered less self-interested and more candid than corporate spokespersons. In a 2005 Columbia University survey, 49% of journalists indicated that they had lost trust in corporations and their representatives over the last year. Seventy-six percent of the journalists polled did not trust corporate spokespersons in times of company crisis.[31] When reporters turn away from corporate sources, they turn toward individuals representing nonprofit and other community advocacy organizations. Nonprofit practitioners have a tremendous opportunity to use their newfound influence to increase their organizations' visibility and power, but in so doing they must keep the principles of responsible advocacy in mind. Practitioners must be held accountable for ethical decision making, lest the reputations of their nonprofit organizations become as tainted as those of some of the most notorious corporations.

Lack of Ethical Role Models

Practitioners in the nonprofit and advocacy world might expect to find role models for responsible advocacy in the campaigns conducted by other nonprofit organizations and by government agencies, most of which are working for public interest causes. However, a number of recent high-profile cases have revealed that practitioners in both the nonprofit and government sectors can and do resort to unethical practices. In recent years, several U.S. government agencies, including the Education Department, the Department of Health and Human Services, and the Department of Agriculture, along with the well-known advocacy group People for the Ethical Treatment of Animals (PETA), have conducted campaigns that violate the principles of responsible advocacy. In each situation, practitioners used irresponsible tactics to achieve particular goals, risking organizational reputation and bringing negative public scrutiny.

Government Missteps

In the spring of 2004, the *New York Times* published an exposé that revealed that a federal government agency had used propaganda-style techniques to win public support for new Medicare legislation. The Department of Health and Human Services (HHS) hired Ketchum, Inc., a powerful public relations firm, to produce and disseminate VNRs that uniformly praised President George Bush's controversial Medicare reform program.[32] These prerecorded segments applauded the availability of new Medicare drug discount cards for low-income senior citizens and portrayed this change as a victory for America's aging population and a concrete way to reduce seniors' out-of-pocket prescription drug costs.[33] One scene showed Bush in the presence of members of Congress, triumphantly signing the Medicare reform bill into law. Other scenes featured seniors engaged in leisure and health-related activities, including a consultation with a pharmacist who explained that the new law would "help you [seniors] better afford your medications."[34] The segments did not address serious concerns voiced by opposition groups who feared that private insurance companies might respond to caps on drug reimbursements by creating restrictive drug formularies that would keep essential medications out of the hands of patients, and interfere with physicians' efforts to deliver effective health care.[35]

In addition to presenting only those elements of the story favorable to the Bush administration, the VNRs lacked any information that would allow viewers to discern that a government agency had funded or produced the stories. The segments were indistinguishable in format and tone from objective news stories, and they seemed to feature actual reporters. The public relations practitioners who created the VNRs hired actors to pose as journalists who were reporting "facts" about the new Medicare law, and gave them scripts to read that had been prepared by government workers. The story packages were produced in both English and Spanish, and each ended with a traditional reporter's sign-off (e.g., "In Washington, I'm Karen Ryan reporting" for the English-language version; "In Washington, I'm Alberto Garcia reporting" for the Spanish-language version), reinforcing the perception among viewers that the material was independent journalism arising from a nongovernmental source or a neutral party. Forty television stations in 33 markets aired some portion of the VNRs between January 22, 2004, and February 12, 2004. Many stations aired the story packages in their entirety, including WBRZ in Baton Rouge, Louisiana, WMBC-TV in New Jersey, and WAGA-TV in Atlanta.[36]

The VNRs created an uproar among opponents of the Medicare law and prompted a federal investigation. Critics lambasted the television segments as irresponsible and unethical, and as part of a duplicitous public relations campaign orchestrated to mislead the public. The General Accountability Office (GAO), a nonpartisan agency controlled by the U.S. Congress that analyzes how the federal government spends taxpayer dollars, initiated an inquiry. The GAO issued a report in May 2004 that described the VNRs as a type of "covert propaganda" intended to deceive viewers and obscure the government's role as the source of the material.[37] The report described the

VNRs as "not strictly factual news stories" that were marred by "notable omissions and weaknesses" in their explanation of the provisions of the Medicare law.[38] The agency report noted that the story packages and accompanying anchor lead-in scripts were designed to be seen and heard directly by the television audience, and that HHS purposely disguised its involvement. The VNRs were crafted to make viewers think the story had been produced and reported by an independent third party. As such, they violated the 1913 Gillett Amendment, which prohibits the use of federal money for publicity or propaganda purposes not authorized by Congress.

Other current examples of the use of unethical public relations tactics by government organizations abound. When the Education Department sought in 2004 to build support for its education reform law, No Child Left Behind, it improperly funneled public funds to a prominent conservative journalist. Once again using the Ketchum public relations firm as a middleman, Education Department officials paid the commentator Armstrong Williams $240,000 to promote No Child Left Behind on his nationally syndicated television show and in his newspaper column, and to use his contacts with African American journalists to encourage them to portray the law favorably.[39] And in June 2005, the *Chicago Tribune* reported that the U.S. Department of Agriculture (USDA) successfully aired three dozen radio and television news segments that promoted a trade agreement with Central America that had been opposed by labor unions, the sugar industry, and many members of Congress. The reports were distributed to broadcast outlets for insertion into newscasts between January and June 2005, prompting a front-page story in the *Tribune* that observed that the Bush administration had taken the practice of public relations "to aggressive levels on issues ranging from the war in Iraq to education and trade policy."[40]

These intensive efforts to produce favorable opinions among key publics have fueled debates as to whether it is ethical for public relations practitioners to try to exert control over news content and public opinion.[41] Can practitioners working for the USDA be considered "responsible advocates" when they present political statements as objective news, disguising the agency's intent to advance a specific trade agenda and silence the voices of its opponents? Can representatives of HHS claim to be acting ethically when they authorize the creation and dissemination of biased news segments that misrepresent the facts surrounding new legislation? Can Education Department officials credibly claim to be protecting the public interest when they buy favorable media attention for specific programs and policies? Responsible advocacy requires that public relations professionals pay as much attention to the public interest as they do to their own organization's interests. The agencies described above violated the principles of responsible advocacy when they presented news organizations with incomplete accounts of public response to new and proposed legislation, and when they paid a journalist to try to influence African American audiences to support No Child Left Behind. Responsible advocates respect their publics and strive to provide them with accurate and complete information regarding organizational decisions. In each of these cases, public relations practitioners fell far short of the bar.

The concept of responsible advocacy carries with it the presumption that a public relations practitioner will recognize and honor obligations to both a client organization and the public at large. The "responsible" portion of "responsible advocacy" disappears whenever the public is purposely misled. As such, any attempt to exert control over public discourse or monopolize public conversation through the use of biased news reports, undisclosed paid spokespersons, or similar abuses of power is fundamentally at odds with its core principles. Responsible advocacy also demands that public relations practitioners clearly identify the source of all communication; in the case of the Medicare VNRs, this meant that either the anchor lead-in scripts should have mentioned that the story originated with a government agency, or a disclaimer should have been superimposed on the visuals to alert viewers to the partisan nature of the report. In recent years, nonprofit and advocacy groups looking to government agencies for role models for ethical practice would have found disappointing mentors. The risk to the public relations profession is grave; when highly respected public agencies flout the basic rules of ethical conduct, they suggest to other organizations that such behavior is entirely appropriate, and worth the relatively small risk of media scrutiny and exposure.

Nonprofit Missteps

Nonprofit and advocacy groups often champion important social causes, such as environmental conservation or disease awareness, but their principled stances on issues of the day do not always translate to responsible and ethical public relations campaigns. In July 2004, the animal rights organization People for the Ethical Treatment of Animals (PETA) successfully called attention to abuses in commercial poultry plants, but did so using unethical tactics that were inconsistent with responsible advocacy. Nonprofits may be less likely to raise public ire for employing such tactics because their goals serve the greater social good—as opposed to the financial self-interest that motivates most corporate actions—but there are consequences nonetheless. Nonprofit practitioners who employ irresponsible practices must recognize that they run the risk of undermining their organizations' reputations and accomplishments, and violating the rights and interests of stakeholders.

Determined to shed light on inhumane conditions, PETA hired an investigator to infiltrate one of the nation's largest poultry plants and to work undercover as a plant employee for eight months. This individual secretly recorded a video that showed employees kicking and stomping live chickens. The graphic footage from the West Virginia plant revealed that workers were "ripping birds' beaks off, spray-painting their faces, twisting their heads off, spitting tobacco into their mouths and eyes, and breaking them in half—all while the birds are still alive."[42] PETA sent copies of the video along with news releases to major newspapers and television stations around the nation, and distributed a digital version of the video to electronic news outlets. The organization also made the video available on its Web site. Many major news outlets, including the *New York Times* and *USA Today*, carried the story. A number of online news sources created links from their reports to the PETA video, which helped to turn the poultry plant abuse story into national news.[43]

Without question, PETA achieved impressive results. The concentrated media attention and public outcry forced the plant's major customer, the fast food giant KFC, to suspend its purchasing contract. Pilgrim's Pride, owner of the plant and one of the largest poultry producers in the United States, terminated three managers and eight workers allegedly involved in the abuse. Pilgrim's Pride also hired quality assurance monitors to supervise all shifts, instituted mandatory employee education about animal welfare policies, and agreed to the placement of a full-time KFC plant inspector to safeguard against further abuse. PETA was also able to gain the support of another nonprofit organization, the Humane Society, whose president went on record urging Congress to hold hearings on the incident and to draft new federal laws to protect live poultry.

PETA may have received the media attention it desired, but the organization's approach clearly fell short of the standards of responsible advocacy. When PETA members devised a campaign that required an individual to conceal his true identity and purpose in order to record an unauthorized video, the organization did not behave ethically toward the plant's employees or owners. Whereas some might defend PETA's actions using situational ethics, arguing that the ends in this instance (shedding light on animal abuse) justified the means (secretive tactics), responsible advocacy demands that attention be paid at all times to the rights and interests of all publics. The German philosopher and ethicist Immanuel Kant suggested that one could gauge whether a particular behavior was ethical by applying the following question: "Would I be willing to be the recipient of my action?"[44] Few people would acquiesce to being secretly videotaped on the job, particularly when the video would bring about termination and public humiliation.

Responsible advocacy requires public relations practitioners to figure out what action might be fair to all involved in a given situation, as opposed to that which might generate the most publicity, and to act accordingly. This is not always a simple task, as it requires practitioners to rise above self-interest and the interests of any one particular client or group, and potentially to reject tactics that might very well bring about dramatic effects, as they did in the PETA case. At the point that advocacy communication, such as PETA's attempt to inform the world about animal abuse, becomes dishonest communication built on secrecy and deception, responsible advocacy is lost.

Despite the social significance of responsible advocacy, ethical campaigns are rarely reported by the media. Instead, unethical public relations campaigns—when discovered—tend to receive the lion's share of public attention. Although news coverage generally portrays such campaigns unfavorably, practitioners can still be influenced by reports of the effectiveness of deceptive tactics. This in turn may have the undesirable result of promoting such practices and encouraging practitioners to adopt them. When practitioners are confronted by examples of powerful organizations that have successfully used unethical public relations to monopolize the marketplace of ideas and exert influence over public opinion, the temptation to behave similarly may be difficult to resist. In this environment, public role models for responsible advocacy are in short supply.

Public Relations Practices that Encourage Responsible Advocacy

Nonprofit organizations may lack prominent role models for responsible advocacy, and market forces may tempt some practitioners to overstep the bounds of ethical practice, but there are a number of public relations approaches common to nonprofits that tend to encourage ethical practice and accountability. Relationship management, resource sharing, and dialogic communication structure the practice of public relations within many nonprofit organizations and provide a framework for responsible advocacy. Nonprofit practitioners who use these strategies can serve as true advocates for their organizations and can enhance the reputation of their organizations as a whole.

Relationship Management

The view of public relations as relationship management conceptualizes the practitioner's key responsibility as using strategic communication to manage the relationships between an organization and its key publics. In this model, public relations is a process of continuous and mutually beneficial exchange between the organization and its publics, and practitioners work to develop long-term relationships that feature dimensions of trust, openness, involvement, and mutual investment.[45] This model is particularly well-suited to nonprofit organizations; members of the public are predisposed to react positively to a group whose main purpose is environmental conservation, workers' rights, or school improvement, as opposed to amassing capital, which is the primary goal of large corporations. This positive predisposition provides fertile ground for relationship building.

The idea that nonprofit groups can use relationship management strategies to advocate responsibly for their organizations has been confirmed by a recent study of the British trade union movement. The public relations scholar Aeron Davis found that British labor unions lacked favorable news coverage and a base of public support in the 1970s and 1980s.[46] He attributed these problems to their failure to conduct a sustained public relations program to communicate the union point of view to journalists and other key publics. In the 1990s, union officials hired professional public relations practitioners to improve the organization's communication operations and increase public support. The union practitioners focused their attention on relationship management and initiated strong, ongoing relationships with journalists, civic groups, social action organizations, and local and national politicians. They positioned the union members as a working-class constituency concerned with such public-interest issues as workplace safety and employment discrimination, providing the basis for a strong bond with nonunion publics. Davis concluded that a majority of the unions that deployed these relationship-building strategies were able to achieve important political and economic objectives, such as increasing their membership and blocking anti-union legislation. Public relations operations are now considered "a standard requirement" for larger unions in the United Kingdom, and have become an important priority for smaller ones.[47]

Organized labor in the United States has also recognized the importance of public relations in achieving organizational goals, and many unions have established ongoing programs. This trend accelerated in the late 1990s following a highly publicized Teamsters Union strike against United Parcel Service (UPS). During that strike, union representatives turned to key publics, such as journalists, to tell their side of the story, and the favorable news coverage helped sway public attitudes in favor of the striking workers.[48] Union representatives in that instance functioned as responsible advocates, leveraging the strength of long-term relationships with organizational publics to communicate their members' needs.

During this period, a smaller union—the 2,300 member Independent Pilots Association (IPA)—also relied on relationship management to weather a series of difficult contract negotiations with UPS. Through its comprehensive public relations program, IPA leaders developed a strong, trustworthy relationship with their union members, the professional pilots who fly the UPS jet fleet.[49] As negotiations soured, union leaders turned to the pilots to get the IPA story out to business reporters and other key publics, believing that these individuals could deliver a persuasive union message. With the help of the public relations firm Manning, Selvage & Lee, the IPA trained more than a hundred "spokespilots" to talk directly to journalists about their working conditions. The spokespilots increased the news value of the IPA situation by telling journalists that UPS would face back-to-back walkouts because of reciprocity agreements between members of the IPA and the Teamsters. In the end, the pilots secured a 29% pay increase and the campaign earned the attention of public relations professionals nationwide.[50] The Public Relations Society of America awarded Manning, Selvage & Lee a 1999 Silver Anvil Award for its work with the IPA.[51]

Successful relationship management is a key element of responsible advocacy. Positive relationships with key publics offer organizations a "credit balance" of sorts that they can draw on in times of need. In the case of the IPA, union leaders built a strong relationship with members that centered on mutual investment and commitment, and were subsequently able to count on those members when the organization required help. When organizations lack these kinds of relationships, they are more likely to turn to unethical means of reaching publics, as was the case when the Education Department paid Armstrong Williams to promote No Child Left Behind. The Bush Administration could not rely in that instance on genuine relationships built on trust and commitment, and instead tried to insinuate itself through Armstrong into the good graces of African American journalists and audiences. The result was fairly disastrous for all involved, and the ethics scandal is likely to tarnish reputations for years to come. Responsible advocacy through relationship management requires practitioners to take the time to build thoughtful and lasting relationships with key publics; such relationships can never be bought.

Resource Sharing

In an effort to overcome financial limitations, many nonprofit organizations have chosen to form resource-sharing partnerships. Instead of each group having to build and maintain its own public relations infrastructure, including paid staff, quarterly publications, and the like, many nonprofits are creating umbrella organizations with like-minded groups and consolidating their public relations efforts.[52] Their joint efforts typically result in cosponsored Web sites, newsletters, and special events, as well as media training for spokespersons. Recent studies indicate that such arrangements can enable smaller groups to extend their cultural and economic capital, and to have an impact on media coverage, even in the face of resource inequality.[53] This approach also follows the recommendation of scholar Aeron Davis, who argues that collective action among nonprofits is the best way to improve "access, legitimacy, and the ability to set agendas."[54]

From an ethical standpoint, nonprofits that create resource-sharing public relations partnerships are likely to enhance organizational commitment to responsible advocacy. When organizations join together and present themselves as a united public front, their sense of accountability to one another, and joint responsibility to the public, increases. These partnerships create, in effect, a "checks and balances" system in which practitioners working on behalf of a particular group, or for a coalition of groups, know that their actions and public statements reflect on and can have consequences for allied organizations. The temptation to step over the line in terms of ethical practice may be quelled by the knowledge that fellow practitioners are keeping close tabs and the health and welfare of sister organizations is at stake. In this way, nonprofits can lead the way in establishing a practice model for responsible advocacy; resource-sharing arrangements are likely to promote a commitment to ethical public relations as the reputation and well-being of any one group is tied to those of its partners.

Earth Share of Washington is a Seattle-based nonprofit organization that has pioneered the resource-sharing model, bringing together 65 local environmental groups in a coalition dedicated to environmental education and charitable giving. As part of its cooperative public relations program, Earth Share maintains a blog that offers information relevant to all its member organizations' publics, such as the dedication of a new bicycling trail or a summary of a new study about pesticides, as well as information particular to each organization, such as an upcoming volunteer opportunity or an award received. As noted previously, greater numbers of journalists are turning to blogs as a source for day-to-day reporting, but most nonprofits lack the manpower to establish and update them.[55] By pooling the resources of dozens of smaller environmental groups, Earth Share has been able to maintain its blog since 2003, increasing the visibility of all its member organizations and establishing its presence as a major Internet site for environmental education and information.[56]

Earth Share's blog is the cornerstone of a public relations program that has been successful from both practical and ethical standpoints. On the practical side, the organization's practitioners credit the blog for driving more traffic to the Web site and increasing public involvement in the member groups' programs.[57] Earth Share's communication coordinator described the Web site prior to the introduction of the blog as "static and stale," and as failing to attract media attention or to engage people concerned with the environment.[58] Now, Earth Share's Web site registers as many as 12,000 hits per month, more than four times the average number recorded before the addition of the blog.

Dialogic Communication

From the ethical standpoint, the Earth Share blog encourages members of the public to engage in an open dialogue with one another and with the leaders of member organizations, a condition that is necessary for ethical public relations practice.[59] When individuals post comments to one of the Earth Share forums, they are participating in what is known as *dialogic* communication, a means of interaction between organizations and publics in which all participants have an equal chance to contribute and no participant exercises control over another.[60] Dialogic communication is recognized by scholars of public relations as a fundamental precondition for ethical relations between organizations and publics, as it is the sole means of arriving at shared truths and mutually acceptable practices.[61] Blogging allows for a true peer-to-peer conversation in which members of the community can communicate their concerns about organizational practice directly to organization leaders, and organization leaders can respond in kind. Three scholars of public relations ethics recently noted the need for such dialogic communication, observing that "ethical practice for the field of public relations will require practitioners to be facilitators of dialogue and listeners as much as speakers."[62] In this regard, nonprofit organizations are ahead of corporations in establishing practice guidelines for responsible advocacy; few corporations engage in truly dialogic communication, and many have gone so far as to fire employees who have divulged any connection to the corporation in blogs.[63]

Conclusion

This chapter has described the opportunities and challenges that public relations practitioners who work for nonprofit and advocacy groups face as they strive to become responsible advocates for their organizations. Nonprofit organizations are enjoying unprecedented opportunities to participate in the public sphere due to the convergence of high-impact electronic communication and a shift among journalists away from traditional corporate sources. These factors give nonprofits new voice, but can also lead to missteps if practitioners place the organization's primary cause or issue, such as animal rights or environmental conservation, ahead of their responsibility to advocate ethically for the organization and its various publics. Many nonprofit organizations, however, are creating public relations programs that encourage ethical practice and accountability. As this chapter shows, nonprofits are particularly well-suited to relationship management strategies, resource sharing, and dialogic communication models—all of which are considered to be building blocks of responsible advocacy.

6

Truth and Transparency

Karla K. Gower

I n the fall of 2001, corporate America was stunned when the Securities and Exchange Commission (SEC) announced that it was investigating the energy company Enron for financial improprieties. From there, the news only got worse. Worldcom, Tyco, Global Crossing, Arthur Andersen, Health-South, and even Martha Stewart all faced investigation for unethical, and in some cases illegal, business practices. Some see the financial scandals as a product of the dot-com era of the 1990s, when business leaders became more interested in their own net worth and the stock price of their companies than in the profits. The single-minded focus on shareholder value meant that stock price was the sole measurement of success for a CEO.[1] Some buckled under the pressure, "cooking" the books to ensure the stock price remained high. Whatever the cause, a surge of anticorporate sentiment swept the country.

This chapter will address issues of ethics and responsible advocacy in public relations from primarily a corporate perspective. It will explore the elements of corporate trust, truth, and transparency, and examine how responsible public relations professionals can assist corporations in working through a crisis, restoring trust after a crisis, and maintaining that trust for the long term.

Scandal Fallout

The financial scandals at the beginning of the twenty-first century were not the only factors fueling anticorporate public opinion. Bankruptcies, the failing of employee pension funds, and rising compensation levels of corporate executives have contributed to a loss of trust in corporate America, both at home and abroad. Klaus Kleinfeld, CEO of Siemens Corporation, noted that "the erosion of confidence in corporate governance in the United States has put at risk the reputation of business on an international scale."[2] In the 2004 Edelman Barometer of Trust survey of international opinion leaders, the scandals that resulted in the greatest reduction of trust in organizations were unethical business practices by accounting firms, misappropriation and underfunding of pension funds, and misleading communications, including financial performance.[3]

Investors, employees, the media, and activists demanded that corporations be held accountable for their actions, which have threatened livelihoods and ruined lives. Government agencies responded to the pressure by increasing scrutiny over corporate affairs.[4] Even before the financial scandals, the SEC had approved Regulation Fair Disclosure, which prohibits corporations from privileging financial analysts with access to material information. As a direct result of the scandals and the unethical behavior of corporate executives, the New York Stock Exchange took steps to restore investor trust by issuing new rules for corporate governance, and Congress enacted the Sarbanes-Oxley Act, which requires CEOs to certify the accuracy of financial statements.[5] The act also calls for management and external auditors to regularly assess the corporation's internal controls or security measures for effectiveness.

The purpose of the act is to prevent accounting errors and make it harder for executives to "fix" the numbers. But it also forces CEOs to take more direct responsibility for the actions of their corporations. CEOs cannot claim they had no knowledge of the unethical behaviors of those under them, as Bernard Ebbers, former CEO of WorldCom, did. Ebbers was found guilty of fraud, conspiracy, and making false regulatory filings in the WorldCom accounting scandal and sentenced to twenty-five years in prison.[6]

Although CEOs will now have to pay a price under the Sarbanes-Oxley Act for bad corporate behavior committed under their watch, unethical and irresponsible behavior on the part of even a few corporations harms many. Direct victims of corporate fraud, such as investors and employees, can lose their life savings, pensions, jobs, and even homes. The companies themselves, if they survive financially, have to deal with the fallout of a damaged reputation and loss of trust with all of their stakeholders. Even those not directly involved can be harmed by corporate scandals. For example, organizations that have named buildings or other structures in honor of donors have their own ethics and reputations called into question when they do not remove the names of disgraced donors. Harvard University, Brown

University, and the University of Missouri have had benefactors who later faced criminal charges. Seton Hall University in New Jersey boasted a Kozlowski Hall, named after Dennis Kozlowski, the former Tyco International CEO who was found guilty on twenty-two counts of grand larceny, conspiracy, securities fraud, and falsifying business records and later sentenced to eight to twenty-five years in prison.[7] Kozlowski Hall, which was home to the university's school of business, has since been renamed.[8]

In addition, all companies pay the price for the actions of a few "bad apples" by having to comply with regulations imposed on them by the government in response to public cries for accountability. When ethical breaches appear widespread, as in the recent financial scandals, when company after company seems to be engaging in fraud, the government often propagates regulations or passes laws that codify ethical norms. The SEC itself was established following the 1929 stock market crash that triggered the Great Depression. As a result of the Securities Act of 1933 and the Securities Exchange Act of 1934, publicly traded companies are forced to be more transparent. For example, before new issues of stock can be made, a registration statement that discloses financial and other information about the issuing company must be filed with the SEC. In addition, companies are required to release quarterly earnings statements and annual reports. And Regulation FD (Fair Disclosure) forces a company to publicly disclose any material information simultaneously with its disclosure to a securities analyst.

The Sarbanes-Oxley Act continues the process of regulating transparency. Although responsible organizations will have no problem with being more open and accountable as required by the act, it can be costly and burdensome to meet such regulations. In a recent survey of corporate financial officers, 64% found compliance with the Sarbanes-Oxley Act difficult or very difficult.[9] The problem with such regulations is that they force companies, even those already acting responsibly, to comply in specific ways, creating a new layer of bureaucracy and oversight within organizations. Thus, instead of an organization choosing the manner in which it will provide information, the laws mandate that it be released in a particular way, and failure to do so can result in fines or other sanctions.

Despite the cost and the increased levels of bureaucracy that regulations impose, some companies go even farther than the laws require. For example, some companies have instituted continuous monitoring as a result of Sarbanes-Oxley to alert them to even the smallest problem early on.[10] Truly responsible corporations, then, have taken the scandals and regulations as an opportunity to reassess and reaffirm their commitment to truth and transparency.

The push for transparency today is similar to an earlier push for the same thing. At the beginning of the twentieth century, reformers called for increased scrutiny over the trusts and big businesses that had arisen in the late 1800s. Reformers demanded corporate openness and sought to shine the spotlight of "pitiless publicity" onto what until then had been private matters. Those calls for greater regulation and oversight of corporate affairs led to the development of public relations as a business policy as corporations recognized the need to address the concerns of the public.

Today, the push for corporate accountability again offers public relations the chance to lead the way in restoring trust. The demand for openness in the early 1900s has become a demand for truth and transparency in the 2000s. The dictionary defines *transparent* as "transmitting light rays so that objects on the other side may be distinctly seen."[11] As with the earlier notion of the light of "publicity," corporate transparency is seen as a deterrent to illegal or unethical behavior.[12] The assumption is that unethical behavior thrives in the dark, like mold, and that light prevents mold from growing and spreading. Transparency lets in the light, preventing unethical behavior. Thus, embracing the concept of transparency improves a company's reputation and helps restore trust.[13] Laws and regulations attempt to force transparency but can only act as a deterrent. True transparency occurs when a corporation respects the integrity of all its stakeholders and does not seek to manipulate them by controlling access to information.

Because of the Internet, people today can uncover vast amounts of information. This situation has fostered a constant expectation of access. Prior to the Internet, companies would prepare annual reports and mail them to shareholders, the financial community, and financial media, a relatively small group of people. Now, annual reports are posted on corporate Web sites and can be read by millions of people worldwide. Barriers to transparency, such as the cost of producing materials and the inability to reach all potential stakeholders with that material, have disappeared. The Internet has created the expectation of transparency and provided the ability to be transparent.

Trust, Truth, and Transparency

According to Al Golin, a public relations executive, "Trust is the most basic element of social contact—the great intangible at the heart of truly long-term success."[14] Trust is the basis of every relationship—husband/wife, patient/ doctor, attorney/client, organization/stakeholder. Organizational trust has been defined as "the organization's willingness, based upon its culture and communication behaviors in relationships and transactions, to be appropriately vulnerable."[15] Elsewhere, it has been defined as "the extent to which a company is thought to be honest, dependable, and sensitive to consumer needs."[16] Golin puts it even more succinctly, "Every stakeholder—from analysts to community citizens—has expectations of an organization. In a general sense, trust is the belief that a company will do its utmost to meet those expectations."[17]

Stakeholders develop expectations in part from their previous interactions with an organization. Social exchange theory suggests that people gauge the outcomes of interactions and rationally choose the action that will provide the best result for them based on the track record of past exchanges, shared values, and communication strategies.[18] The frequency of interactions encourages trust and trustworthy behavior. For example, the more often Wal-Mart meets a shopper's expectations for a certain level of quality at a low price, the more the shopper will come to trust the company.

Obviously, unrealistic expectations cannot be met, and trust will either not develop or be broken. In fact, "a scandal can be defined as a betrayal of expectations based on normal conditions of mutual interpersonal trust in social relations of community."[19] Enron, for example, faced a discrepancy in society's expectations of its behavior. Enron created false expectations about its viability by lying in its financial statements, breaking whatever trust it had developed with investors, employees, and the media. Therefore, to ensure a stakeholder's expectations can be met and trust maintained, an organization must be truthful about its circumstances.

The "truth" is "the whole story (if that were possible), with all its innumerable justifications, explanations and excuses."[20] But as the quote indicates, the "truth" is not possible. Therefore, when people talk about the truth, what they really are referring to is an account. In that sense, being truthful means "being accurate and factually correct."[21] From an ethical standpoint, being truthful means not lying. From a legal standpoint, it means that the information can be verified and is not misleading. For example, when the Texas Gulf Sulphur Company issued a news release in 1963 announcing that rumors regarding its discovery of a major sulphur mine were untrue, the SEC claimed the company was misleading investors. The company had made a potentially significant find but was still conducting tests to confirm the size of the ore deposit. In its defense, Texas Gulf Sulphur argued that it had issued the release to quell the rumors that were playing havoc with its stock price and that it had intended to announce the find as soon as it had completed testing. The SEC and the court did not buy the argument and found the release not truthful. Although other factors were at work in the case that determined the outcome, the point is that once an organization decides to make a statement, even to say it cannot talk about something, it must carefully craft the statement so that it is truthful and does not mislead.

Of course, a fact is a fact—or is it? It is easy to prove whether some facts are true. The football team has seven wins, or it doesn't. Diet soda has zero calories, or it doesn't. But it can be difficult to prove the truthfulness of other facts. Not all facts are necessarily easily verifiable. State Farm is a good neighbor, or is it? The Atkins diet is a healthy lifestyle, or is it? A company is environmentally friendly because it meets the minimum legal requirements, or is it? One of the problems with "facts" is that sometimes they are subjective and value laden.

The scholars Robert Heath and Richard Nelson argue that it is difficult to apply the legal standards of substantiation and verifiability used to determine the veracity of advertising claims to image advertising, for example, because claims in image ads are often subjective. In an image ad, for instance, an organization may claim that it is a good corporate citizen because it engages in community service work. Whether the organization does in fact engage in service work can be readily verified. Whether that work means that it is a good corporate citizen is another matter. Values such as corporate social responsibility may change, which requires a change in the facts that support the values.

Nike discovered the impact of truth on corporate reputation and the impact of changing values on what constitutes truth when activist Marc Kasky sued the company under the California false advertising law. Kasky alleged in part that Nike did not ensure that workers in its overseas factories were paid a "living wage," whereas Nike alleged that its subcontractors were bound by a signed Memorandum of Understanding to pay their workers a "living wage." The truth of such "facts" on both sides of the debate is open to interpretation as to what constitutes a living wage. Nike initially used its Code of Conduct and Memorandum of Understanding as evidence that it was a responsible corporate citizen. When those two documents were first introduced, those facts were sufficient. But, the value of what constituted good corporate citizenry then changed. Requiring compliance without anything more was no longer sufficient to support the new value. Nike was faced now with a legitimacy gap—a discrepancy in Nike's behavior and society's expectations of Nike.

Thus truth alone is not sufficient today for a trusting relationship. An organization can be truthful and tell its employees that it is laying them off, but that information alone does not mean the employees trust the organization. Truthfulness must be combined with transparency. A study of Enron's communication strategies and the media coverage of its downfall reveals that the media did not trust Enron when it said it was cooperating with the SEC, although that may well have been true, because the organization had not been transparent with the media in the past.[22]

Although transparency is often discussed in terms of governments, when it is used in connection with an organization, it refers to information transparency. It is a measure of the degree to which organizational actions and decisions are ascertainable and understandable by a party interested in those actions or decisions.[23] Although most of the legal and administrative reactions to the financial scandals have involved financial transparency, corporate transparency is broader than just finances.

For example, technology companies in the past tried to hide or ignore software flaws in their products. For instance, in 1994, Intel ignored the complaints of a few mathematicians that its newly introduced Pentium chip had a computational flaw until those complaints garnered media attention. Increased media attention to that kind of issue has turned what is essentially a product problem into a software industry problem. Today, companies cannot wait until a third party discovers a flaw. They must announce it themselves; they must be transparent. As Eric Armstrong, a public relations practitioner in the technology industry, notes, "while vendor disclosure of flaws will not negate responsibility, only through transparent dealings with its public will a tech company be able to build and retain the consumer trust upon which it depends."[24]

Intel's problem, from a public relations perspective, was not that it had produced a flawed product, but that it had ignored consumers who were trying to help the company by telling it about the flaw. Those consumers saw themselves in a relationship with Intel, but Intel failed to recognize that relationship as anything more than contractual. Stakeholders have complex relationships and interactions with organizations today, which means that simply producing a quality product is not sufficient to generate and keep trust. Stakeholders demand more. Transparency, then, is an organization's willingness to disclose all of its business, social, and political activities, in other words to be open, so that stakeholders can see what it is doing and understand the reasoning behind its actions.

Transparency carries with it an implication of accountability—that executives will be held accountable either to the legal system or to their stakeholders if they violate the law or act in ways that adversely affect stakeholders' interests.[25] In that sense, it involves "the willingness and responsibility to try to give a meaningful and accurate account of oneself, or of circumstances in which one is involved."[26]

Such openness is characterized not just by the information itself, but also by the perception of how it is delivered.[27] The legal adage, "Justice must not only be done, it must be seen to be done," can be applied to the concept of transparency. The adage suggests that although a defendant may in fact get a fair trial regardless of, say, prejudicial pretrial publicity, the public must also believe that the defendant received a fair trial given that publicity. In the business context, it is not enough for an organization to simply disclose financial information in a timely and clear manner and claim to be open. Today's stakeholders demand that corporations and their leaders be open, candid, and engaged.[28] That is, stakeholders must perceive or believe that the organization is transparent and that they are being told everything they need to know. To be transparent, it is not sufficient for an organization to announce to its employees that it is laying off many of them without also explaining why and how it reached its decision. The employees do not necessarily have to agree with the decision, but they must understand the decision and believe the organization has told them the truth about its reasoning.

Transparency should be seen as a process because it involves not just making information available, but also "active participation in acquiring, distributing and creating knowledge."[29] Transparency is an unending process because there is always new information to disclose, new stories to tell. How much information and what information to share will depend on whether the information significantly affects stakeholders. Transparency should be guided by the relationship between the organization and its various stakeholders.

Failure to be perceived as transparent can be damaging to an organization's reputation. In Enron's news releases during the SEC investigation into its finances, it attempted to be transparent.[30] It announced the investigation, promised to cooperate fully with the SEC, and indicated that it was taking corrective action by establishing a special committee of its board to assist the SEC. But the media did not perceive Enron as being transparent. The media saw Enron's actions as attempts to defend itself and shift the blame. They described an Enron that was not forthcoming even with its own employees and that had tried to deceive analysts. The *Economist* summed it up best with the comment, "transparency was never Enron's strong suit."[31]

WorldCom, on the other hand, received more favorable media coverage during its SEC investigation even though its news releases were not substantially different in message from Enron's. The difference appears to have been that WorldCom's CEO, John Sidgmore, worked the telephones, making himself available to the media. He promised to take responsibility for WorldCom's actions and committed the company to transparency. In other words, although he did not take personal responsibility for WorldCom's past actions, he did take control of the situation and make himself accountable for the company's future behavior. Sidgmore's actions fostered a perception of transparency. The difference between media coverage of the two companies can be attributed to the fact that Enron said they were transparent, while Sidgmore said they would be. Thus, not only being transparent, but being perceived as transparent, is vitally important for an organization's reputation.

But transparency is not without its problems. Some scholars have argued, for example, that the demand for increased transparency is based on assumptions that may not be true. First, it is assumed that the demand for transparency is coming from the public, that the public wants more communication from organizations. But, some argue, most consumers are not interested in organizational attempts at greater transparency. Except for a few activist groups that seek disclosure into organizational practices, most people really are only interested in some assurance that organizations are behaving properly.[32] What stakeholders want to know most is how an organization's actions will impact them positively and negatively.[33]

Second, it is assumed that the public has unlimited information-processing capacity, that the public has the time and ability to absorb all of this information. Again, critics argue that the public is not really interested in everything corporations are disclosing. While it is certainly true that consumers are probably not interested in all the information a corporation discloses in an effort to be transparent, it is also true that people become upset when they discover that corporations have been behaving badly. Therefore, although people may not be monitoring organizations on a constant basis, they expect those organizations to be responsible and transparent. As Fred Cook, CEO of the public relations firm GolinHarris, says, "The average American demands that the companies they do business with communicate every detail about their products and practices. And when things go wrong, they automatically blame the company."[34]

Third, it is assumed that more information leads to greater trust and credibility.[35] Information per se, however, does not equate with transparency nor necessarily lead to trust. Unethical organizations can use transparency to obscure and obfuscate reality by presenting a mass of information that hides rather than illuminates. "It is a form of transparency that is not transparent at all," as legal scholar J. M. Balkin put it.[36] Lawyers use such tactics in the discovery process when they have to disclose documents at the other side's request. Rather than providing the pertinent documentation, they submit volumes of documents, forcing the other side to spend hours finding the relevant information among the mass of papers. The result is the effective hiding of information under a claim of openness and cooperation. Thus, transparency and the disclosure of information must be coupled with the intent to act responsibly and be open and accountable.

Another problem with the concept of transparency is that sometimes information cannot be disclosed. Despite the ideal of transparency, as a practical matter there are times when confidentiality is required of an organization. It can be difficult, then, to balance "the absolute need to be transparent in a way that gives all constituencies of the corporation an opportunity to act with maximum information counterpoised against the absolute requirement to hold some matters—for legal, competitive, and other purposes—in strict confidence."[37] The balance between transparency and confidentiality varies on a case-by-case basis. For example, when dealing with proprietary matters such as competitive intelligence and trade secrets, confidentiality will take precedence. Similarly, during negotiations leading to mergers and acquisitions and the quiet period before an initial public offering, confidentiality is not just required but legally mandated by the SEC.[38] But, while there are times when confidentiality may be required, the overarching and guiding principle must be transparency. Thus, confidentiality should be the exception and not the rule. The answer is to "have a perceptive, ethical and knowledgeable general counsel, who can explain what can, and cannot, be revealed, according to current regulations and business practices."[39]

Public Relations During Crisis

The importance of being truthful and transparent is magnified in times of crisis. Often, the damage from a crisis occurs not because of the incident itself, but rather because of the way the company handles it.[40] The Institute for Crisis Management defines a crisis as "a significant business disruption, which stimulates extensive news media coverage. The resulting public scrutiny will affect the organization's normal operations and also could have a political, legal, financial, and governmental impact on its business."[41] As the definition suggests, a crisis can have a profound effect on a company and its future. Exxon's reputation suffered for years from the company's handling of the 1989 Exxon Valdez oil spill in Alaska, even though other companies have had larger spills, because the public perceived Exxon as arrogant and uncaring. Thus, a crisis has two components: the incident itself and the organization's public response to the incident.

A crisis can occur suddenly and unexpectedly. For example, a natural disaster can destroy a business, a disgruntled former employee can return and shoot others on the premises, or terrorists can blow up a building. More often, however, a crisis is not completely unexpected. It is something that has been building for some time but has existed under the media's radar. In either case, because a crisis is public in nature, it demands a statement from the organization, a statement "that is a wise, ethical, and strategic response" to the crisis.[42]

An ethical response to a crisis will take into account stakeholders' expectations of the organization. Because stakeholders may be harmed by a crisis, they want to be reassured that the organization is capable of taking control of the crisis, resolving it, and taking steps to prevent a recurrence in the future. An ethical response will help stakeholders understand what happened and why, and what actions have been taken or will be taken. Thus the response must be credible and foster "trust, openness, commitment, identification, and aligned interests."[43] To be credible, the statement must meet stakeholders' expectations and must match the organization's actions. Enron's responses to its crisis were not credible because the media did not expect Enron to be transparent. And Enron's actions—first stonewalling and then stopping communication entirely—belied its promises of openness.

In determining the appropriate strategic response, the nature of the crisis must be taken into account. Factors such as the amount of personal control the organization had over the crisis and the severity of the crisis must be considered.[44] Experimental studies have shown that "image damage increases with perceptions of organizational responsibility for the crisis."[45] Case studies of response strategies suggest that when the organization is perceived as bearing responsibility for the crisis, accepting responsibility for the crisis and apologizing (mortification) and a combination of bolstering (reminding publics of the organization's existing policies), shifting blame, and taking corrective action may be the most effective.[46] The problem with accepting responsibility, however, is that it may open the organization up to legal action. And shifting blame goes against the ethical tenets of responsible advocacy in that it can be used to obfuscate reality. Shifting the blame to another party is an attempt to take the focus off oneself and direct attention elsewhere. But being truthful and transparent requires one to be open and accountable for one's own actions.

Corrective action and bolstering may be better strategies because they are just as effective and not as legally dangerous as accepting responsibility.[47] Studies have also found that the most important strategy is victim oriented and demonstrates that the organization has learned its lesson and will not repeat the crisis.

Being open and truthful about a crisis can be difficult to achieve when the crisis may lead to a lawsuit. The old crisis communication adage, "Tell it first, tell it fast, and tell it all," while certainly having merit, must be tempered with careful analysis of the situation, especially when it comes to the "tell it all" part. There are times when telling it all is not only unadvisable, it may even be negligent. According to the Institute for Crisis Management, labor disputes, class action lawsuits, defects and recalls, and workplace violence are among the most prevalent crises faced by organizations.[48] Because each of these involves questions of legal liability, legal and public relations counsel are often brought together in times of crisis. Both lawyers and public relations professionals have the best interest of the organization at heart, but they have different methods of protecting the organization. Lawyers are focused on avoiding conflict and then on winning the litigation or courtroom fight once conflict becomes unavoidable. They know that any pretrial messages put out in behalf of an organization could well come back to haunt the organization in court.

Public relations professionals, on the other hand, operate in the court of public opinion. They also seek to avoid conflict and keep the organization's reputation intact with its various stakeholders, but in a situation of conflict, they seek to communicate the organization's position openly and quickly. Public relations practitioners know that a win in the courtroom at the expense of public support may still be a loss. As crisis communication expert Jon Bernstein put it, "If after months or years of excellent legal work, you obtain positive results for a client—but the client's business is still irrevocably damaged due to rumor, innuendo, misperception and competitors taking advantage of same," the courtroom win may have come at too high a price.[49]

Denial of guilt or responsibility for the crisis, a traditional legal response, has been shown in studies to have limited effectiveness as a strategy in corporate image restoration. The literature suggests that only corporations that are truly blameless, as in the cases of Johnson & Johnson's Tylenol tampering scare and Pepsi's syringe crisis, have been able to use denial of guilt successfully. Of course, in both of those cases, the companies were innocent victims in the crisis and thus were able to credibly deny responsibility.[50] Similarly, the fast food restaurant Wendy's was able to effectively deny responsibility when someone found part of a finger in a cup of its chili because it was able to quickly ascertain that the finger did not come from any of its employees or food suppliers.

When an organization is a victim or is being wrongly accused, a strong response to the charges can help protect the organization's image. For example, crisis manager Steven Fink has argued that Wendy's should have defended itself more strenuously in the media when it became clear that the finger-in-the-chili incident was a hoax. "If Wendy's doesn't defend itself, why should leery customers trust them and frequent the restaurant?" he notes.[51] Staying quiet in the face of attacks allows others to frame the issue and set the discourse around that issue.

Lawyers, of course, have long used the mass media to get their clients' side of the story out to the public, especially in high-profile court cases, but the formal practice of litigation public relations, a subspecialty of crisis communication, first emerged in the early 1980s.[52] Litigation public relations has been defined as the management of the communications process "during the course of any legal dispute or adjudicatory proceeding so as to affect the outcome or its impact on the client's overall reputation."[53] One of the goals of litigation public relations is to influence the outcome of the court case, perhaps by encouraging early or favorable settlement or by pressuring the prosecution into bringing lesser or no charges.[54] Another goal is to protect the client's reputation before and during the trial. These goals are achieved by

- counteracting negative publicity,
- making a client's viewpoint known,
- ensuring balanced media coverage,
- helping the media and the public understand complex legal issues,
- defusing a hostile environment, and
- helping resolve the conflict.[55]

Although most scholars appear to accept the need for litigation public relations, others question the ethics of the practice, concerned that it could easily cross the line into extrajudicial speech, comments made about a trial to the public, including potential jurors, outside the courtroom.[56] Extrajudicial speech by attorneys is regulated by state bar associations, but there is no similar constraint on public relations professionals.

While some scholars equate the practice with pretrial publicity and question whether such publicity serves to defeat the fairness of the judicial system,[57] others suggest that attempts to influence the outcome of a trial are broader than focusing on potential jurors.[58] Prosecutors and plaintiffs work to de-legitimize defendants in the eyes of the media, investors, legislators, and other stakeholders. For their part, defendants seek to de-legitimize the case against them. For example, prosecutors in the criminal case against Richard Scrushy, former CEO of HealthSouth, who was indicted on conspiracy, false reporting, fraud, and money laundering charges, painted a picture of Scrushy in the media as the mastermind of a scheme to defraud small investors and employees out of their life savings. Scrushy, through his Web site and attorneys, portrayed himself as an innocent victim of conniving subordinates and an overzealous prosecuting attorney. The jury ultimately found that although fraud had indeed occurred at the company, the prosecutors had not established beyond a reasonable doubt that Scrushy knew about the fraud.

One answer to effective crisis response is to have legal and public relations counsel work together to craft a strategic communications crisis plan before a crisis hits. Then, should a crisis arise, the parameters for reacting to it will already have been developed. It is possible to send a message of compassion and action to stakeholders, for example, without accepting responsibility for the crisis. Such an approach could well satisfy both public relations practitioners and their desire to be forthcoming and legal counsel and their desire to say nothing.

The most effective crisis response is to identify the real cause of the crisis and rectify it. The author Curt Bechler notes rightly that most of the crisis communication literature examines crisis response strategies in neutral terms. A crisis is described as an obstacle that must be overcome by the organization. The focus of the literature is on finding the most effective way to do that, to restore the status quo. But, Bechler argues, that approach does not address the "internal problems that prompted the event in the first place."[59] In other words, counseling Enron on how best to overcome the financial scandal in terms of rhetorical strategies ignores Enron's role in the scandal. Enron's executives were not innocent victims of a terrorist plot. They were active participants in the creation of the culture that permitted the behaviors resulting in the scandal. The culture at Enron, and the other companies involved in the accounting irregularities, permitted the scandal to occur because it legitimized lying as a means to an end.

An ethical and responsible advocate, then, would not be so concerned with restoring the status quo in times of crisis, but in convincing an organization that it needs to put its own house in order to prevent a future recurrence of the problem. Advocates, whether legal or public relations, provide an organization with objective advice, forcing decision makers to see the effects of their decisions on others so that the right decision can be made. Public relations professionals serve as liaisons between an organization and its stakeholders and, as such, play a boundary-spanning role.[60] They not only advocate for the organization before the stakeholders, but they advocate for the stakeholders before the organization. A responsible public relations advocate will help an organization understand its responsibility to its major stakeholders.

Restoring Trust After a Crisis

It is not sufficient to just call a crisis at an end. An organization must work to rebuild any trust that it lost during the crisis. Once lost, trust cannot be regained overnight. Rebuilding trust is a long-term and continuous venture that requires a commitment from an organization's leadership. According to an industry coalition, "It requires injecting a philosophy of social responsibility and ethical behavior into the company's culture and then demonstrating a willingness to open up the company to scrutiny."[61]

In building an organization's capacity for openness or transparency, public relations professionals play an important role. Although other departments, such as human resources, marketing, and investor relations, engage in communication with stakeholders, the public relations department is in a unique position in terms of building trust because it is concerned with an organization's various stakeholders, both external and internal. While human resources deals with employees, marketing with consumers, and investor relations with investors, public relations must consider the range of stakeholders—employees, consumers, the community, government, suppliers and distributors, investors, and even activist groups. Competent public relations counsel, then, serves "as a strategic integrator, champion, bridge builder, catalyst, facilitator and record keeper for appropriate transparency."[62] Such counsel ensures that a company's external and internal strategies are fully integrated so that its communications are clear and consistent.[63]

Given the extensive rules and regulations regarding financial transparency, investor relations and public relations must work closely together to ensure that a responsible message is being communicated to stakeholders. Similarly, because laws and regulations make being truthful and transparent not always possible, it is imperative that legal and public relations counsel understand each other's contributions and work together to ensure that organizations do the right thing. Research suggests that more collaboration between the two professions is occurring, and that process needs to continue. Consistent dialogue between the two is essential so that a strategic communication plan can be developed that protects the organization from a legal and a reputation standpoint. Mutual understanding comes from continued contact. Public relations professionals need to understand legal counsels' priorities and concerns, while the lawyers need to also understand the importance of communication.

One factor that works against collaboration between legal and public relations counsel is a lack of understanding between the two, although one study has found that lawyers actually have a more accurate view of public relations practitioners than public relations practitioners do of lawyers. Such misunderstanding on the part of public relations professionals can be problematic, especially in times of crisis. As the authors of the study note, "If public relations counselors assume that lawyers are going to usurp their turf, when lawyers may actually be quite open—desirous, in fact, of public relations input—a collaborative crisis-solving relationship is difficult at best."[64]

Maintaining Trust into the Future

Once the organization has made the changes necessary to protect itself from recurrences of the crisis, the public relations professional must communicate those changes to the stakeholders and make it clear that the organization has changed and is commited to transparency. Because many Americans harbor a distrust of large corporations, corporations must work hard to prove they are worthy of trust.

Klaus Kleinfeld of Siemens Corporation suggests that the key to maintaining trust is keeping all stakeholders in balance.[65] Troubles arise when one group of stakeholders is favored over another. For example, some of the corporate scandals were caused by emphasizing rewards to the top executives at the expense of other stakeholders, such as other employees and investors. Other scandals were caused by the focus on investors to the detriment of employees and customers.

Maintaining trust requires the strengthening of relationships with people whose perceptions are vital to the organization. The author Gerald Baron writes that "the ability of the organization to develop and strengthen relationships and leverage strong existing ones into powerful new ones is perhaps the most critical factor in evaluating the future prospects of an organization."[66] And it is the role of the public relations department to maintain and leverage those relationships. When people form opinions about an organization, they do so based on their experience with that organization. The more credible and trustworthy an organization seems, the more the organization is better able to withstand allegations of wrongdoing. The first step in maintaining trust, then, is deciding on the most important stakeholders; the second step is listening to those stakeholders.

Listening to stakeholders permits the public relations professional to find out the needs and expectations of those stakeholders so that the organization can meet them. It also sends the message that the organization respects and values the stakeholders. The information received by listening should be used to take action and craft messages that show stakeholders the organization seeks to meet their needs.

Public relations professionals can begin the process of rebuilding trust and maintaining it into the future by practicing responsible advocacy. Ethics scholars Kathy Fitzpatrick and Candace Gauthier have set out three principles for the practice of responsible advocacy.[67] Responsible advocacy requires public relations professionals do the following:

- Consider the harms and benefits to an organization's stakeholders that can reasonably be expected to result from the organization's actions.
- Maintain respect for stakeholders and treat them with dignity. Stakeholders must be provided with the information necessary to make informed decisions about the organization or to make an informed assent regarding the organization's actions.
- Distribute fairly among the stakeholders the benefits and harms of any action.

Conclusion

The financial scandals that began the twenty-first century caused many to lose trust in American organizations. The scandals seemed to serve as proof that something was wrong with corporate America, that large corporations were arrogant, unethical, and uncaring. Congress reacted to public pressure by enacting laws holding executives accountable for their organization's actions in an effort to restore trust. Transparency became the new buzzword.

The financial scandals were the public face of the problem, but they were not the only factor leading to the demand for transparency. The accessibility of information that the Internet has permitted also created a demand for transparency and the ability to be transparent. Transparency, however, is not without its problems. It can be difficult to balance the need for transparency with the need for confidentiality, for example. And unscrupulous organizations can hide behind a façade of transparency by burying important information under a mass of irrelevant data.

Public relations professionals can assist organizations in rebuilding trust through truth and transparency by practicing responsible advocacy. Responsible advocacy requires public relations professionals to become true advocates for their organizations. That is, they must provide their organizations with objective advice regarding the effect of the organizations' actions on stakeholders and develop consistent messages to stakeholders that respect their dignity and provide them with the appropriate information to make informed decisions regarding the organization. In being responsible advocates to their organization, public relations professionals will also develop strong relationships with the legal and investor relations departments, among others, to ensure that the organization's communications are integrated to be clear and consistent.

Transparency alone will not solve the problem of corporate ethical breaches of behavior. As one scholar put it, "The corporation needs to reaffirm the importance of honesty and propriety in its dealings with its employees and the public at the highest executive levels to truly make a change in current practice.[68] Transparency will only be effective when executives have internalized the norm of transparency; that is, when they have internalized the obligation to disseminate all relevant information in a clear manner to stakeholders. Effective transparency also requires that external stakeholders internalize a norm of acceptable corporate behavior and become willing to act on revelations of breaches of that norm.[69]

7

Responsible Online Communication

Kirk Hallahan

During the presidential elections in 2004, a wild rumor circulated throughout the United States that the federal government planned to reestablish a military draft. Fully one-half of all eighteen- to twenty-nine-year-olds surveyed in one public opinion poll said that they thought the rumor was true.

In fact, no such plans existed.

Many news reports attributed the rumor to the Web site and e-mail campaign conducted by an activist group called MoveOn.org Student Action. The group was an affiliate of a liberal activist group that had gained notoriety because of its efforts to unseat President George Bush and for its adroit use of the World Wide Web to raise political campaign funds online.

Similar to most rumors, the story about a prospective military draft was partly based on fact. In spring 2003, a full year before the invasion of Iraq, legislation had been introduced in Congress to reconstitute the military draft if needed. But leaders of neither major political party favored such a controversial action, even though presidential candidates John Kerry and Ralph Nader both made oblique references to the need for a draft in their campaign rhetoric.

The draft rumor thrived for several months while frustrated government officials tried unsuccessfully to squelch it. The agency that eventually would be responsible for registering prospective draftees was forced to post a message on its Web site that said, "Notwithstanding recent stories in the news media and on the Internet, Selective Service is not getting ready to conduct a draft for the U.S. Armed Forces."[1]

Although another watchdog group, Congress2004.org, had conceived and championed the claim, MoveOn.org Student Action picked up on the antidraft argument and was successful in making the issue visible to a far larger audience because of its savvy use of the Internet.

New Frontiers of Ethics and Responsible Advocacy

In many ways, this incident illustrates the impact that the Internet has had in modern society. Web sites, e-mail, bulletin boards, newsgroups, chat rooms, and wireless telecommunications are now potent forces that must be reckoned with—and are being adroitly used by organizations ranging from loosely organized social movements to large Establishment organizations.

Yet, the effects of these new online media are not yet fully understood—and it is all too easy to fear, criticize, or overstate their impact. Indeed, the Internet was only one part—albeit an important one—in MoveOn.org's campaign to oppose continued military intervention in Iraq. Other activities included ads in college newspapers and special events on college campuses.

The Internet has transformed the techniques and technology of advocacy by enabling individuals and organizations with relatively modest resources to reach a global audience instantaneously twenty-four hours a day, seven days a week.[2] Many practitioners have embraced Internet technology,[3] while others have pointed to the Internet's potential to equalize power relationships in society and to provide a "voice" to otherwise marginalized groups.[4]

Yet, along with opportunity comes responsibility.

Once messages are created, the speed and ease with which online communications can be distributed, stored, duplicated, and redistributed pose new challenges for responsible communicators. In the case of the military draft rumor, for example, much of the "buzz" resulted from thousands of Internet users who forwarded e-mails and news stories to others. People also posted comments on message boards and Web logs (blogs) and forwarded links to Web sites that featured stories about a prospective draft.

Joint Statement of Principles on Public Relations and the Internet

Despite widespread adoption, surprisingly little attention has been paid in the professional public relations literature to the many ethical issues that confront public relations practitioners as users and operators of online communication systems. These include problems that are exacerbated in an online environment (such as false claims) as well as a variety of ethical dilemmas peculiar to the Internet.[5]

For example, none of the codes of ethics promulgated by the principal professional organizations in the field—the Public Relations Society of America (PRSA), the International Association of Business Communicators, the International Public Relations Association, or the National Investor Relations Institute—specifically mention online communications.[6] Yet, all the organizations agree that the general principles embodied in their guidelines for professional conduct apply to practitioners who use the Internet.[7]

Since 2001, the principal source of guidance for public relations practitioners has been a somewhat obscure statement of ethical principles issued under the leadership of the Arthur W. Page Society, an organization of leading corporate communications executives. Members of the Page Society had become concerned about anonymous postings in chat rooms and bulletin boards, as well as the failure of practitioners to disclose the credentials of experts quoted online and potential conflicts of interest. The group worried that inaccurate or misleading information would lead to a loss of credibility for Internet communications.

The Page Society drew upon the classic principles outlined by the pioneer public relations professional for whom the organization is named, and obtained endorsements from ten other organizations for the resulting statement.[8]

Joint Statement of 11 Public Relations Organizations*

Establishing Principles for Public Relations on the Internet[9]

All public relations associations and news organizations share a common understanding for the need to adhere to ethical standards in communications with the public. Although statements of values regarding communications principles may take different forms, they are founded on certain basic tenets. Seek the truth. Minimize harm to others. Be accountable for your actions. Such unalienable principles are the underpinnings of honesty and fairness in everything we do as communicators.

As the newest communications tool, the Internet presents tremendous opportunities to build positive, productive relationships with a variety of publics. It also presents tremendous challenges to professional standards and ethical practices. The digital world is open and transparent. Erroneous or misleading information can be posted on the Internet and instantly and widely disseminated. Anonymity on Web sites can cause irreparable harm. The news media, which increasingly uses the Internet as an information

(Continued)

(Continued)

source, demands accuracy. Public relations practitioners risk losing credibility for themselves and their clients if they violate that trust.

The following principles, developed by the Arthur W. Page Society, are presented as a vehicle for public relations to attain and maintain the highest possible standards in the digital world.

1. Present Fact-Based Content
- Tell the truth at all times.
- Ensure timely delivery of information.
- Tell the full story, adhering to accepted standards for accuracy of information.

2. Be an Objective Advocate
- Act as a credible information source, providing round-the-clock access.
- Know your subject.
- Rely on credible sources for expert advice.
- Offer opportunities for dialogue and direct interaction with expert sources.
- Reveal the background of experts, disclosing any potential conflicts of interest or anonymous economic support of web content.

3. Earn the Public's Trust
- Simultaneously contact multiple stakeholders with relevant and accurate information.
- Disclose all participation in online chat rooms and conferences.
- Correct information that is online.
- Provide counsel on privacy, security and other online trust issues.

4. Educate the Public Relations Profession on Best Practices
- Compile case studies on the best use of the new media.
- Advance and encourage industry-wide adoption of best practices on the Internet.
- Practice principled leadership in the digital world, adhering to the highest standards.

---

*Organizations: Arthur W. Page Society, Corporate Communications Institute, Council of Communication Management, Council of Public Relations Firms, The Conference Board's Council on Corporate Communications Strategy, Institute for Public Relations, International Association of Business Communicators, Public Affairs Council, Public Relations Society of America, Public Relations Society of America Foundation, Women Executives in Public Relations. Adopted December 2001.

The joint statement was predicated on three ethical principles: practitioners should tell the truth, minimize harm to others, and be accountable for their actions. The joint statement identified fifteen guidelines for practitioners to follow in four broad areas: providing fact-based content, being objective advocates, earning public trust, and educating the profession.

Although the 2001 statement was a useful beginning, most of its tenets represent practical advice that ought to be followed whether practicing public relations offline or online. Among its few Internet-specific guidelines was the admonition that practitioners should avoid anonymous participation in chat rooms and discussions. In addition, the statement called on practitioners to become prepared to advise clients on ethical concerns such as online privacy, security, and trust. Although the statement called for the profession to develop and promote "best practices," no specifics for doing so were provided. And as of early 2006, no subsequent efforts have been undertaken by any of the participating organizations to do so. The statement is further limited because it carries no authority to monitor or enforce compliance.

Efforts Outside Public Relations to Promote Responsible Online Communications

The lack of emphasis on online ethics in the public relations field is partly explained by the fact that public relations practitioners use many communications tools, not just the Internet. Only two small groups within the field focus specifically on technology concerns: PRSA's Technology Section and the new International Association of Online Communicators.[10] Furthermore, many practitioners still view the Internet as a set of tools only for *outbound* communication. Most practitioners have been only minimally involved in the *inbound* collection of data from users—the greatest public concern about online ethics today.

Various initiatives outside public relations, stemming from both the private and public sectors, are shaping the standards of conduct for online communications. These are defining best practices and undoubtedly will influence future public relations practices.

Private-Sector Initiatives. Various organizations—ranging from the Catholic Church to local school boards—have issued position papers and policy statements related to online ethics.[11] Similarly, a number of professional and trade associations in fields ranging from appraising to medicine and psychology have incorporated provisions related to the Internet in their codes of conduct.[12]

Organizations whose members are directly dependent on online communications have taken the leadership to regulate themselves and to foster responsible online communications using four principal mechanisms:

Standards and guidelines have been promulgated by several of the leading trade associations in advertising and marketing. Examples include the American Marketing Association, the Interactive Advertising Bureau, and the Direct Marketing Association (DMA) in the United States; and the International Chamber of Commerce.[13]

The DMA's general guidelines, for example, address precautions about promotions to children and the collection, use, and maintenance of all user data. For its members involved in online marketing, the DMA outlines specific recommended disclosures that should be placed on Web sites to explain an organization's online practices. In addition, the DMA states that commercial e-mail solicitations should be sent to only a marketer's own customers, or people who have consented to receive mail and/or who have been given the opportunity to "opt out." The DMA also addresses the improper use of names referred by third parties without the permission of addressees. Finally, the DMA prohibits appending an individual's e-mail address to other electronic records unless specific requirements are met.[14]

Educational programs and organizations have been launched to promote ethical standards of conduct and public understanding of online communications. Many public relations practitioners work for organizations that subscribe to standards promulgated by these groups. Among the most prominent examples are the Electronic Frontier Foundation and the Electronic Privacy Information Center.[15] WiredSafety.org was created to help consumers protect themselves from abuse.[16] Other specialized groups include the Email Service Provider Coalition, the Coalition Against Unsolicited Commercial Email, and the International Council for Internet Communication—all formed to fight spam while protecting the delivery of legitimate e-mail. Meanwhile, the Network for Online Commerce has devoted itself to promoting ethical behavior among firms that provide paid entertainment and information services through telemedia worldwide.[17] Separately, the ePhilanthropy Foundation promulgated a Code of Ethical Online Philanthropic Practices.[18] Two examples in the health field include the Internet Healthcare Coalition and Internet Health Ethics (Hi-Ethics).[19]

Accreditation programs for Web sites involve examinations by third-party organizations to ensure compliance with established guidelines.

Organizations whose Web sites pass scrutiny are permitted to display insignias designed to assure users that sites meet established criteria for protecting users and for maintaining content reliability. The two most prominent examples are Truste and iCop.[20] In the health arena, accreditation of Web health sites is conducted by URAC in the United States and by the Health on the Net Foundation worldwide.[21]

Professional certification or *credential programs* enable online communicators to demonstrate their knowledge, professionalism, and commitment to ethical conduct. Examples include testing programs sponsored by the International Association of Privacy Professionals and the Organization of Search Engine Optimization Professionals.[22]

Public-Sector Efforts. Public policymakers at the federal and state levels also have been pressed to guard against questionable online practices. The resulting rules for behavior contained in laws and regulations represent *minimum* standards of online conduct that organizations and individuals must follow to avoid civil or criminal prosecution.

In the United States, the communications activities of organizations can be regulated as part of the government's oversight of activities in which it has a *compelling state interest* as long as that regulation does not impose

---

Selected U.S. Laws Shaping Responsible Online Communications[23]

Fair Credit Reporting Act, 1970. Pub. L. 91–508, 15 USC 1601. Governs the collection and distribution of electronic credit reports. Strengthened most recently by the Fair and Accurate Credit Actions Act, 2003. Pub. L. 108–59, 15 USC 1601.

Family Educational Rights and Privacy Act, 1974. Pub. L. 93–380, 20 USC 1232g. Prescribed policies about the public disclosure of student information to be followed by educational institutions that receive federal funds.

Computer Software Copyright Act, 1980. Pub. L. 96–517, 17 USC 102, 117. Curtailed pirating by affirming copyright protection for computer software.

Computer Fraud and Abuse Act, 1986. 18 USC 1030(a). Prohibited unauthorized access to particular computer systems with intent to steal or

---

(Continued)

(Continued)

commit fraud. Strengthened in No Electronic Theft Act, 1998 Pub. L. 105–47, 17 USC 506.

Electronic Communications Privacy Act, 1986. Pub. L. 99–508, 18 USC 2510. Prohibited unauthorized access to specified electronic communications and disclosure of private communications.

Health Insurance Portability and Accountability Act (HIPAA), 1996. Pub. L. 104–191, 42 USC 1302(d). Outlined safeguards for protecting patient confidentiality, including electronic disclosures.

Children's Online Protection Act, 1998. Pub. L. 105–217, 15 USC 6501–650. Made it a federal crime to transmit harmful information to minors. Passed in response to the Supreme Court's overturning of the Communications Decency Act of 1996, Pub. L. 104–104, which had outlawed distribution of all online pornography. Complemented by the Protection of Children from Sexual Predators Act, 1998. Pub. L. 105–134.

Digital Millenium Copyright Act, 1998. Pub. L. 105–304, 17 USC 1201–1205. Extensively revised the Federal Trademark Act of 1947 (Lanham Act) to address digital media issues; guaranteed and protected the use of encryption systems.

Workforce Investment Act, 1998. Pub. L. 105–220, 20 USC 794d. Section 508 of the law requires that Web sites must be accessible to the disabled if paid for with federal funds.

Anti-Cybersquatting Consumer Protection Act, 1999. Pub. L. 106–113, 17 USC 1125 to strengthen the Federal Trademark Dilution Act, 1995. Pub. L. 104–98, 15 USC 1125c to protect against trademark misuse and dilution by others in an online environment.

Electronic Signatures in Global and National Commerce Act, 2000. Pub. L. 106–229, 15 USC 7001. Permitted and encouraged use of electronic signatures in commerce.

USA Patriot Act—United and Strengthening America by Producing Appropriate Tools to Interrupt and Obstruct Terrorism Act, 2001. Pub. L. 107–56, 28 USC 994(p). Expanded CPAA (1986) and provided exemption from prosecution for hardware, software, and firmware companies whose equipment might be used by terrorists. Allowed government to use wiretaps to monitor Internet users and permitted police to intercept communications of computer trespassers.

CAN-SPAM—Controlling the Assault of Non-Solicited Pornography and Marketing Act, 2003. Pub. L. 108–187. Authorized the FTC to curtail delivery of undesired commercial messages.

undue prior restraint on free speech. An examination of the debates leading up to the adoption of each of these laws and regulations is informative because advocates invariably called for legislation and regulation based on public concern and examples of egregious violations of the public's expectations about ethical behavior.

Administrative regulations also are beginning to subtly influence how organizations conduct online activities. For example, the Federal Trade Commission (FTC) promulgated an advisory to businesses that effectively places Web site designers in the same category as advertising agencies. Both groups are now responsible for reviewing online information to substantiate claims and to avoid information that is misleading. To help Web site sponsors determine whether required disclosures are clear and conspicuous, the FTC provided a series of guidelines for ethical communication. According to the FTC, disclosures should be in close proximity to relevant claims or should be easily found through the use of clearly labeled markers and links; disclaimers must be prominent and not overshadowed by distracting material; audio messages must be presented with adequate volume and cadence to be heard; visual disclosures must appear for a sufficient duration; and the language used needs to be understandable by the intended audience.[24]

A second federal agency, the Food and Drug Administration (FDA), is also concerned with unethical online activity, particularly misleading claims and outright fraud involving the sale of drugs and medical devices. (The agency is still formulating a position about whether drugs ought to be sold online at all.) Unlike the FTC, the FDA has issued no specific guidelines related to the production of online content. However, the agency routinely issues "cyber letters" to Web sites believed to engage in questionable activities. The FDA also encourages legitimate Web site operators to display public service messages (banner and button ads) that lead consumers to precautionary information on the FDA's site.[25]

Separately, the Securities and Exchange Commission (SEC) proactively encourages use of the Internet to meet its mandate that publicly traded companies engage in prompt and full disclosure of material information that could influence investment decisions. Since 1984, the SEC has required the electronic submission of SEC filings by regulated companies. In 2002, the agency broadened the list of material information that should be provided on company Web sites, either directly or through links to the SEC's Electronic Data Gathering and Reporting (EDGAR) system. At the beginning of 2005, the SEC promulgated proposed rules that would change the procedures for initial public offerings (IPOs). The SEC proposed that companies be allowed to use Webcasts to distribute analyst presentations ("road shows") to a broad array of audiences and to forego distribution of final offering prospectuses if the documents were available online.[26]

Ethics and Computing: A Broader Perspective

As computing became increasingly prominent in people's lives during the twentieth century, computer engineers and operations professionals found themselves grappling with the questions of ethics and social responsibility.[27] In part, this reflected the increased sense of professionalism among computing professionals and culminated in the adoption of a joint code of ethics by two of the largest computer associations, the Association for Computing Machinery and the Institute of Electrical and Electronics Engineers.[28] Other specialized organizations were formed, such as the Computer Ethics Institute, an affiliate of the Brookings Institute in Washington, D.C. The Computer Ethics Institute, most notably, published a widely quoted "Ten Commandments of Computer Ethics."[29]

Ten Commandments Of Computer Ethics[30]

1. Thou Shalt Not Use A Computer To Harm Other People.

2. Thou Shalt Not Interfere With Other People's Computer Work.

3. Thou Shalt Not Snoop Around In Other People's Computer Files.

4. Thou Shalt Not Use A Computer To Steal.

5. Thou Shalt Not Use A Computer To Bear False Witness.

6. Thou Shalt Not Copy Or Use Proprietary Software For Which You Have Not Paid.

7. Thou Shalt Not Use Other People's Computer Resources Without Authorization Or Proper Compensation.

8. Thou Shalt Not Appropriate Other People's Intellectual Output.

9. Thou Shalt Think About The Social Consequences Of The Program You Are Writing Or The System You Are Designing.

10. Thou Shalt Always Use A Computer In Ways That Insure Consideration And Respect For Your Fellow Humans.

SOURCE: Copyright 1991. Computer Ethics Institute. Written by Dr. Ramon C. Barquin. Reprinted with permission.

Computing professionals quickly recognized their need to be accountable and have largely rejected the notion of what the author Richard T. DeGeorge calls the "myth of amoral computing and information technology." Computers obviously are not moral beings; people clearly are responsible for the design, function, and consequences of technology.[31] Yet, as social critics—including Jacques Ellul, Neil Postman, and others—have pointed out, modern societies embrace new technologies almost unquestioningly and without considering the moral and social consequences.[32]

The increased reliance on communications technology results from both increased demand for information and the slavish promotion of new technologies, motivated by the desires for productivity among users and for profitability among suppliers. These two "pull" and "push" forces have multiplied the "moments of truth" where people make critical decisions about how technology will be used.[33]

In principle, online communications are no different from any other human activity. However, the Internet features some peculiar characteristics that pose particular ethical challenges. These include its instantaneous speed, global scale, anonymity, interactivity, reproducibility, and uncontrollability.[34] One leading Internet ethicist, Jerden van den Hoven, suggests the application of traditional applied ethics is inadequate in the age of cyberspace. He cites the loss of territorial base for comparison when making judgments, the redefinition of moral concepts, problems in attributing responsibility, and ignorance among both computer operators and users about the consequences of their actions.[35]

A widely cited expert, Lawrence Lessig, argues that regulation of cyberspace is driven as much by the architecture of Internet technology itself (the "code") as by laws, the market, and social norms.[36] But Richard Spinello, a leading ethicist who specializes in technology issues, argues that ethics are more than merely social norms. Instead, Spinello contends that ethics serve as *metanorms* that represent universal values that ought to play a directive role in influencing all the factors Lessing cites—laws, the market, system architecture, and social norms.

Spinello organized the moral quandaries in the electronic frontier into three categories. He suggested the following operative moral questions:

Consequences-based morality: Which action or policy promotes the best overall consequences or the greatest utility for all parties?

Duty-based morality: Can the maxim underlying the course of the action being considered be universalized? Is the principle of fair play being violated? If there appear to be conflicting duties, which is the stronger duty?

Rights-based morality: Which action or policy best protects the human and legal rights of the individuals involved? Does the proposed action or policy impede the basic requirements of human flourishing?[37]

Spinello's model reflects major approaches to ethics commonly cited in the public relations literature and elsewhere.

Consequences-based ethics involves, among other things, the principle of *enlightened self-interest* (also known as *egoism*), which suggests that an action is morally right if it promotes a party's long-term interests.[38] Thus, the operator of a Web site might think a particular practice is justified if it results in online traffic or transactions. Consequences-based ethics also incorporate a *teleological* approach to ethics, which suggests that the obtained result is what's important. *Teleos* is the Greek word for "the good" or "the end." Using this rationale, the end justifies the means because the benefits exceed the costs. This is particularly true if the results produce happiness, pleasure, or the greatest social good. The utilitarian ethical approach, first suggested by writers such as John Stuart Mill and Jeremy Bentham, might suggest that knowingly deceptive online practices are acceptable because they contribute to attaining larger, even socially desired, goals.[39]

Duty-based ethics are grounded in *deontological* ethics, which rejects utilitarianism and argues that people must employ proper means and act with good intentions regardless of outcomes. *Deontology* is based on the Greek word *deon,* for "duty" or "obligation." The philosopher Immanuel Kant popularized this idea in his notion of the *categorical imperative,* in which he argued that all human actions must be fair and honest.[40] Judeo-Christian and other cultures around the world embrace the notion that people are not merely means toward ends and emphasize values such as respect for the individual, choice, freedom, and justice. A number of modern-day ethicists have outlined typologies of the values that thus constitute ethical behavior.[41]

Rights-based ethics go beyond deontological obligations to emphasize that people are *entitled* to fair and equitable treatment. One approach, which was popularized by Joseph Fletcher in the 1960s, argues that ethics are rooted in the notion of *community.* These ethicists argue that ethical maxims (or expectations) vary by community and are not absolute—although love, human welfare, and happiness appear to transcend most communities as bases for ethical decision making.[42] Another example involves *communitarianism,* which has received attention as a possible framework for public relations.[43] Similarly, *distributive justice* draws upon the notion of the contractual rights that exist between the individual and civil society. The philosopher John Rawls suggested in the 1970s that people often operate in a "veil of ignorance" and don't fully understand their position in a social system or their own capabilities. As a result, a moral society must consider the needs and rights of all members. Justice requires that people have (a) equal claim to basic rights and liberties, and (b) equal access to opportunity.[44]

Although all of these approaches to ethics might be applied to groups or organizations seeking to conduct responsible online communications, the latter-day approaches based on duty and rights—and that emphasize community, respect, and equal access—have particular appeal. This is especially true when considering the contemporary emphasis on Internet users as a *virtual community*.[45]

One application of this rights-based approach is the call for a *new social contract* to govern our information society. The information ethicists Richard Mason, Florence Mason, and Mary Culnan identified six key tensions that provide a framework for considering ethics in an information management context. These included ownership and use of intellectual property, privacy, the quality and accuracy of information, information justice (access), gatekeeping (restrictions on the free flow of information), and technological implementation that avoids social disruption, dislocation, and human misery.[46]

According to Mason, Mason, and Culnan, four parties play principal roles in the information society: *Information givers* provide information. *Information orchestrators* gather, process, store, and disseminate information and serve as information gatekeepers. *Information takers* receive and use information for their own purposes. (In a public relations context, clients are information takers whereas practitioners often serve as information orchestrators). Finally, *stakeholders* are people (and organizations) affected by the information-based actions in which information takers engage. The responsibilities of each can be summarized as follows:

- Information takers should collect information only for legitimate purposes that are just and beneficial to givers and to stakeholders.
- Information takers and orchestrators should use the information only for the purpose for which it is taken and obtain consent from givers.
- Information givers ought to supply the source information because it is necessary in order for takers to take action or benefit shareholders.
- Information orchestrators or gatekeepers should handle information with fidelity to source while shaping, limiting, or expanding it to best meet the takers' needs.[47]

Eight Core Concerns: A Framework for Ethical Online Public Relations

Thus far, this chapter has examined the limited effort to delineate principles of responsible online public relations. It also reviewed steps taken in the private and public sectors to curb abuses and foster responsible online communication more generally. Finally, within the emerging context of information management, it has explored key concepts in ethics.

Ethics in public relations (or any other activity) can be defined as establishing and following criteria to be used when making decisions about what is right or wrong.[48] The late Supreme Court Justice Potter Stewart, in a frequently cited quote, defined ethics as "knowing the difference between what you have the right to do and what is the right thing to do."

Importantly, ethics are *social constructions* that are negotiated. People concerned with particular social problems (such as abusive online practices) come to agree on what are accepted rules through a process of deliberation. Indeed, Aristotle's principle of the "golden mean" suggested that in every situation there are two extremes and that the ethical choice is in the middle.[49]

The remainder of this chapter integrates these various ideas by identifying eight broad areas of ethical concerns for online public relations practitioners. The discussion identifies overarching areas of concern, but also points out particular practices that are problematic. Importantly, defining ethical online behavior is an ongoing process, and acceptable standards of practice continue to evolve.

Access and Choice

Ethical online public relations begins by providing publics with the opportunity to communicate. A decade following the popularization of the Internet, people have come to *expect* that organizations and groups have an online presence and that users can communicate with them online if they choose to do so.

Access involves offering users the choice of tools (Web sites, e-mail, newsgroups, games, etc.) and delivery options that best meet their needs (personal computers, wireless, personal digital appliances, interactive television, etc.). In the coming years, this will require organizations to make an increased commitment of resources to offering a variety of access options.[50]

Despite the ostensibly ubiquitous presence of the Internet, only two-thirds of Americans have Internet access, and adoption rates vary considerably based on age and socioeconomic status. Penetration rates also differ widely worldwide. The public debate about this "digital divide" requires public relations practitioners to be sensitive to problems of equal access consistent with duty- and rights-based approaches to ethics. In a few instances, such as the promotion of topics inappropriate for children, access might need to be limited on ethical grounds.

Moreover, not all constituents necessarily will *want* to use the Internet in every situation to communicate with an organization. Despite efforts to be on the cutting edge (and to reduce costs by shifting constituent contact to the online environment), prudent organizations must continue to allow (and encourage) alternative forms of contact—the telephone, correspondence, and personal visits—if they are truly committed to serving constituents. In short, giving people *choices* is important.

Accuracy of Content

Ethical online public relations cannot be misleading. Depending on the circumstances, content might be subject to governmental oversight (by agencies such as the FTC, FDA, or SEC in the United States) to guard against fraud. However, content needs to be accurate, complete, and current to maintain the confidence and trust of users—as a matter of duty and users' rights.

Public relations practitioners must be vigilant about the accuracy of content, whether produced by a public relations unit or others in their client organizations. The broad and rapid-speed dissemination of information requires practitioners to avoid distributing inaccurate information that can be stored, reproduced, and redistributed unwittingly by recipients who assume the veracity of information. The real-time nature of the Internet allows for the easy updating of information on Web sites and e-mails. Ethical practice requires making every effort to correct and acknowledge errors quickly.

Accuracy applies to both verbal and visual messages. One of the unintended consequences of new digital technologies is the ability to digitally manipulate photos and graphics. Although photographers and graphic artists have always employed a variety of techniques to enhance pictures, electronic editing systems now make it tempting for practitioners and others to alter the *material* accuracy of images and thus alter the representation of reality. This problem is further exacerbated on the Internet because intermediaries and end users have the same capabilities to alter images.[51]

The fragmented and decontextualized nature of online communications (evidenced by the layering of content on multiple Web pages and people's propensity to use cryptic language and sometimes ambiguous references in e-mails) demands that each communication be complete so it can be understood on its own.

Also of concern is the consistency of messages—an important contributor to a message's believability. Online communications must engender verisimilitude (a sense of realism) and resonate with a person's offline experience. To do otherwise can mislead audiences, interrupt message processing, or discourage message acceptance. A lack of believability raises doubts about the trustworthiness of the message, the source, and online communications itself. Thus, public relations practitioners are posed with new responsibilities to monitor their organization's online presence as a critical element in reputation management.

Deceptive Practices

Ethical public relations involves the avoidance of deceptive practices related to the design and functionality of online communication. Practitioners can unwittingly engage in deception whenever otherwise accurate information is presented in a way that misleads users.

Obvious examples of unethical conduct include the *misappropriation* of content from another source. Practitioners must not misrepresent themselves by using the intellectual properties of others. This includes reproducing copyrighted material without acknowledgement or beyond the established rules of fair use. This also includes reproducing editorial matter from newspapers and magazines that favorably mention a client, unless permission is granted and it is clearly labeled. Similarly, practitioners should not use another party's trademark unless authorized and permission to do so is acknowledged.

In the case of Web sites, more subtle ethical problems involve including textual links to another's Web site without permission and using screen frames to enclose another organization's Web pages within another without permission. The effect of these techniques is to suggest an endorsement or relationship that might not exist.

Deception also can occur in the layout of Web pages, where information is so fragmented that it becomes difficult for a user to fully comprehend the context in which an idea or offer is presented. As the FTC's guidelines suggest, material disclaimers must be both in close proximity and sufficiently prominent so that users are not misled. Users also can be deceived into thinking that they have no other option for communicating with an organization when addresses, telephone numbers, and e-mail addresses are omitted.[52]

Deceptive misrepresentation of online sources is probably the most egregious ethical problem in the online environment today. Not identifying a source and using false-front organizations (where the real identity of sponsors is purposefully withheld) are prohibited under the PRSA Code of Ethics. However, many organizations operate online without fully disclosing their identity, which places a burden on users to check the veracity of information and sources.[53]

Participating in chat rooms and bulletin boards without identifying one's connection to an organization that might have a vested interest in a topic under discussion is one of the few ethical violations specifically identified in the "Joint Statement on Public Relations and the Internet." However, a more difficult question is whether a chat room participant should even eavesdrop on conversations. Some proponents of this practice argue that monitoring discussions is the legitimate equivalent to watching a public debate or employing an electronic clipping service. On the other hand, critics of the practice point out that many chat rooms are considered private conversations among participants in a community of common interest. Depending on rules that might explicitly be stated when registering, or that might be implicitly understood by participants, lurking in chat rooms to collect intelligence could be an unethical breach of duty or the violation of the rights of participants.[54]

Other identity-related problems involve the branding of Web sites. Competitors or opponents often create sites with similar names (such as whitehouse.com versus whitehouse.gov). These *rogue sites* (which include *attack sites* as well as *spoof sites*) divert traffic from legitimate site operators for financial or political gain. Although such sites are legal as long as they do not create initial confusion of intent, such branding practices are questionable. Similarly, purchasing Web addresses so that legitimate potential users cannot use them (or must purchase the rights to do so at a hefty charge) has been labeled *cybersquatting*—an unethical practice that is now illegal in the United States.[55]

Tracking technologies that might be used by a client organization similarly give rise to ethical issues. The least invasive of these involve the use of *cookies,* short fragments of identifying computer code placed on a user's computer in order to track and facilitate future Web site use. Cookies are a somewhat questionable form of attendance taking, but have become generally accepted because computer users can alter the settings on their Web browsers to not accept cookies. A more invasive and clearly questionable practice is the placement of *adware* or *spyware,* software remotely installed without permission, on a user's computer. The intent is usually to track Web site visits and to then direct compatible content to the users. But spyware can also be used to eavesdrop on correspondence, steal electronic files, or even disarm or disable computers.[56]

A growing, but less known, set of deceptive practices involves manipulating the prominence with which sites are listed on search engines (euphemistically referred to as *search engine optimization*).[57] Yahoo!, Google, and other search engines now generate considerable advertising revenue through "featured site" programs where sponsors pay for prominent placement.

However, such financial arrangements are not readily evident nor disclosed to users. Public relations practitioners ought to question whether their client organizations want to engage in this kind of Web site promotion, which relegates Web sites to being perceived merely as advertising.

Other unscrupulous activities involve tricking the *remote agent software* (also known as *crawlers, spiders, ants, robots,* and *intelligent agents*) that search engines deploy to catalog content on the World Wide Web. Web site operators are stuffing extra or inappropriate keywords in metatags, inserting hidden text and links that are read by the search engines but are invisible to users, employing *bogus referral pages* to inflate visitor counts, and using *cloaked* pages where Web sites serve up one page to a search engine for indexing and another to users.[58] All are efforts to make Web sites appear to be more popular than they really are—and thus more relevant to searchers and attractive to advertisers.

Deception can occur when paid content appears on other Web sites. Besides search engines, there has been a recent trend toward the use of undisclosed product placements on Web sites, which reflects the more general ethical problem that hybrid messages represent in movies and on television.[59] Since 2000, the American Society of Magazine Editors (ASME) and the Magazine Publishers Association have promulgated voluntary guidelines designed to differentiate editorial matter from advertising and "sponsored content." Among ASME's eight standards, all online magazine pages should disclose whenever an advertiser pays for a link embedded in editorial content, *advertorial* sections should be clearly labeled as such, and e-commerce and other affiliate fees should be reported on a disclosure page.[60]

In a similar way, the posting of patently promotional messages on computer bulletin boards and on opinion blogs (known as splogging) and the distribution of promotional messages via e-mail (spamming) and instant messaging (spimming) have generated outcries about deception, particularly when the identity of the sponsor is not disclosed.

Dependability

Ethical online communication is dependable. People with Internet access increasingly rely on online information to make critical decisions and to flourish in their personal lives. Thus, sponsors and operators of online systems have a duty to meet people's performance expectations, if not a responsibility to fulfill their right to information. Responsible online public relations practitioners also must concern themselves with reliability issues.

Dependability includes twenty-four-hour access, timely updates, a minimum of downtime, and the proper functioning of software and hardware.

Dependability is particularly critical during crises, the time of uncertainty that follows natural disasters or other extraordinary events. People naturally seek up-to-date and accurate information about how the crisis might affect them and what actions they should take to avoid risks. Ethical PR practice requires organizations to anticipate such circumstances and to prepare for them.[61] For example, many crisis response teams now include online communications specialists. Crisis plans now include alternative methods to provide Web and e-mail access during system outages or during periods of high demand following extraordinary events. These techniques include maintaining backup or off-site computer servers known as *hot sites*.

Interactivity and Involvement

Ethical online public relations takes maximum advantage of the inherently interactive nature of online communications.

Among all the communications tools available to public relations practitioners, online communications are uniquely equipped to allow organizations and their constituents to engage in *two-way* communications. Normative theories of public relations practice equate ethical behavior with the degree to which organizations engage with and involve their publics. The ideal and most ethical model of public relations practice is posited to involve *symmetrical* communication, in which the organizations and constituents share power and interact on an equal basis.[62] This approach has also been defined as engaging in dialogue. A growing line of research has considered how Web site designers can improve *dialogic* characteristics of Web sites and online communication.[63]

Ethical online communications encourage users to become active participants in the communication process.[64] *System interactivity* empowers users to control the online experience itself—by selecting content and choosing to use features inherent in the system. *Verbal interactivity* enables users to express themselves—through written words (e-mail, newsgroups and chats, and fill-in/feedback forms on Web sites), spoken words (*online audio* and *Web conferencing*), and visual images (including personal *Web cams* used in instant messaging, *Webcasting*, and the sharing of *digital images*).

Responsible organizations that invite verbal interaction must be prepared to respond in timely and meaningful ways when users communicate opinions, ask questions, or request information, products, or services. Effective and ethical responses involve prompt acknowledgement of inbound messages, personalized (versus generic) answers, and the timely fulfillment of requests.

In addition to promoting dialogue *between* an organization and its constituents, organizations also can facilitate conversations *among* members of stakeholder groups. Tools can include interactive chats, bulletin boards and newsgroups, and Web conferences on the public Internet or limited-access intranets (for employees) or extranets (for suppliers, distributors, or allied organizations). By capitalizing on such tools, public relations practitioners and their client organizations can foster a sense of community.[65] However, such efforts can only be successful (and ethical) if they encourage and foster the free expression of ideas. This requires tolerance for comments that challenge or question an organization's policies or practices and the elimination of fears about reprisals. At the same time, however, sponsorship of such activities also places upon sponsoring organizations the ethical responsibility to police users' actions that might be abusive, dangerous, illegal, or threatening to other participants.

Personalization and Customization

Ethical online public relations takes advantage of personalization and empowers users to shape their online experience through customization—features of online communications that public relations practitioners have yet to fully exploit.

One of the great strengths of online communications, particularly Web sites, is the ability to tailor information to the needs and interests of users. *Personalization* entails providing information based on the known interests or characteristics of a user. *Customization* enables users to knowingly select and organize categories or channels of content based on their interests. Examples of customization include the "My . . ." tab found on some commercial Web sites and portals set up on organizational intranets.

However, personalization raises ethical concerns regarding both how information is obtained and how information is used. Many organizations *ask* users to complete registration forms or surveys that give users the option to receive or not receive particular kinds of information ("opt-in" or "opt-out"). Some systems, however, tailor the information provided by tracking and recording the user's online behaviors. Online merchandisers, for example, use cookies to impute a user's interest about particular categories of products based on searches conducted or visits to particular topical areas—and then prominently promote related merchandise. Beyond the fact that the user was not asked, the result can often lead to erroneous or potentially embarrassing assumptions.

Customization, while presumably rooted in actual choices made by the user, can also raise ethical questions. Most customization systems limit the choices that can be made to a range of options prescribed by an organization and prohibit certain forms of content from either being customized or even being accessible. In the workplace, for example, access to pornographic

Web sites or e-mail flies in the face of providing people with a choice of content and raises the perplexing questions of when such limitations are appropriate and ethical.

Both personalization and customization raise ethical concerns about how data and systems settings might be used to *profile* users—a form of electronic stereotyping. Profiling clearly is illegal if used to discriminate against a user based on race, color, creed, religion, national origin, or marital status. However, people are often unaware of when their rights to equal opportunity are violated. Other data, such as age, education, or income, might appropriately be used as a basis for segmenting audiences. However, audience segmentation based on personalization or customization (or other online behaviors, such as visits to pornographic sites or sites advocating the overthrow of a government) also are wrought with potential problems of discrimination, recrimination, or reprisals in violation of a user's rights.

Privacy and Security

Ethical online public relations respects user privacy and maintains data security. Both privacy and security involve guarding the confidentiality of *personally identifiable information* about users.

Privacy focuses on the questionable use of provided or imputed personal information by an organization itself. *Security* involves the potential theft and/or misuse of the data by others (such as computer *hackers* or unscrupulous employees) who might gain unauthorized access as a result of breaches in an organization's systems.

Nearly two-thirds of Americans have expressed serious concerns about online privacy.[66] Consumers fear they can be harmed, embarrassed, disadvantaged, or annoyed. Organizations that collect data are expected by users (and watchdog groups and lawmakers) to exercise care in using information available to them about users. Special care is required when collecting data from protected classes, such as children, but the problem applies to all users who might be treated unfairly.

With increased frequency, public relations practitioners are asking for personally identifiable information from users. Requests might be as simple as asking a journalist to register in a pressroom or to provide an e-mail address in order to receive news releases or electronic newsletters via e-mail. However, many general queries from consumers and citizens also ask for name and contact information that are stored in an organization's database. More detailed information is frequently acquired from users such as donors, customers, or employees.

Public relations practitioners must examine both the policies and practices of their own units and of their organizations to consider the establishment of formal guidelines, such as those recommended by other groups in the field.[67] Although the specifics may vary, ethical online database management involves providing *notice, choice,* and *redress.*

Notice usually involves providing a privacy statement on Web sites or in initial e-mails that discloses the nature of information that might be requested and how that information will be used. Although sometimes implied, ethical organizations should provide an explicit promise that information will be used only for the purpose for which it was obtained and that the organization will exercise care to protect all information provided.

Choice involves giving people the option to provide or not provide personally identifiable information or to put limits on how data about them are be used. For example, some users might not object to receiving future e-mail communications. Yet the same users might object to the sharing of data with third parties (including an organization's public relations consultant!).

Redress entails maintaining procedures so users can know about and correct errors in whatever information about them might be in an organization's files. Ethical organizations are also obligated to publish and to follow established procedures to quickly and appropriately disclose and remedy breaches of privacy.

These principles of notice, choice, and redress make sense, but also are consistent with public relations principles related to duty and the rights of publics on whom a group or organization depends for its success. Not surprisingly, public concern about online privacy and security has evolved into a major public issue that public relations practitioners must address on behalf of clients in their dealings with consumers, the media, and government.

Usefulness and Usability

Finally, ethical online public relations involves supplying meaningful content in a functional format that is usable by both novice and experienced online users.

Usefulness and usability are important if only to improve the communications effectiveness between an organization and the user constituents. For that reason, the U.S. Department of Health and Human Services has launched an initiative to improve the effectiveness of online health communications by promoting usability standards. Yet, providing information that is pertinent and relevant (through techniques such as personalization) also contributes to user satisfaction and the quality of the online experience—a right to which users might be entitled ethically.

Research on usability suggests that content is critical to assessments of satisfaction by users. However, Web sites, cellular phone screens, and personal data appliances (PDAs) also should feature functional designs that are easy to navigate so people find the information they need with a minimum of errors.[68] Special accommodations are required to serve the growing number of online users who might suffer from disabilities, and practitioners can confirm that Web sites comply with established standards using HTML validator software.[69]

Conclusion

From this discussion, it is readily apparent that a wide range of ethical concerns confront public relations practitioners who use online communications. Many of these concerns focus on protecting individuals as matters of duty. Others are based on the rights of users. Clearly, the Internet is here to stay as a fixture in modern life, and organizations and users alike must adapt to the changing technologies. Both must learn and develop trust about new ways of communicating while discerning what constitutes ethical practice.[70]

Adhering to this burgeoning array of ethical concerns is a daunting task. However, any discussion of ethical online public relations also must take into account problems created for organizations by the unethical actions of users. Organizations, groups, and causes of various kinds are themselves the targets of unethical and unscrupulous detractors and competitors who will take whatever action they can to resolve a dispute or promote a cause. Ethical online behavior is a matter of good citizenship in a democratic society. But abuses can take place in the form of attacks, libelous or scandalous accusations, hate speech, fraud, misrepresentation, subterfuge, and stealing of intellectual properties. Scoundrels can be classified as attackers, hackers, lurkers, rogues, and thieves.[71] Practitioners must become aware of this "dark side" of online ethics and take steps to protect their organization's reputation and other digital assets in cyberspace.

As an activity that inherently attempts to influence people's behavior—what they know, how they feel, and why they act—public relations practice is inextricably intertwined with ethics. The motives of organizations in general (and public relations in particular) are continually called into question. As a result, public relations practitioners must strive for professionalism and high standards of ethical practice online.

But defining what is ethical is sometimes difficult in a rapidly changing environment where traditional benchmarks do not apply. Similarly, as Lawrence Lessig suggested, the forces of the marketplace, technology, and social norms are reshaping how online public relations will and ought to be conducted.[72]

Elsewhere, I have drawn on earlier public relations theory[73] to argue that online communications can help build organizational-public relationships.

In that context, key outcomes that shape ethical online communications include perceived *commitment,* a shared sense of *communality, mutual control* of the relationship, *satisfaction,* and *trust.*[74] To the extent that online public relations practices contribute to achieving these relationship-based outcomes, they can be deemed ethical.

Public relations practitioners must be concerned with both the ethical conduct of the public relations unit itself as well as the ethical online conduct of the entire organization and anyone involved in helping an organization achieve its goal. This is particularly critical because online communication, such as the operation of a Web site, is a *shared* organizational activity where responsibility transcends individual organizational units such as marketing, operations, human resources, or public relations. Online stakeholders do not differentiate between different parts of an organization when their only frame of reference is a Web site or bulletin board. Even more so than in an offline environment, organizations must speak responsibly with a "single voice" in cyberspace.

Table 7.1   Useful Web Resources on Ethics and Responsible Online Communications

Centre for Democracy and Technology	www.cdt.org/
Computer Ethics Institute	www.brook.edu/its/cei/cei_hp.htm
Computer Scientists for Social Responsibility	www.cpsr.org/
Direct Marketing Association	www.the-dma.org/
Electronic Frontier Foundation	www.eff.org/
Electronic Privacy Information Center	www.epic.org/
ePhilanthropy Foundation	www.ephilanthropy.org/
Ethics Resource Center	www.ethics.org/
Internet Healthcare Coalition	www.ihealthcoalition.org/
U.S. Department of Health and Human Services	www.usability.gov/
U.S. General Services Administration	www.section508.gov/
Online Ethics Center for Engineering and Science	www.onlineethics.org/
PR-education.org	pr-education.org/onlineethics.htm
Society of Technical Communication	www.stcsig.org/usability/topics/ethics.html
Wired Safety	www.wiredsafety.org/

8

Responsible Advocacy Through Strategic Risk Communication

Michael J. Palenchar and Robert L. Heath

Industrialization has been a two-edged sword. Since the latter half of the nineteenth century, as a result of the American Industrial Revolution, large industrial combines have served to create jobs, spawn small support and ancillary businesses, and create innovative products and services that continually reshape lifestyles. Industrial combines have shifted wealth to the hands of a few, created new social classes, increased population and urbanization, and formed at times poor working conditions and labor unrest, as well as fostered productive working conditions, neighborhoods, and natural environments that have sometimes taken advantage of and sometimes strained people's risk tolerance.

Among this progression, industrial refining, specifically chemical manufacturing facilities, has been one of the most significant and controversial human inventions. Manufacturing facilities coordinate human and environmental resources to achieve notable and safe, and at times insignificant and hazardous, objectives. These facilities create constructive and responsible, as well as destructive and irresponsible, products and services. With the continuous expansion of products and services comes the challenge of efficient production embedded in the strategic management of health, safety, and environmental risks related to manufacturing. In essence, the production and consumption of risks has become equally, if not more, important as the production and consumption of goods and services.[1]

In this context, public relations and risk communication discussions center on responsible advocacy. Well beyond any communication model that might adequately rest on what has often been called "sharing information," the sides—and there are many—engage in advocacy in a marketplace of perceptions and opinions. People make claims, and support and refute those claims in many ways. A variety of innovative processes has come to the fore-front as companies and residents has engaged in dialogue intended to exam-ine, weigh, and mitigate risks associated with working conditions, industrial processes near residential areas, and product designs.

Community residents who live near manufacturing, storage, and trans-portation facilities have legitimate reasons to be concerned for their own and others' health, safety, and environmental quality. Life hazards are a part of everyday existence in a modern, industrialized society. Concerns ranging from the safety of influenza vaccines to genetic engineering remind people of the perceived, potential, probable, or likely dangers and risks. Life hazards reflect the increasing size and complexity of modern science, technology, and industrial and chemical manufacturing. Indeed, as symbolic anthropologist Mary Douglas has argued, society is organized for the collective manage-ment of risk, which can be more functional through responsible advocacy in open contest.[2]

Alarm, anger, and outrage can result when people believe they are exposed to technologies that distress or harm themselves or others, whether they live and labor near the risk or encounter it while using or consuming a product. A primary motivator of activism is people's desire to be safe and healthy coupled with their vigilance for problems of that sort that need rem-edying. They are sensitive to the fairness and equality of risk distribution. They don't like to bear risks that primarily benefit others. When organiza-tions are seen as abusing the privileges given to them by their constituencies and other publics who affect and are affected by them, individual and com-munity responses and governmental controls and regulations can and should sanction the capacity of organizations to continue to operate. "The emer-gence of the powerful consumer and the critical public is not coincidental but a symptom of the emergence of the risk society."[3]

Safety, fairness, equality, and aesthetics are motivators people use when deciding whether a problem exists that affects them and deserves their atten-tion, and when considering the option of making personal responses or collaboratively seeking collective solutions by engaging in public policy struggles. All four motivators have been at the forefront of the public policy debates regarding risks over the past three decades. Translated into consid-eration of the benefits and harms of technologies, these motivators play a major role in the discipline called risk communication.[4]

The Environmental Protection Agency (EPA) established risk communication as a means to open, responsible, informed, and reasonable scientific and value-laden discussion of risks associated with personal health and safety practices involved in living and working in proximity to harmful activities and toxic substances.[5] Defined this way, risk management, including communication about risks, is successful to the extent that people who fear that they may be or are demonstrably harmed by a risk can become more knowledgeable about and confident that sufficient control is imposed by the sources of the risk and by government or other external sources that are responsible for monitoring the risk generators.

In this equation, control first needs to be responsibly exerted by industry in the public interest. To the extent that such control is not proactively achieved, health, safety, and environmental concerns will remain at the forefront of media and public policy discussions. Community residents will continue to bear the risks of living near manufacturing facilities, outcries from community activists will continue to be fueled, and the credibility of the industry will continue to be challenged. This is the crux of responsible advocacy—the engagement of concerned and interested parties.

Strategic and ethical risk communication entails science and information within dialogic advocacy, the framing and interpretation of facts, values, and policies. Does ethical communication end with and become defined by public policy—that which is legally required—or is there a higher standard to be borne by the good company/industry behaving and communicating well? In the scope and purpose of mandated community-right-to-know legislation, people are supposed to be alerted to the potentiality of a risk occurring that could affect their health, safety, or environment. Thus, responsible risk communication calls for effective, continual, expert, and honest communication about risks and the best way of responding to prevent or mitigate each one. Risk communication professionals should serve as internal voices for external interests, helping organizations interpret publics' perceptions of risk and fostering trust through open dialogue.

Within this framework, the purpose of this chapter is to consider the ethical mandates of public relations in the context of risk communication. A rhetorical rationale for responsible advocacy in risk communication is proposed, including guidelines for ethical risk communication practices. Emphasized topics include the need to address the people's "right to know" and to involve key publics in risk assessment and decision-making processing. The chapter demonstrates that public partnership, shared control, uncertainty environment, community decision making, trust and collaboration, individual values, community relativism, and community narratives are at the heart of ethical and responsible public relations and risk communication advocacy.

The Evolution of Risk Communication

Few management and communication challenges loom as ominously as those that arise from risks people fear they suffer in their places of work, neighborhoods, and daily activities. History is a drama of people assessing, communicating about, and creatively preventing or adapting to risks.[6] The history of risk management and risk assessment can be traced back before Greek and Roman times.[7]

Explicit, modern-era interest in risk communication can be traced back to the 1950s and the "Atoms for Peace" campaign, and the later development of the antinuclear movement (focused on opposing weaponry and electrical generating with nuclear fuel) in the 1970s, which helped bring risk communication to the limelight.[8] The term *risk communication* was coined in 1984,[9] but from a regulatory perspective, risk communication began with marketing by the EPA and the organizations it regulates.

Strategic approaches to risk communication, including ethical considerations, have changed significantly within the past thirty years. The early information-based, linear model advocated by numerous scholars, including the National Research Council, defined risk communication as "an interactive process of exchange of information and opinion among individuals, groups, and institutions. It involves multiple messages about the nature of risk as well as other messages, not strictly about risk, that express concerns, opinions, or reactions to risk messages or to legal and institutional arrangements for risk management."[10] The risk communication scholar Vincent T. Covello provides an oft-quoted definition of risk communication as "the exchange of information among interested parties about the nature, magnitude, significance, or control of a risk," which is similar to the one offered by the National Research Council because they both focus on the transmission of information and do not specify an outcome.[11]

William Leiss, who studies risk management and communication, has identified three unique eras in his review of the historical evolution of risk communication.[12] The initial phase, which according to Leiss began around the mid-1970s, was marked by the certainty that risk estimates should be expressed quantitatively and that "priorities for regulatory actions and public concerns should be established on the basis of comparative risk estimates."[13] However, numerous scholars challenge both the ethical and strategic effectiveness of this approach because information about risks is not adequately communicated solely through the use of quantitative risk estimates for numerous reasons, including the public's distrust of technical experts.[14]

Is being informed the goal of risk communication? That seems to be a limiting sense of the total process. What about the abatement of risks thought to be intolerable? What about the values that guide assessments of when each risk is tolerable? What about the sociopolitical forces that bring a balance in each community between personal and organizational interests? Questions such as these suggest that factors are missing from this definition, particularly the desire on the part of key publics to politically control intolerable risks—their source, their likelihood, or their consequences. Questions such as these demonstrate how responsible advocacy is a more accurate and useful paradigm for risk communication. Enhanced standards of corporate responsibility and community commitment do more to assuage fears of risk than does the sharing of technical data that often are beyond the educational capacity of community residents and employees to comprehend and interpret.

Leiss contended that the second phase of risk communication started around 1985 with the realization that risk messages should be persuasive messages with the intent to transform and lower people's risk estimations and thus increase their support of industry.[15] This phase was based on marketing communication practices and took into account the psychometrics of how the target audience perceived the messages. It focused on enhancing trust by improving source credibility. This phase was valuable to the development of risk communication because it took into account people's perceptions about risks, and initiated the concept of community dialogue among stakeholders. Limitations of this era included a lack of resources and commitment by industry and other involved organizations to appreciate and acknowledge the unique decision heuristics employed by community residents in their perception and understanding of risk, and to develop messages and public policy/manufacturing protocols that effectively addressed community concerns. This perspective was regarded as "potentially dangerous, for it could result in any rational content in the message being subordinated or even dissolved by those excessively clever techniques."[16]

The third and current phase of risk communication began around the mid-1990s with the realization that risk communication should not solely focus on persuasive techniques because there is a profound lack of trust, uncertainty, and lack of control in risk issues. The current model, one advocated in this chapter as responsible advocacy through strategic risk communication, places an emphasis on social context, that is, on the social interrelations among the stakeholders in the dialogue and resulting actions within risk management.[17] The present era should be and at times is marked by a commitment to communicating risks responsibly—through information and advocacy. Ideally this process entails values consensus building through dialogue, compliance with industry and governmental regulations, and meaningful stakeholder interaction.

Overall, the current version of risk communication advocated in this chapter features complex social relations operating within community infrastructures where multiple voices weigh in from all sides of contestable issues of fact, values, and policy. People often decide what levels of risk are acceptable not based on technical data analysis, but rather based on a question of values, such as fairness.[18] "Risk communication requirements are a political and ethical response to popular demand. The main product of risk communication is not informed understanding as such, but the quality of the social relationship it supports. Risk communication is not an end in itself; it is an enabling agent to facilitate the continual evolution of relationships."[19] Shared responsible control and demonstrated commitment outweigh endless tables of performance data and toxicology reports.

Responsible Advocacy

Philosophers and scholars have defined ethics as the study of what is right or wrong, fair or unfair, just or unjust. Others have argued that ethics is, in essence, morality. While a thorough review of ethical orientations is not the scope of this chapter, such models are based on historical philosophical perspectives such as Aristotle's golden mean and normative perspectives such as utilitarian considerations.

Aristotle's golden mean advocates that a person of moral maturity would naturally seek the action that would further moral character. Moral maturity is defined as one who is of good character, which comes about by developing the habits of good character, thus gaining sound moral reasoning. This moral mean lies somewhere between excess and deficiency, though that does not advocate starting with extremes and identifying the mean—this would lead to mediocrity rather than excellence. The moral mean is different for each person, and is acquired through good character, moral maturity, and the ability to perceive a situation accurately as it pertains to the individual.[20] Within risk communication, this approach can be taken to form the basis of a good organization communicating well based on the developing habits of good character (behavior).

Utilitarian considerations are grounded on a theory of ethics based on quantitative maximizations of some good for society or humanity. Utilitarianism, originally proposed by Jeremy Bentham and others in the eighteenth century in England, can be traced back to ancient Greek philosophers such as Parmenides. At the core of this philosophy is the concept of utility: that the good is whatever brings the greatest happiness to the greatest number of people. John Stuart Mill, in his classic work *Utilitarianism,* considered cultural and spiritual happiness to be of greater value than physical pleasures alone.[21] From a risk communication perspective, society is justified in affecting behavior of an organization to prevent injury to others, but it is not justified when the behavior is deemed simply immoral or harmful.

Within the field of public relations, numerous scholars and practitioners study and advocate various perspectives of viewing or incorporating ethics into the study, pedagogy, and practice of public relations. Numerous public relations scholars, such as Tom Bivins and Ron Pearson, have advocated for an ethical paradigm for public relations based on moral philosophy.[22] Kathy Fitzpatrick and Candace Gauthier reviewed previously suggested theories of public relations ethics ranging from attorney-adversary to the two-way symmetrical model, ultimately modeling their own professional responsibility theory of public relations ethics that is based on practitioners' dual obligations to serve client organizations and the public interest.[23]

One public relations model that receives considerable attention is the two-way symmetrical model. Scholars James Grunig and Jon White noted that "public relations should be based on a worldview that incorporates ethics into the process of public relations,"[24] while Grunig and Todd Hunt summarized that public relations and social responsibility are interconnected. "Public relations managers should be 'inside the door' of management in all kinds of organizations where they can provide internal social reports on the organization's public performance."[25]

The public relations scholars Robert Heath and Michael Ryan suggested that public relations' ethical role is about responsible, professional, and strategic communication management, and can include elements such as monitoring and analyzing issues; making companies cognizant of prevailing ethical standards; defining concepts of organizations' social responsibility; helping develop codes of ethics; working to integrate such codes and standards into the research, planning, and operations of organizations; working to integrate such codes into the organizational culture; developing strategies; and helping to avoid crises that can damage organizational reputation.[26] In essence, public relations practitioners can incorporate ethics as an element of the brand management of organizations: good organizations working and communicating well.

Such a rhetorical perspective on public relations originated from the writings of ancient Greeks and Romans. As Heath explains, this rhetorical heritage of Western civilization offers rationale for the ethical practice of public relations:

> It explains how public relations participates in the creation and implementation of value perspectives that shape society. It supports the practice of public relations in the marketplace and public policy arena, where values are brought

to bear on economic and sociopolitical matters. The rhetorical heritage of public relations features the role of public discourse through which ideas are contested, issues are examined, and decisions are made collaboratively. In this way, concurrence is achieved to guide personal and societal decisions.[27]

Within risk communication, the ethical dilemma may lie within people's struggle to control risks, seek and responsibly contest facts, evaluate premises, and form conclusions derived from those facts and premises. The ethical public relations dilemma is no different from the management dilemma; the challenge is how to understand, manage, and control risks, as well as gain acceptance for these measures in ways that foster the wisest outcomes in any community of interests.[28] Heath writes,

> Corporate actions are evaluated by key publics. For this reason, corporate social responsibility is value-informed choice making. Ascertaining appropriate ethical responses is a rhetorical problem vital to strategic planning used by excellent organizations that aspire to build and maintain mutually beneficial relationships. Public relations persons enjoy an ideal position to counsel executives on which values fit best with the interests of their markets, audiences and publics.[29]

Responsible advocacy occurs when senior counselors make a case that reflects the arguments and claims of concerned citizens and employees. This is an internal voice for external interests. This management positioning of public relations does not demand that it is contentious toward management preferences but gives fair and honest vetting to concerns voiced by employees, customers, and neighbors.

Concern centers on organizational strategies that abide by the organization's standards of ethics and resulting behaviors that are perceived and recognized by stakeholders and the market as credible, ethical, and positive. These standards should be based on genuine attitudes and actions of the organization, rather than on an image that is inconsistent with organizational operations. "The character of this market recognition is therefore largely one of social agreement, i.e., one constructed by shared communication."[30] This perspective is consistent with Pearson's contribution to public relations ethics that maintaining a communication relationship with the public is essential and that the quality of those relationships is improved through dialogue.[31]

What is the balance between the public's right to know and the prevailing interests of the corporation? How does one assess the ethical dimensions of risk communication? Many of the Greek philosophers, especially Plato and Aristotle, chose not to ask what is the right thing to do. Instead, they focused on what traits of character make one a good person.[32] For the purpose of this chapter, a better question may be what traits of character make an organization a good member of the community, and what traits of strategic risk communication plans make one a good organization communicating well.

Strategic Risk Communication

If exposure to risk is not new, then why is there a renaissance in risk communication research and communication? According to Baruch Fischhoff, a professor of decision sciences, "What is new in their [stakeholders and general public] response to the risk of modern technologies is their insistence on having a role in deciding how those risks will be managed."[33]

Another reason for the expansion of risk communication and risk communication research is people's feeling of entitlement; key publics hold government and business officials accountable for their policy decisions and actions.[34] Public distrust of industry and government officials is readily apparent. Research has demonstrated that industry and government regulatory officials (excluding plant managers) are not considered the most trusted sources of risk information. One recent study of a Houston ship channel community, dominated by manufacturing facilities, examined whether over a ten-year period increased awareness of industry health and safety efforts by community residents increased support and trust for the industry. While residents were more supportive of the industry in relation to these efforts, it did not necessarily translate into trust for the involved industry and government officials nor awareness of specific communication efforts or sources of information.[35]

At times, the behavior of industry and regulatory agencies that oversee industrial production, storage, and transportation has failed to match the public policy requirements and risk bearers' expectations. The authors Napoleon K. Juanillo, Jr., and Clifford W. Scherer have noted this decline in the public's confidence in the ability of government and industry to act responsibly in risk assessment and risk management.[36] This lack of confidence has created a public that is no longer the passive receiver of risk information. "Large segments of the public now demand more involvement in debates over risk issues and challenge conclusions and recommendations from scientists and experts."[37] Members of the lay public want to be a part of the risk communication process but often have difficulty understanding risk messages, participating in risk discourse and trusting information sources, and gaining access to decision makers. They also perceive a lack of internal and external control over risks and lack an overall awareness of some risk communication protocols.[38] Addressing these and other shortcomings, the following responsible advocacy guidelines are posited within the context of strategic risk communication to guide ethical choices and strategic actions by public relations and risk communication practitioners, scholars, and students:

- Work with community residents to develop and use emergency response measures that can mitigate severe outcomes in the event of a risk event.
- Acknowledge, research, and appreciate the depths of desire on the part of stakeholders to exert control over factors they perceive to have a negative effect.
- Acknowledge uncertainty in risk assessments, and do not trivialize this uncertainty but use it as an incentive for constantly seeking better answers to the questions raised by members of the community.
- Work with community members to effectively participate in decision-making systems that they are a constructive part of the risk assessment and risk management process.
- Build trust over time through community outreach and collaborative decision making.
- Feature legitimate benefits while acknowledging harms in communications, but do not assume that all persons' decision heuristics or values lead them to the same weightings of risk harms and benefits.
- Participate in the risk assessment and communication process through dialogue, and understand concerns in terms of the experiences and values of community members.
- Recognize the value-laden, personalized decision process community residents apply, and frame the risk assessment accordingly.

Public Partnership

During the 1980s, iconic industrial chemical production crises, such as Union Carbide India Limited's toxic methyl isocyanate gas spill in Bhopal, India, and the oil tanker *Exxon Valdez* running aground on the Bligh Reef in Prince William Sound, Alaska, tested the abilities of local, national, and industrial organizations to prepare for, and respond to, disasters of crisis magnitude. It also tested the role of risk communication as an integral part of strategic preparation, issues management, community relations, and crisis response.

Federal public policy, such as the Emergency Planning and Community Right-To-Know Act of 1986, which is section three of the Superfund Amendments and Reauthorization Act of 1986, or SARA Title III, and industry policy, such as the Responsible Care Program, have defined much of the development of risk communication programs and community right-to-know protocols. By codifying environmental risk communication, these communication policies require chemical companies to inform citizens regarding the kinds and quantities of chemicals that are manufactured, stored, and emitted in each community. SARA's underpinning assumption was that, as companies report the toxic and hazardous materials they produce, transport, and store, people could become informed of the level of risk in their neighborhood. Such information could assuage concern or be the substance of responsible advocacy for higher standards of performance.

The lack of strategic risk management and communication caused many people to distrust and, therefore, to oppose industry.[39] Specifically, worries that what happened in India would happen in the United States prompted federal legislators to create the Superfund Amendments and Reauthorization Acts of 1986 (SARA), which included community right-to-know provisions (SARA Title III). SARA Title III gives the EPA oversight of risk communication efforts related to the formation of local emergency planning committees (LEPC) in communities near high-risk facilities. LEPCs are designed to plan for manufacturing emergencies, but they are also designed to serve as community forums where nearby residents, government officials, industry representatives, health and safety officials, and any other concerned individuals and organizations could request information and voice concerns.

Responding to these federal and state initiatives, the American Chemistry Council (formerly the Chemical Manufacturers Association) developed and implemented Responsible Care, a program established to meet at a minimum the requirements of SARA Title III. The Responsible Care Program includes the formation of community advisory panels (CAPs) to serve as forums for public dialogue related to manufacturing safety concerns and risks.

Developed in response to the terrorist attacks of September 11, 2001, the Responsible Care Security Code focuses on safeguarding against potential terrorist attacks, expanding industry relationships with law enforcement and the community, and providing a model for chemical site protection. The security code chapter in the American Chemistry Council's *Responsible Care Practitioner's Site* manual stated that chemical companies should constantly work to improve their security processes, and that companies should communicate as openly as possible without giving away information that would "pose a threat in the wrong hands."[40] Thus, the industry as a concerted effort, as well as individual companies, have given attention to developing risk communication plans that include components sensitive to terrorism.

Positive impact of such measures is not a given. For instance, research has led to mixed reviews of LEPCs' and CAPs' ability to communicate environmental information to citizens. In a recent study, Robert Heath, Julie Bradshaw, and Jaesub Lee found a lack of awareness of the existence of LEPCs and CAPs and low use of such organizations, while at the same time found that more than two-thirds of the residents surveyed approved of their intended functions. Overall, their findings suggested, "a fully functioning communication infrastructure leads to a healthier community that responds to risks as manageable uncertainties."[41]

The risk communication scholar Susan Hadden found that institutional barriers often stand in the way of meaningful dialogue in communities where people experience risks that they worry are intolerable.[42] Such barriers result, at least in part, from statutes that do not specify what technical data are crucial and, therefore, should be collected. Even when data have been collected by industry or governmental agencies, institutional barriers prevent citizens from gaining access to them. People often encounter a maze of agencies, do not know where to acquire information, and suffer data dumps that provide huge amounts of information in ways that make it difficult to interpret. Thus, the paradigm of "sharing information" is naïve and perhaps even dysfunctional. Among other fallacies, it does not recognize how data are often meaningless until transformed into interpretive arguments and asserted claims that can be compared, weighed, and debated.

Encountering such barriers, people become frustrated or unsure that they have the data they need or want. Even when information is obtained, people run into barriers as they seek to exert changes they hope will mitigate the risks they believe they have discovered.

Along these same lines, proactive companies strive to inform community members about emergency response systems that are in place to warn them of an emergency and to assist their efforts to be safe. Proactive firms such as these, often in conjunction with local government, formulate personal response plans that people can use to shelter in place—to go or stay inside a residence or business, close the building to outside air, and monitor the emergency by using special radio frequencies and emergency-response-activated telephone systems. Extensive research has been conducted on the effectiveness of such campaigns. Strategic risk communication programs have been found to have a strong relationship with awareness of health and safety issues in the community, knowledge of how to appropriately respond during an emergency, increased sense of internal and external control, and increased sense of trust, while also decreasing, sometimes intuitively, dangerous behaviors such as evacuation.[43]

Is this good communication policy? It conforms to principles offered by the health communication scholar Kim Witte, who reasoned that when spokespersons for ostensible sources of risk attempt to downplay a risk—either its probability or severity—without addressing ways to increase people's self-efficacy, public response is likely to be outrage or denial.[44] To avoid raising the public's fear, such information must be accompanied by procedures that offer a constructive, proactive response to that concern.[45] Without measures for responding safely in the event of an emergency—which reasonable people acknowledge could happen—community members are likely to engage in outbursts of rage; resort to denying that an explosion or toxic release will happen or will affect them (or reason that they will die quickly); or resort to measures of self-efficacy, such as deciding to attempt to evacuate in the event of an emergency. For this reason, communities where risks exist do well to stress the expertise and preparedness of manufacturing plant personnel and community fire/police officials to respond during an emergency.

Companies find reason to implement programs whereby they increase publics' understanding of technical processes as a means for lessening the fear of the threatening unknown and of increasing trust. To do so requires that the companies consider public interest in how they operate and communicate. They often have the best information to determine whether or how some commercial process should be conducted. If that information is hidden or otherwise withheld from the public, it cannot serve the wise formulation of public policy. Overall, responsible advocacy works to empower relevant publics by helping them develop and use emergency responses that can mitigate the severe outcomes in the event of a risk event.

Shared Control

Many studies have demonstrated that control is a key variable in risk communication.[46] The social psychologist Suzanne C. Thompson defined control as the belief that an individual or organization can influence an event, or at least has the ability to do so if it chooses to influence the aversive situation.[47] Control can be exerted to reduce the likelihood of a risk event or to minimize its impact.

As such, control can be divided into two distinct types. Internal control is where a person feels control over his or her own destiny, and external control is where outside forces have control over a risk source. Based on these findings, it is reasonable to assume that people respond to the uncertainties of risk occurrence and outcome by attempting to increase personal or community control over the source of the risk. Risk communication processes and statements are more likely to be effective to the extent that they empower citizens of a community of risk. That observation is relevant to the ways in which public relations is practiced in risk situations. Is the risk too great, too high—particularly in proportion to the benefits that might be derived from it? This dimension of risk assessment is not only a matter of science and economics, but of ethics.

Covello argued that an individual's control was a key determinant of people accepting risk, and other studies have found that people's perceptions of industry control affected their risk estimates related to chemical cleanups.[48] Economic controls affect risk tolerance levels,[49] and a relationship exists between people's belief that they can control the gathering of information and their support for risk communication programs.[50] Residents' perception of a lack of control can lead to public opposition to hazardous facilities, while several researchers determined that risk communication is likely to fail if it does not increase residents' control in the decision-making process regarding the risk.[51]

Community-based control means that members of a community seek to exert corporate responsibility standards on organizations that generate risks and their watchdog counterparts (including government and nonprofit organizations). In this regard, studies show that the more people feel in control, the less they feel that local chemical plant activities will affect their lives.[52] Personal control extends to perceptions of speed of onset, scope (area), and duration of impact of the risk, as well as the quality of emergency preparedness.

The primary outcome of stakeholders' belief that sufficient or insufficient control exists is their support or opposition for the source of the risk and the governmental agencies that are expected to act on behalf of community members. If people believe that the agency of control can and will effect lowered risk or foster appropriate emergency response to it, they tend to support that agency. If the agency, such as a business, has demonstrated that it understands the risk, knows the appropriate responses, and is willing to enact the proper control, it should enjoy support instead of suffer opposition. "In turbulent times, uncertainty and distrust soar. Highly involved people struggle to control sources or risks that affect their self-interests. Information and knowledge become less relevant to the need to exert control because they are only loosely related to risk tolerance."[53] Lacking this control, people turn to other agencies of control and voice opposition to the source of risk. Thus, advocacy is a paradigm of risk communication, at least from the outside in, but organizations can join the dialogue in responsible ways to manage uncertainties that are inherent in risk. Overall, responsible advocacy strives to research, appreciate the depths of, and accept the desire on the part of stakeholders to exert control over risk factors.

Uncertain Environment

Uncertainty can be viewed "as the perceived lack of information, knowledge, beliefs and feeling necessary for accomplishing organizational tasks."[54] In this vein, uncertainty has been defined as the lack of attribution confidence about cause-effect patterns.[55] Aristotle, in discussing *enthymene*, suggested that people do not have to deliberate the notion of certainty, that no human action is inevitable.[56] Rather, people have to deliberate upon what is uncertain, and on that which their judgments are based on no more than probabilities. The very nature of risk prohibits absolute definitions and knowledge.

Uncertainty motivates information seeking because it is uncomfortable. Using that principle, uncertainty reduction theory explains the human incentive to seek information.[57] Publics want information to reduce their uncertainties about the subjects under consideration and about the people who are creating those uncertainties.

Risk assessment and uncertainty are interrelated; risk is a product of the uncertainty relating to two dimensions: whether an event will occur, and the possibility/probability that its consequence will be good or bad—rewarding or harmful.[58] To complicate matters, uncertainty thrives in risk communication issues. It has been suggested that when policy decisions regarding technological risks need to be made, that is the time when scientific knowledge is often the most uncertain.[59] Thus, sharing information may be a dysfunctional paradigm if the crux of the issue is the need for more and better information.

Within risk perception and risk communication discussions, uncertainty has been related to estimating risk information about technical risks,[60] assessing the impact of a new or unfamiliar technology,[61] and calculating the degree of confidence to communicate knowledgeably about risk issues[62] to highlight a few. In general, unknown and unfamiliar risks are seen as riskier.[63]

Risk messages related to complex manufacturing issues can be confusing: they come from a variety of sources that involve multiple parties and often reflect competing scientific conclusions. Experts and regulatory agencies often operate on the assumption that they and their audiences share a common framework for evaluating and interpreting risk information. This confusion also stems from the fact that prominent government officials take different and, often, opposing viewpoints about environmental, health, and safety risk matters and participate in highly public debates about risk estimations.[64] Such dialogue by nature consists of advocacy. The challenge is to assure that it is responsibly used to the mutual benefits of the engaged parties.

Numerous views of communication, however, continue to identify understanding as the final dependent variable. For example, people may intuitively understand what each color of the U.S. Department of Homeland Security's Homeland Security Advisory System stands for, or at least perceive the red fifth stage as the most severe. However, some people will not be satisfied that those assessments achieve or constitute the proper levels of risk. People will also agree or disagree with recommended risk management activities such as being vigilant, taking notice of their surroundings and reporting suspicious items or activities to local authorities immediately, establishing an emergency preparedness kit as well as a communications plan for themselves and their family, and staying informed about what to do during an emergency situation.[65] Agreement may have less to do with risk certainty and more to do with risk uncertainty derived from personal experience, economic standard of living, cultural or religious variables, education, and psychometric variables such as trust and control. This line of reasoning makes explicit the fact that risk communication is not merely a scientific or knowledge-based activity. It entails responsible advocacy where agreement builds on understanding. Responsible advocacy acknowledges the uncertainty in risk assessments and uses it as an incentive for constantly seeking better answers to the questions raised by members of the community.

Community Decision Making

Responsible advocacy works to empower community members by demonstrating to them through their participation in decision making that they are a constructive part of the risk assessment and risk management process. This approach seems ideal for such studies to assist corporate and governmental planning as well as reinforce or alter the plans as they are implemented. In a time when critics caution against public communication because it could aid terrorist planning, advocates of effective risk communication need reinforcement that their efforts can lead to an empowered rather than cowed community. To this end, communication has a value unto itself, apart from the utility of information it generates.[66]

By making the information available, even in formats unsuited to making rational risk choices, it still addresses key concerns regarding the imposition of and discontent regarding terrorism security efforts. Increasing research in risk communication demonstrates the tangible value of dialogue in the community. Benefits can range from increased perception of individual control by community residents, increased perceptions of more vigilant external control by industry and regulatory agencies, increased cognitive involvement, and more vigilant awareness of community risk, as well as more knowledge about what to do in case of a chemical emergency in their community.[67]

The act of dialogue that includes discussion and negotiation based on honest, clear, transparent, and appropriate information from the perception of all the different parties' perspectives is essential to responsible advocacy and effective risk management. At a time of heightened concerns related to risk from terrorist attacks in the industrial chemical sector, open yet cautious discourse of site, cyber, and transportation security may be even more important.

Trust and Collaboration

For effective and responsible risk communication, the source of information and advice needs to have a satisfactory level of trust in the judgment of each public.[68] People tend to be less afraid of risks that come from places, people, and corporations or other organizations that they trust, and more afraid if the risk comes from a source they don't trust.[69] If expert risk estimates conflict with one another, the decision to be made becomes more complex and requires greater amounts of trust.

People in each community where risks occur must be able to trust the efforts to achieve reasonable levels of safety security. Such levels need to withstand the "smell" test of the area residents that they could and should trust industry to exert reasonable amounts of security and communicate in ways that increase rather than decrease citizens' security.

Industry would like to say, "Trust us because we have planned and put policies into place that will reasonably protect your interests, your security and safety." Yet trust is ultimately demonstrated in word and deed. It is groomed and maintained. It can be lost or destroyed. It is a precious ingredient in community relations. If citizens cannot trust individuals or organizations to be responsible, they will turn to other entities—such as government and activists—to force appropriate operating standards. Thus, industry has a moral and strategic business-planning obligation to motivate and guide its planning and operations based on trust built through strategic risk communication.

Individual Values

One of the daunting findings of risk assessment studies is the recurring theme that risks are a tradeoff of costs and rewards. Although technical knowledge may have little effect on risk tolerance, other types of knowledge, especially perception of benefits, may be relevant to risk tolerance. For instance, a study of environmental health risks found that the judged benefits of the hazard were ranked first among other variables in correlation with risk tolerance.[70] Fischhoff and his colleagues found a consistent relationship between perceived benefit and acceptable risk level.[71] However, in a different study, researchers discovered that benefits played a significant role in the risk acceptability of only two of six risky technologies they tested (and not for industrial chemicals).[72] In general, people tolerate higher risks from activities seen as beneficial, especially if benefits extend beyond economic to include qualitative variables such as basic needs, safety, security, and pleasure.

Considering questions by citizens during environmental reviews of incinerators, one author has argued for a risk-benefit analysis and not just a prediction of upper-bound risks.[73] Often-repeated questions at hearings include: What are the risks compared to the benefits of the project? How is the risk calculated? Does the design of the facility make the risk as low as possible? Who in the community bears the burden of the risk? What are the chances of a serious accident? Are the risks identifiable? Can the public influence how the facility is designed and operated? An ideal risk-benefit approach should evaluate alternative risks, examine catastrophic potential, and assess ways that enable those affected to control the risk in meaningful ways.

Several studies have shown significant relationships between perceived economic benefit and support for hazardous industries.[74] James Flynn, William Burns, C. K. Mertz, and Paul Slovik suggested that the local community would support hazardous facilities as long as the benefits of the facility outweigh the possible risks.[75] For example, their study of the Yucca Mountain and the U.S. Department of Energy's geologic repository measured the perceptions of positive economic benefits resulting from the siting of the nuclear waste repository. Their research hypothesis was that those who felt the repository would bring economic benefits to the area would be more inclined to support its siting. Surprisingly, no statistically significant relationship was found between perceived economic benefit and support for the site. On the other hand, they also discovered that those respondents who felt the siting of the plant would stigmatize Nevada as a nuclear waste dump site, and thus negatively affect the state's image to potential tourists, were significantly opposed to the site.[76]

In a study of a plastics plant near two small Texas towns, evidence supported some of Flynn's findings. Residents who perceived economic harm from the facility were significantly more likely to oppose it.[77] For risk communication practitioners, responsible advocacy and good community citizenship requires the featuring of legitimate benefits while acknowledging harms. Risk communication that assumes all persons' decision heuristics or values lead them to the same weightings of risk harms and benefits is contrary to dialogic decision making by community residents who receive both the benefits and harms of such facilities. Responsible dialogue features legitimate benefits while acknowledging harms. It does not assume that all persons' decision heuristics or values lead them to the same weightings of risk harms and benefits.

Community Relativism

At least three theoretical options guide the way in which risks are calculated, evaluated, and controlled: (1) scientific positivism, whereby data and methodologies of scientists dominate efforts to ascertain the degree of risk—once the decision has been reached, an elite manages and communicates about the risk on behalf of the community; (2) constructivism/relativism, which assumes that everyone's opinions have equal value so that no opinion is better or worse than anyone else's; and (3) dialogue—through collaborative decision-making processes, scientific opinion becomes integrated into opinions which are vetted by key publics' values.[78]

Some scientists, regulators, and members of risk-producing industries scoff at any risk assessment and decision-making approach other than the first option, but proactive risk communication practitioners acknowledge that community-based relativism should not be dismissed. The stabilizing force in risk decisions is the collective judgment of the community crafted through dialogue. People feel that they enjoy more control when they have a say in the formulation of the factors that seem to lead to the control of risks.

Favoring an approach to risk which takes into consideration key publics' concern, Fischhoff and some of his colleagues initiated expressed-preference research, which involves measuring a wider array of attitudes than merely weighing the benefits in the effort to ascertain tolerable risk levels.[79] These researchers found lay people's risk ratings, unlike those of experts, are not just influenced by fatality estimates, but also by their judgments of several qualitative factors. Of particular note, the public evaluates an activity or technology as more risky if it is involuntary, unfamiliar, unknown, uncontrollable, controlled by others, unfair, memorable, dreaded, acute, focused in time and space, fatal, delayed, artificial, and undetectable, as well as if individual mitigation is impossible.

Rather than a purely scientific and actuarial approach, a dialogic view stresses the likelihood that people's fears as well as their expressed desires for the benefits accrued from risks become part of a community of thought, the culture of a neighborhood or even a profession. A communication plan that fosters responsible advocacy builds on and may go well beyond one that merely advises exchanging information.

Because scientific data are hard to interpret and risk decisions are value laden, differences of opinion are not easily reconciled. Policy often is not the product of shared points of view but, rather, negotiated resolution of conflicting opinions examined through responsible advocacy. Such communication is likely to be disproportionately shaped by key players, industry, government, media, and activists. Although no group actually represents the public—because there are many publics—each of the dominant groups strives to speak and act as though it were the advocate and champion of the public interest. Such outcomes may leave all parties dissatisfied. Conflicting interests and epistemologies unique to the battlefield of risk often prevent communicators from finding "common ground between the social world of risk perceptions guided by human experience and the scientists' rational ideal of decision-making based on probabilistic thinking."[80]

A responsible and strategic approach to risk assessment, management, and communication aims to empower the persons in a community, rather than to deny them access to information and interpretive processes that they do not have the technical knowledge and expertise to understand and evaluate. Dialogue and decision making may be more important than the ability of people to play constructive roles as participants. Even if they cannot understand the scientific assessments, they know when they feel that their concerns and interests have been responded to and regarded. Responsible advocacy encourages community participation in the risk assessment and communication process through dialogue, and works to understand concerns in terms of the experiences and values of community members.

Community Narratives

Knowing the common narratives of a group, organization, or society allows risk communicators the framework for scanning, analyzing, identifying, and monitoring community residents' perceptions related to living near chemical manufacturing, storage, and transportation facilities. Aristotle pointed out that people do not necessarily experience organizations, but rather they experience the communication organizations use to explain their actions and the communication about organizations.[81] People, especially in more economic-based countries, have become accustomed to companies speaking as individuals, sharing their thoughts and perspectives on a range of issues, and not just those pertaining particularly to their company's or industry's core job functions. Chemical companies often voice their opinions about community affairs in which their plants are situated. A rhetorical view within risk communication perceives that it is a form of social influence, a view that treats persuasion as an interactive, dialogic process whereby points of views are contested in public and socially constructed.

Within this dialogue and contest, words have propositional value,[82] and the selection of those terms affects how information is considered, accepted, acted upon, or altered. These propositions, according to Heath, compete "in ways that help to inform judgments and actions, clarify and order the evaluative (value) dimensions of thought and choice, and justify or deny the expedient wisdom of competing policies."[83] Each idiom reflected in the language and meaning of the community can thus be viewed as a unique view of economic, political, social, corporate, personal, and community interests.

This view of public relations also entails that risk perception is enacted in narrative form.[84] Some communication scholars regard narrative as the paradigm of all communication.[85] People think and act in terms of narratives.

Narrative form and content connect and give meaning to events. In the narrative of oceanic travel, the sinking of the Titanic is an iconic narrative, as is Hanford in the production of nuclear weapons and energy.

Hanford is a 586-square-mile plutonium production complex located along the Columbia River in southeastern Washington State. This site, under the direction of the Department of Energy (DOE), includes nine nuclear reactors and associated processing facilities. The site was developed as part of the Manhattan Project beginning in the 1940s and is the world's largest environmental cleanup project, with numerous overlapping technical, political, regulatory, financial, and cultural issues.[86] In 1989, the DOE, the EPA and the Washington State Department of Ecology agreed to the Hanford Federal Facility Agreement and Consent Order, commonly known as the Tri-Party Agreement, which outlines the Hanford cleanup that is expected to possibly continue through 2035.

According to the DOE, its work has taken a "holistic, multigenerational and integrated approach to long-term stewardship."[87] Long-term stewardship includes the protection of human health and the environment from the risks associated with remaining contamination following cleanup. Part of the DOE's risk communication efforts include resources for reporters on its Web site, including press releases, backgrounders and fact sheets, presentations and archival materials, progress reports, public affairs contacts, and safety statistics.

However, others view the Hanford site differently. Whereas the DOE describes its work as an environmental cleanup project, others see it as "mismanagement of the area." Whereas long-term stewardship is described by the DOE as the protection of human health and environment, others see it as "wreaking havoc on environmental progress." While the DOE discusses its approach to transition from a cleanup mission to long-term stewardship that includes reusing assets such as land, facilities, technologies, and skilled personnel that are no longer required to support the site missions, some argue that the cleanup is nowhere near completion and lacks any plan for unrestricted cleanup, which is not a goal of the DOE. At the core of this discussion lies the difference in total cleanup advocated by some community residents and activists, as opposed to long-term plans to address permanent, long-term contamination from the perspective of the DOE.[88]

Not only do such events happen over time, as narrative, but they also are part of larger narratives of transportation and industrial activities. Each news story frames events, characters, and meaning in terms of who, what, when, where, why, and how. These narrative elements correspond to how people think. For this reason, public relations and risk management statements made by organizations are more likely to be meaningful and agreeable when they address the narratives key publics use that are reflected in their particular cultures. People think, communicate, and behave in accord with their narratives.[89]

The narrative paradigm assumes that "there is no genre, including technical communication, that is not an episode in the story of life (a part of the 'conversation')."[90] From an enactment perspective, the communication scholar Walter Fisher has argued, "A narrative perspective focuses on existing institutions as providing 'plots' that are always in the process of recreation rather than existing as settled scripts," while stressing that "all forms of human communication need to be seen fundamentally as stories— symbolic interpretations of aspects of the world occurring in time and shaped by history, culture, and character."[91]

Conclusion

This chapter has demonstrated how risk communication managers can ethically enhance strategic communication and increase support for their organizations when they help key publics become a part of the decision and information sharing/interpreting processes, work with the needs (information, advice, decision heuristics) of publics, and deliver information and advice, as well as help shape interpretative heuristics people think are useful.

Confidence in open communication is vital, not only so the community ensures industry is doing the right thing but also so community residents are willing to know and comply with the emergency response protocols. Risk communicators should understand the dynamics of the risk communication process, work to participate in it rather than dominate it, and seek to help people control their lives rather than challenge that sense of control. Risk communicators dealing with risks should foster trust through dialogue. Dialogue is responsive to people's desire to exert control. For this reason, risk communicators should be prepared to work with the idiosyncratic responses and interpretations people make in regard to whether risks exist and are likely to lead to harm.

The historical realities of risk management as the essence of society have once again become front-page and top-of-the-hour news hooks. The events of September 11, 2001, have placed a renewed emphasis on the role of risk communication efforts related to industrial chemical production. In an era of terrorism, too much transparency can have negative consequences; information could fall into hands that might be able to use it against the industry and the people whose interests must be served. However, organizations should be concerned that this strategically dampened flow of information about health, safety, and environmental planning might harm their relationship with community residents.

Companies engaged in risk communication face obstacles as they work to form, change, or reinforce opinions and behaviors regarding risks. "Risk behavior is a function of how human beings, individually and in groups, perceive their place in the world and the things that threaten it."[92] The rightness of decisions depends on which versions of their self-interest key audiences need to advance. Corporate managers and governmental officials make a grave mistake when they miss that point, arguing that some action is legal—as though that will satisfy the critic's sense of ethics, health, safety, and security. "The issues around which publics form and which they support are used as vehicles for the expression of their identity"[93] is a fundamental concept of public relations and risk communication that is not often considered in ethical discussions. The consequence is that in dealing with stakeholders and publics, it is not necessarily the risk itself that is the issue but the identity of the public in relation to the risk. Risk communication becomes a tool for communicating values and identities as much as being about the awareness, attitudes, and behaviors related to the risk itself.

Ultimately, the risk communication process is more than just the sharing or exchanging of information. Numerous researchers have argued that for public relations to mature and perform the role of ethical counsel of organizations, practitioners must be well versed in ethics and trained in ethical analysis. While this is surely true, ethics more importantly demands strategic business and communication decisions based on understanding and working with publics while appreciating their unique decision heuristics within responsible advocacy. It is through responsible and professional practice, and working for good organizations that communicate well, that ethics and public relations build equity.

9

The Ethics of Public Diplomacy

Philip Seib

Public diplomacy can be defined in various ways. It may be an effort
by a government to bring an honest view of the world to people in
countries where their own governments obstruct access to information. Or
it may be nothing more than self-serving, manipulative messages of questionable truthfulness. However it is defined, there is no doubt that public
diplomacy will be an increasingly significant part of international relations,
particularly as advances in communications technology enhance the global
flow of information. With public diplomacy's importance increasing, its
ethical standards deserve scrutiny.

Public diplomacy is one facet of governmental public relations.
Governments are unrelenting in their pervasive public relations efforts. To
see how this takes shape, consider the work of the White House Press Office
on any given day as it churns out its usually sophisticated versions of
policies and events, all designed to shine the most flattering light on the
president and perhaps others in the government.

As the political scholar Stanley Kelley observes, "Any system of government, autocratic or democratic, owes its life to some kind of support in
public opinion."[1] Within the U.S. government, public relations specialists
work to influence the opinions of diverse intragovernmental and external
publics.[2] The stakes are often high, ranging from the apportionment of
appropriations to the outcome of elections. On a global level, particularly
since the September 11, 2001, attacks on the United States, public diplomacy

has been a vital manifestation of "the war of ideas," and the "client" for this public relations effort is America itself.

Ethics issues related to public diplomacy can best be considered within the context of governmental public relations. Despite complexities arising from the transnational nature of the work, the country that is the source of public diplomacy efforts has a duty to maintain carefully considered ethical standards. In public diplomacy, as in other tasks, public relations professionals serve as a vital link in the communications process as they promote understanding and coexistence among individuals and institutions.[3] To be effective as an ethical enterprise, public diplomacy not only must be well grounded in the source country's ethical standards but also must conform to ethical norms of the people and states that are the recipients of the public diplomacy message. This is similar to the general ethical principles of domestic governmental public relations: the integrity of the democratic process depends on the dissemination of truth, and the framing of truth—through various mechanisms of emphasis—must be done carefully to avoid distortion.

Although the publics who constitute the audience for public diplomacy may be physically distant and culturally different from domestic audiences, they nevertheless deserve to be recipients of communication that adheres to a high standard of truthfulness. To conduct public diplomacy without maintaining such standards would not be merely unethical in an abstract sense, it would also likely prove counterproductive (especially over the long term). In public diplomacy, as in other kinds of governmental public relations, good ethics is good business. Despite the desire of public diplomacy practitioners to deliver a politically useful message, responsible advocacy remains a practical necessity.

This chapter illustrates the challenges facing American public diplomacy professionals in terms of the tasks they undertake and the ethical standards they should meet. These practitioners should serve as the collective conscience of the foreign policy process, a role that requires an embrace of the principles of ethical public relations.

The Mission Defined

During the autumn of 2004, the young Yemeni spent weeks maneuvering with friends and smugglers to get into Iraq. By the time American forces began their advance into Fallujah in November, he was waiting for them, with an AK-47, in a small house filled with other jihadis. As the U.S. troops came closer, he prayed: "Oh God, you who made the prophet victorious in his wars against the infidels, make us victorious in our war against America. Oh God, defeat America and its allies everywhere. Oh God, make us worthy of your religion."

When a visitor mentioned coming to see him and his family back in Yemen after the fighting in Iraq finally ended, the young man snapped, "The only place I am going from here is heaven."[4]

That young man's fierce willingness to fight and die is by no means the common sentiment among Middle Eastern Muslims, but he is not alone. In varying degrees, anger at the United States is pervasive and is presumed to contribute to the growth of terrorism. It is this knot of anger that public diplomacy must help unsnarl.

In the face of the harsh realities of international relations, public diplomacy may seem to be an exercise in wishful thinking. But as its doubters—at least among American policymakers—grow more uneasy about the ramifications of widespread anti-American sentiment, public diplomacy is increasingly recognized as an essential tool of foreign policy. A baseline definition of public diplomacy is to inform, engage, and influence foreign publics.[5] In practice, that can involve "giving timely news to foreign journalists, providing information on America directly to foreign publics through pamphlets and books, sponsoring scholarships and exchanges to the United States, exhibiting American art, broadcasting about U.S. values and policies in various languages, and simply transmitting balanced, independent news to captive people who have no information source independent of a repressive government."[6]

The principal difference between public and traditional diplomacy is that the traditional approach is based on a government-to-government relationship, while public diplomacy builds links between a government and foreign publics. Joseph Duffey, former director of the United States Information Agency, said that public diplomacy is "an attempt to get over the heads or around diplomats and official spokesmen of countries and sometimes around the press to speak directly to the public in other countries and to provide an interpretation, [an] explanation of U.S. values and policies."[7]

Duffey's point about getting around the press underscores the fact that public diplomacy in some ways competes with the news media. It is an advocacy medium—that is why it exists—but it still presents itself as operating within the boundaries of truth. As such, it conforms to the ethical requisites of the larger field of public relations. Its proponents may defend the use of slant or spin as being part of their craft, and that may lead to questions about how far the public diplomacy product can stray from objectivity before it becomes dishonest. This question is at the heart of consideration of the ethics of public diplomacy. Emphasis within the bounds of truth is a core practice/value of public relations; it is advocacy constrained by responsibility.

As a practical matter, the amount of attention paid to such ethical issues is affected by the task at hand. A principal mission of American public diplomacy professionals since the 2001 attacks on the United States has been to address the question, "Why do they hate us?" The 9/11 Commission report urged the government to become more fully engaged in the "struggle of ideas" against Islamic radicalism, and then national security advisor Condoleezza Rice observed, "The hearts-and-minds issues are back, maybe in an even more real way than they were in the Cold War."[8]

The urgency of this task may tempt public diplomacy practitioners to cut corners as they shape the messages that are supposed to reduce existing hatred and prevent the development of further antipathy. As a matter of professional ethics, shortchanging the truth should be avoided, and as a matter of efficacy, departing from truth would almost certainly prove counterproductive over the long term. Champions of public diplomacy present it as an alternative to propaganda, which is not by definition untruthful although the word tends to have pejorative connotations. (The word is derived from the Latin verb *propagare*, meaning "to spread.") Propaganda is widely perceived as self-serving information that is not necessarily truthful, and critics of public diplomacy argue that the difference between propaganda and public diplomacy is merely the label. One argument advanced by those who say that there *is* a distinction is that public diplomacy always relies on "the known facts," while propaganda is based on falsehoods mixed in with facts.[9]

Ethics scholar Jay Black cites some of the common themes appearing in definitions of propaganda: "A presumption of manipulation and control, if not outright coercion, that dehumanizes the audiences or intended 'victims' of propaganda; a power imbalance—rhetorical, political, economic, and so forth—between propagandists and propagandees; and a presumption that principles of science, rhetoric, semantics, and enlightened or open-minded education serve as powerful antidotes to propaganda."[10] Black also notes concerns about propaganda not being compatible with the responsibility of a democratic media system to not be manipulative and to "encourage an open-minded citizenry—that is, a people who are curious, questioning, unwilling to accept simple pat answers to complex situations."[11] Propaganda generally does not aim for open-mindedness among members of its audience but rather seeks adherence to the particular viewpoint being promoted.

Black does, however, offer a cautionary note about sweeping judgments concerning propaganda being "an inherently immoral enterprise." He points out that propaganda can be part of the "open marketplace of ideas." Nevertheless, he says, balance in discourse must be maintained, which means that both the providers and consumers of information have responsibilities. "A fully functioning democratic society," wrote Black, "needs pluralism in its persuasion and information, not the narrow-minded, self-serving propaganda some communicators inject—wittingly or unwittingly—into their communications and which, it seems, far too many media audience members unconsciously and uncritically consume."[12]

Perceived commonality with propaganda makes public diplomacy vulnerable to challenge about its being an ethical enterprise. When the pressures of the war on terrorism are combined with a record of naïveté and other flaws in approaching target audiences, public diplomacy specialists face the temptation of choosing the expedient over the ethical as they chart a new course. Given the complex political context in which public diplomacy is being reshaped, it is important to distinguish between errors made in good faith and purposeful ethical lapses. The record of American ventures in the first several years since the 9/11 attacks featured more of the former than the latter.

Soon after the 2001 attacks, veteran advertising executive Charlotte Beers was named Undersecretary of State for Public Diplomacy and Public Affairs. She appraised Middle Eastern attitudes toward the United States in this way: "We are talking about millions of ordinary people, a huge number of whom have gravely distorted, but carefully cultivated, images of us—images so negative, so weird, so hostile that I can assure you a young generation of terrorists is being created. The gap between who we are and how we wish to be seen, and how we are in fact seen, is frighteningly wide."[13]

Beers's tenure produced mixed results. One of her major projects was a "shared values" television advertising campaign showcasing achievements of American Muslims. But by the time the $15 million campaign aired, the Arab world was less concerned about domestic American attitudes toward Muslims and more interested in the looming invasion of Iraq.[14] Television officials even in the relatively friendly governments of Egypt and Jordan refused to air the ads. Only four countries—Indonesia, Kuwait, Malaysia, and Pakistan—were willing to run the "shared value" spots on their state-operated channels.[15] Similarly, criticism arose when the U.S. government printed 300,000 copies, in ten languages, of a pamphlet titled "Muslim Life in America." Muslims could rightly argue, "Now you're even trying to co-opt our religion and tell us that 'the American way of Islam' is best." That was not the intent of the pamphlet—it was designed to show that Muslims are not persecuted in the United States—but regardless of intentions, ingenuousness is not a useful ingredient in public diplomacy. This incident also underscores the importance of maintaining an ethical standard of sensitivity toward audiences. Failure to do so is likely to foster and reinforce stereotypes, which can lead to exacerbation of cultural tensions. Once again, ethical behavior—defined with substantial breadth—is both desirable as a matter of principle and as a way to enhance chances of success for public diplomacy efforts.

The principal U.S. television project as part of public diplomacy efforts has been Al-Hurra ("the free one"), a satellite channel designed to offset the influence of Al-Jazeera and Al-Arabiya, which prominent U.S. government officials have criticized as consistently reflecting an anti-American bias. President George W. Bush said Al-Hurra was to be part of an attempt to "cut through the barriers of hateful propaganda" generated by Arabic television stations and provide "reliable news and information across the region."[16] This is a White House definition of the distinction between propaganda and public diplomacy.

Al-Hurra is owned by Middle East Television Network, Inc., a nonprofit corporation, with editorial policy set by the Broadcasting Board of Governors, a federal agency that also oversees the Voice of America. When it began broadcasting in February 2004 with a $62 million budget for its first year, Al-Hurra received mixed reviews. (In late 2003, Congress added $40 million to the Al-Hurra budget for a sister station broadcasting solely to Iraq.) Critics referred to it as "Fox News in Arabic" and noted its U.S.-grounded political leanings were obvious in semantic usages such as referring to "coalition forces" in Iraq, rather than Al-Jazeera's preferred "occupation forces."

The news judgment of Al-Hurra's journalists has also been questioned. In March 2004, when Israeli missiles killed Hamas leader Sheik Ahmed Yassin, most Arab news channels covered the story as it developed; Al-Hurra stayed with its regular programming, a cooking show. Al-Hurra apparently learned from that misstep; when another Hamas leader was killed, Al-Hurra immediately reported it and followed with five hours of live coverage. But later in 2004, when other Arab channels were airing video with the last words of an Arab journalist killed by a U.S. helicopter attack in Baghdad, Al-Hurra told the story without the graphic images.[17]

Al-Hurra also lagged behind the Arab networks in the prominence and quantity of coverage of Palestinian issues. This was one factor that led Hussein Amin, a mass communication professor at the American University in Cairo, to observe of Al-Hurra's staff that "their credibility is open to question right now. If they take the position of the United States and color everything with its policies, then people will reject the message and it will not achieve success in any form."[18] Nabil Dajani, a professor at the American University of Beirut, asked, "Can they expect the Arabs to watch them if they don't show Palestinians being killed and don't portray Israelis as oppressors?"[19] Harsher criticism came from a Saudi jurist, Sheikh Ibrahim Al-Khudairi, who said that Al-Hurra was "waging a war against Islam and Americanizing the world. . . . The objective of the channel is to facilitate American hegemony over the world in the religious, political, and social fields."[20]

Competition for the Middle East television audience is intense, with viewers having more than a hundred satellite channels to choose from. Surveys conducted in mid-2004 found Al-Hurra trailing Al-Jazeera and Al-Arabiya. Among 3,300 respondents to a poll in Egypt, Saudi Arabia, Morocco, Jordan, Lebanon, and the United Arab Emirates, no one said Al-Hurra was his or her first choice for news and only 4% picked it as second choice.[21] Another survey of viewers in Saudi Arabia found that 82% of households watched Al-Jazeera, 75% watched Al-Arabiya, 16% watched Al-Hurra, and 12% watched CNN. Only 17% of respondents said they considered Al-Hurra to be very trustworthy or trustworthy, while 20% viewed it as untrustworthy. (The remainder expressed no opinion about its trustworthiness.)[22] Other figures, derived from A. C. Nielsen surveys and cited by Al-Hurra, reflect more interest in the broadcasts and much higher credibility ratings.[23]

Scholar Shibley Telhami observed that part of the problem for Al-Hurra is that its apparent detached objectivity does not match the mood of its intended viewers. "Its aim," said Telhami, "is to be precisely dispassionate while facing a passionate audience."[24] As seen in its reluctance to air graphic images or to use language perceived as critical of U.S. policy, Al-Hurra has sometimes tied itself in knots while trying to do journalism and at the same time trying to advance the U.S. political agenda in the Arab world. Although Al-Hurra's staff includes journalists who pride themselves on their objectivity, their ultimate boss—as their audience well knows—is the U.S. government, and that inevitably affects the station's credibility.

Similar conflicts exist with recent American radio ventures Sawa, broadcasting in Arabic, and Farda, broadcasting in Farsi and targeting an Iranian audience. A preliminary version of a State Department report leaked to the news media in October 2004 said that Sawa, which first went on the air in 2002, was preoccupied with building its audience by emphasizing its music (a mix of Western and Middle Eastern) and was failing "to present America to its audience."[25] Although Sawa's supporters challenged the State Department analysis, concern persisted that even if the station was attracting listeners to its music, its credibility as a news source and a public diplomacy vehicle was limited.

The experience of Radio Sawa illustrates the multifaceted difficulties facing those trying to establish viable public diplomacy media efforts. Concentrating on building audience makes sense if over the long term the station is to be able to effectively deliver its political message. From its listeners' standpoint, the emphasis at this stage on entertainment rather than news allows the station to be perceived as being relatively ethical in that it is not overtly serving as the American government's messenger. Critics in

Congress and elsewhere say that being a messenger is the reason Sawa was created. So, where is the ethical path? Perhaps in building trust at the outset, but then that trust—once established—must not be betrayed. If that is the ethical path, it is a steep and twisting one.

The Importance of "Soft Power"

The high stakes for public diplomacy are based on some traditional assumptions about public opinion that have been altered—if not rendered obsolete—by the increasing diversity and accessibility of information venues. During the Cold War, the ongoing battle for public opinion between the United States and the Soviet Union proceeded on a manageable number of fronts. Each government used its own machinery plus surrogates (some very obviously playing this role, some less so) to reach targeted audiences. With limited resources, independent indigenous media were usually ineffective competitors. The superpowers maintained hegemony in information as in other aspects of their global influence.

From the American standpoint, the demise of the Soviet Union and end of the Cold War should have left the remaining superpower and its associates with a solid monopoly in information dissemination. During the 1991 Persian Gulf War, for example, Western media organizations such as CNN and the BBC were the primary suppliers of war news to the world. They were not official agents of the U.S.-dominated coalition, but they delivered information colored by a Western perspective, which was noticed by audiences in places such as Cairo, Beirut, and Amman, where people had few alternatives to these news organizations that were seen as de facto tools of the coalition.

This began to change in the mid-1990s as satellite television broadcasting became less expensive and more widespread. The birth of Al-Jazeera in 1996 was one of many new arrivals in the Middle East, and it is likely to be a prototype for new regional information outlets around the world. The Qatar-based station's rising influence serves as a good example of the complicating factors that face the architects of American public diplomacy. Strong indigenous voices compete with those from the West and possess credibility that eludes outsiders. Convincing people in the Middle East that the war against Iraq was not really a war against Islam, or that the United States is truly concerned about the interests of the Palestinians, is a much harder sell when many local media voices are presenting the news about these matters in ways that are implicitly (and sometimes explicitly) critical of American policy. This underscores the importance of not only being ethical but also being *perceived* as ethical.

Ethical behavior and credibility are closely linked, which gets to the essence of the mandate for ethical public diplomacy. As with public relations generally and government public relations specifically, how the audience treats the message being sent will depend to a significant degree on the ethical standing of the source. This again illustrates a difference between public diplomacy and propaganda: a firm commitment to ethical practices is important if the former is to be seen as being distinct from and having greater credibility than the latter.

As Arabs increasingly feel besieged by the West, they have become more skeptical about Western sources of information. Palestinian journalist In'am el-Obeidi wrote that during the first Intifada (1987–1993), there was ample coverage of protests against Israel. But, she recalls, the story "was always told by American or European crews addressing Western viewers, even when this reached the Palestinian audience via Arab media, such as the Jordanian or Syrian television channels." A decade later, she said, the second Intifada was covered by Arab satellite channels whose crews

> were formed of locals, as familiar with the history of the conflict as they were with people's feelings and culture. Similarly, they had viewers who knew the history of the struggle, spoke the same language, and shared their feelings and beliefs. For the first time, Palestinians felt that they were no longer subjects of an outside narrator. They felt that their story was being told and narrated by themselves.[26]

When such a story is receiving attention, news coverage and public diplomacy may compete for the attention and trust of a common audience, as when journalists report events and public diplomacy professionals make the case for the policies behind those events. Both face the difficult task of defining *objectivity* and remaining committed to it. The reporter for the Arab satellite news channel might believe that "journalism of attachment" is appropriate, and that it is his or her job to present a sympathetic portrait of the Palestinians. Does that fall within the boundaries of ethical communication, or is opinion overriding facts? For the public diplomacy practitioner, such as an American official justifying U.S. support for Israel during the Intifada, how one-sided may the case being presented be? The jobs of the journalist and the public diplomatist are different, but both are communicators and presumably owe some allegiance to the integrity of the process of communication itself. The ethical foundations of both professions are built on common ground.

Along these lines, journalists and public diplomatists both must consider objectivity as an idealized goal vis-à-vis objective approaches that may be more pragmatic and feasible in practice. As a practical matter, objectivity—if defined as uninfluenced by personal prejudice—is an illusion. All humans are influenced to varying extent by personal and cultural factors, even if these are not readily apparent, and to say that a communicator is either biased or unbiased is to just skim the surface of this issue.[27] On another level, objectivity is not feasible because people communicate with a purpose; they want to affect others in some way with their messages. Objectivity and advocacy may seem mutually exclusive, but in public diplomacy—as in other areas of public relations—"objective approaches" are possible. This means exercising intellectual discipline to impose ethical boundaries on advocacy. The alternative—and this is where problems may arise in terms of the public diplomacy/propaganda distinction—is to slide into overt bias.

There is more to all this than semantic hairsplitting. Taking an objective approach implies a fundamental honesty that rises above the most expedient ways of making a case. Advocacy remains, but it is grounded in truth. Members of the public are not stupid; they can spot bias in most cases, and when they do, they tend to disregard the biased message (unless, perhaps, it is one that they are predisposed to agree with), and after that happens, the public diplomacy effort, like other public relations ventures with the same failing, will have diminished chances of being successful. The ethical guideline that emerges from this is to define an objective approach that merges, as best as possible, advocacy and truth. In such a way, ethics and pragmatism may coexist.

The ability to take an objective approach as the path toward convincing audiences is at the heart of *soft power,* a term used most notably by Harvard's Joseph Nye to define noncoercive strength. It is, wrote Nye, "the ability to get what you want through attraction rather than coercion or payments. It arises from the attractiveness of a country's culture, political ideals, and policies. When our policies are seen as legitimate in the eyes of others, our soft power is enhanced."[28] The moral suasion that is at the heart of soft power is a tool getting increased attention not only from the United States but also from others: countries with growing international clout, such as China; countries that want clout, such as France; and nongovernmental organizations, such as Doctors Without Borders, that seek to influence numerous countries' foreign policy. The spreading appeal of soft power is partly a function of communications technologies that allow more players into the game of international relations. The International Campaign to Ban Land Mines, which won the 1997 Nobel Peace Prize, relied heavily on the Internet to organize support for reshaping government policy and public opinion.[29]

The effective exercise of soft power depends largely on its being a part of a comprehensive, well-designed public diplomacy effort. It will not be successful as a facet of U.S. foreign policy, said Nye, "unless the style and substance of American policies are consistent with the larger democratic message."[30] Concerning the highest priority of American public diplomacy, Nye wrote, "The current struggle against Islamist terrorism is not a clash of civilizations; it is a contest closely tied to the civil war raging within Islamic civilization between moderates and extremists. The United States and its allies will win only if they adopt policies that appeal to those moderates and use public diplomacy effectively to communicate that appeal."[31]

This speaks to an important part of the ethical foundation of public diplomacy—the need for such endeavors to be more than blue smoke and mirrors and to be grounded in substantive policy rather than in ephemeral promises. As a matter of professional ethics and long-term effectiveness, public diplomacy practitioners must resist the temptation to rely on lavish promises wrapped in extravagant packaging. The requirement for the ethical practice of public diplomacy is to remain linked as closely as possible to truth.

The Competition for World Opinion

Some critics of American public diplomacy efforts have said that project managers tend to approach their work as if they were simply trying to win a popularity contest. Mark Helmke, a senior staff member of the U.S. Senate Foreign Relations Committee, observed that

> American public diplomacy is about one thing and one thing only, American national security. It's about defending and protecting American interests in a dangerous world. It is not about making the rest of the world "like us" more. . . . At the end of the day, American national security is not threatened by people in other countries not liking us. It is only threatened if they take that dislike and turn it into hatred and terrorist action against us.[32]

As Helmke indicates, ill-defined quests for popularity should give way to more precisely targeted policies. A Brookings Institution study released in early 2004 said,

> An immediate objective for American public diplomacy and foreign policy should be to transform our relationship with Muslim-majority countries, reversing recent steep deterioration in a way that enhances our national security. . . . Given the realities of the September 11th attacks, America needs a broad coalition to protect itself. To build and sustain the alliances necessary, i.e. to make our coalitions both bigger and more "willing," we have to communicate more effectively.[33]

Communicating "more effectively" in this context merits consideration as a matter of public relations ethics. The policy goal is clearly to create and deliver a message that will encourage the creation and maintenance of desired alliances. Doing so involves more than relying merely on "whatever works," which could be manipulative use of information that strays far from the truth. That approach might work temporarily, but disregarding ethical principles is an unwise way to try to build a lasting political relationship. The public diplomacy process needs built-in reminders—perhaps some kind of ethics ombudsman—to help maintain ethical standards.

When building coalitions or moving toward other political goals, public diplomacy does not operate in a political or communications vacuum. It is constantly tested by competing voices, which have been growing in volume as a result of advances in communications technology, such as the increased availability of cellular telephones, regional satellite television, and the Internet. The Brookings study found that "students, journalists, and business leaders across Muslim-majority countries obtain information directly from the digital and satellite TV world, often as fast as Americans," and that the impact of this technology-based access to information has been enhanced by rising literacy in the Middle East, where literacy rates have reached 73% for men and 49% for women.[34]

When considering the pervasiveness of just the Internet, the Muslim world's intriguing prospects for dramatically increased access to information and the effects of that access can be seen. An interactive medium as well as a conventional information provider, the Internet can bring unprecedented cohesion to the most far-flung community. Scholar Gary R. Bunt has noted that "it is through a digital interface that an increasing number of people will view their religion and their place in the Muslim worlds, affiliated to wider communities in which 'the West' becomes, at least in cyberspace, increasingly redundant."[35] As the Internet continues to reduce the significance of national borders and other boundaries, the entire array of global media and information technology may help create virtual communities that are as worthy of coverage as traditional states have been.

During the past few years, Internet usage has increased substantially—in percentage terms—in some Islamic countries, but as of early 2004, actual use still lagged far behind the levels in much of the rest of the world. No predominantly Islamic country ranks in the top twenty-five nations in terms of percentage of population with access to the Internet. In the entire Middle East, minus Israel, only 5% of the population has Internet access. In large, predominantly Muslim countries elsewhere, the rate was even lower: for example, 3.6% in Indonesia and 1% in Pakistan. Statistics about the *growth* of Internet use are more substantial: from 2000 to 2004, use in Iran increased almost 1,200% and in Saudi Arabia 610%. But the figures from Pakistan illustrate how far Internet use still needs to grow. Although usage in that country increased more than 1,000% during the four years, in real numbers the expansion was from 133,900 to 1.5 million users (out of a total population of more than 157 million).[36]

Assuming that Internet use in Islamic countries will grow significantly during the coming years, the *ummah*—the worldwide Islamic population— might become a virtual community with a certain level of technology-based cohesion. Not even technology can erase cultural and political differences within the Islamic world, so virtual unity may be tenuous. Even if some coming together occurs, whether this population will be insular or participate in the larger global community will be a crucial factor in determining the future character of Islam. Those observers who believe that the clash of civilizations will occur might consider any new unification within Islam to be a threat, while those who are skeptical about the clash theory might argue that the Internet will enhance the potency of globalizing and moderating influences that could lead Islamic states and people toward greater integration with the rest of the world.

Information is becoming more of a global commodity, and, as with satellite television channels, the Web could help defuse cultural clashes by providing information that undermines myths and stereotypes and could similarly be a potent tool in public diplomacy efforts. But the high-tech, high-speed flow of information also creates challenges for those who implement public diplomacy. Ease of communication should encourage a reaffirmation of ethical public relations standards because the audience is more extended, messages move more quickly, and these factors combine to enhance the potency of words and images. An example of this phenomenon could be seen in the speed of dissemination of the May 2005 report in *Newsweek* magazine about desecration of the Qu'ran by American personnel at the Guantanamo Bay detention facility. In this case, reaction to the story led to a dozen deaths and more than a hundred injuries, and it undermined much public diplomacy work. *Newsweek* had inadequately corroborated the information in the story before publication, although it later was shown that the basic theme of the story was correct. Regardless of the specifics of this case, the incident underscores the need for a high standard of care in ascertaining accuracy, whether in journalism or public diplomacy. Public relations and journalism share some important professional responsibilities.

A study by RAND, a U.S. policy think tank, noted that "information intended for domestic audiences is frequently received by foreign audiences as well; and conversely, information intended for foreign audiences is also accessible to domestic ones."[37] When such crossovers occur, the reactions of the different audiences may vary greatly. State Department official Christopher Ross wrote that the public diplomacy practitioner "must keep in mind the home truth that it is not what one says, but it is what the other hears that ultimately matters most."[38] The Brookings Institution public diplomacy report noted that international publics may be well informed about "the more extreme parts of the American political landscape," and so when conservative leader Pat Robertson said that Islam "is not a peaceful religion" and Rev. Jerry Falwell called the Prophet Muhammed a "terrorist," even though the comments created few ripples in the United States, there were strong anti-American reactions elsewhere in the world.[39]

Because it is so easily accessed, the Internet is particularly potent in reinforcing misleading information, as shown when students at an elite Saudi Arabian university consider former Ku Klux Klan leader David Duke's strident, anti-Semitic Web site as a reliable source of news about the United States. In general, the din of many voices may be an encouraging sign of diverse discourse, but finding truth amid the noise can be difficult. This is another task for public diplomatists.

The high-speed global pervasiveness of information, as illustrated by these examples, makes public diplomacy more important and more difficult, and it increases the need for professional self-discipline to perform tasks ethically rather than just quickly. As the volume of information available to global publics grows, truth becomes even more valuable.

Ethics and Politics

If U.S. public diplomacy is to be more than a crisis response tool, it will require well-conceived organization and clearly stated operating principles. That is the foundation on which an ethical structure may be built. Most of all, public diplomacy's mission and the method of accomplishing it should be defined in a way that is compatible with ethical practices.

The shortcomings of America's public diplomacy efforts have received serious attention (even though this attention has not always led to serious reforms). The Advisory Commission on Public Diplomacy, chaired by Edward Djerejian, a former U.S. ambassador to Syria and Israel, told Congress in 2003 that "the United States today lacks the capabilities in public diplomacy to meet the national security threat emanating from political instability, economic deprivation, and extremism, especially in the Arab and Muslim world." The commission's report criticized "a process of unilateral disarmament in the weapons of advocacy over the last decade [that] has contributed to widespread hostility toward Americans which has left us vulnerable to lethal threats to our interests and our safety." The report called for strong coordinating leadership from the White House and a "dramatic increase in funding."[40]

Internal improvement in all aspects of public diplomacy is important, and so is adjusting the operating philosophy behind America's way of sending messages to the rest of the world. Distrust of U.S. intentions will not vanish quickly, and information identified as emanating from the U.S. government will probably continue to be viewed with considerable skepticism, if not ignored altogether.

During the Iraq war, American officials worked fairly well at times with representatives of important Arab news organizations such as Al-Jazeera, and such efforts need to expand. Rather than having U.S. agencies directly disseminate information and become competitors of regional news organizations in the Middle East and elsewhere, they might be better off trying to work *with* them while quietly encouraging them to alter the tone of their coverage of American policy and values. Suggestions have also been made that the United States should provide financial support to indigenous media. This might prove more cost-efficient and make more political sense than relying on U.S.-based media because close-to-home news organizations, not distant voices, are most likely to establish credibility with the audience. Shibley Telhami notes that "if you don't trust the messenger, you don't trust the message."[41]

This approach may be effective, but it also could raise ethical concerns similar to those that were recognized, usually belatedly, during the Cold War when various media organizations, foundations, and other channels were co-opted (or, in some cases, created) by the Central Intelligence Agency. Publications that purportedly were independent voices were covertly funded and controlled to varying degrees by that era's version of public diplomacy planners. Frances Stonor Saunders, who wrote a history of this process, stated that its purpose was to "nudge the intelligentsia of Western Europe away from its lingering fascination with Marxism and communism towards a view more accommodating of 'the American way.'" The CIA maintained a "Propaganda Assets Inventory" of conduits and individuals that it used to direct information to targeted publics.[42]

A case can be made that this approach was legitimate as part of pragmatic Cold War foreign policy, but it entails substantial costs in credibility. Can it be called "ethical?" Proponents of public diplomacy like to distinguish their work from propaganda in part by citing its openness and honesty. If that distinction is to be maintained, the manipulative maneuvers of covert information management must not become a part of public diplomacy. A high level of transparency would seem to be a requirement for ethical practice in this field.

Whatever grand strategies and clever tactics are employed, public diplomacy can be successful only if it is part of carefully crafted foreign policy. Barry Fulton of George Washington University's Public Diplomacy Institute said: "Public diplomacy is not, and should not be, somehow considered as camouflage for public policy. Public diplomacy is describing public policy, but it doesn't improve on it, change it, or misrepresent it."[43] When policy information is available to be disseminated and when a well-designed system exists to do so, public diplomacy can be a significant force in the democratization of communication. Its targeting of mass publics counteracts the efforts of governments to control the information that reaches those publics. When specific issues, such as the response to 9/11, are set aside and open communication per se is considered, the importance of ethical standards for public diplomacy becomes clear.

As with other elements of democracy, even robust public diplomacy is susceptible to infection by unethical practices—spreading false information, using communication tools to defame or provoke, interfering with transparency, and other tampering with the foundations of honesty. In public diplomacy, as in other forms of public relations work, truth remains essential. Temptations to stray from truth are plentiful, but public diplomacy must be conducted ethically or else it will certainly fail. Given the stakes involved in today's world, that is an unacceptable outcome.

10

Advocacy Across Borders

Donald K. Wright

Several years ago at an international public relations convention, a large group of delegates from about a dozen different countries dined together at a restaurant. The restaurant did not want to provide individual checks to each diner, so the group decided to order a variety of food and drink and at the end of the evening to divide the bill by the number of group members. When the check arrived, someone suggested that 15% or 20% should be added as a gratuity for the waiters. Diners from some countries understood the request, but others wondered aloud about this unfamiliar procedure. Many did not understand the American custom of restaurants paying low wages to waiters with the expectation that they will earn additional money in tips for good service.

In some ways, the differences between public relations advocacy at home and abroad are similar to the differences encountered that evening in the restaurant. Just as customs such as tipping waiters differ from country to country, so do opinions about what constitutes ethical public relations practice and unethical public relations practice. In the United States, for example, it is considered highly improper for a public relations person to pay a fee to a journalist, or to buy a reporter a gift, in order to ensure that specific information from a news release gets inserted into a newspaper, magazine, or news broadcast. And yet, in various parts of the world, fees and gifts of this nature are very much a part of everyday media relations practice. In China, for example, it is expected that public relations professionals will pay journalists a "transportation allowance," a small cash stipend to cover the cost of attending a client's speech or special event. This custom has evolved as a response to the low salaries paid to Chinese journalists and the fact that many news organizations will not reimburse their employees for expenses incurred on the job.

The situation regarding responsible advocacy is much the same. To determine how familiar international practitioners are with the term *responsible advocacy*, this author conducted a brief survey with officers and national chairs of the International Public Relations Association (IPRA). The IPRA is perhaps the world's most geographically diverse professional public relations organization; it has members from more than a hundred different countries. This author asked more than three dozen practitioners from twenty-five countries if they knew this term. No one responded affirmatively. Although the term responsible advocacy is not one that is familiar to those who practice public relations outside the United States, international public relations professionals are very aware of the need to practice public relations responsibly and ethically.

This chapter examines public relations advocacy from an international perspective. A major focus is on cultural differences that exist among people in various countries and the potential impact on public relations ethics and effectiveness.

Global Public Relations

In practicing public relations globally, it is important to realize that public relations as practiced in one country frequently differs from how it is practiced in another country. It is particularly important that this consideration be taken into account in a chapter of this nature, especially one written by an American. As the public relations scholars Krishnamurthy Sriramesh and Jon White have explained, public relations is mainly a Western concept, and so much of the research about public relations—and even more of the public relations research in the area of ethics and advocacy—has been conducted by Americans.[1]

The Excellence research project of the International Association of Business Communicators (IABC) initiated several significant global studies that analyzed how public relations is practiced in various parts of the world.[2] This research found that in some parts of the world, the practice of public relations is underdeveloped and largely restricted to one-way communication such as press agentry and publicity. In these countries, public relations consists mainly of media relations and promotional work. That is, public relations professionals distribute messages and try to get publicity for their organizations, but rarely counsel those organizations on strategic matters. In many other countries, however, public relations is practiced much more frequently as two-way communication, where public relations efforts play a unique and influential part in organizational decision making. In countries that use the two-way model, public relations professionals function in the public opinion arena in much the same way that attorneys function in courts of law. These practitioners play a substantial role in organizational leadership and help clients solve problems in addition to facilitating communication.

An Ethical Overview

"Ethics—in all aspects of communication study and practice—has attracted a good deal of attention over the past few decades. Many who work in various aspects of communication are bombarded regularly with diverse ethical cues, and too few of these communications practitioners really have developed frameworks for making ethical judgments."[3]

Most scholars agree that four criteria—shared values, wisdom, justice, and freedom—compose the foundation of all systems of ethics. Shared values are essential because a society needs agreement on its standards of moral conduct before ethical judgments can be made. Any mutually agreed-upon standards need to be based on reason and experience, and should harmonize the rights, interests, and obligations of all citizens.

Ethics is the branch of philosophy that deals with questions of moral behavior. It is similar to a set of principles or a code of moral conduct. Making ethical decisions in public relations is easy when the facts are clear and when the choices are black and white. However, it is a different story when ambiguity clouds a situation, or when incomplete information, multiple points of view, and conflicting responsibilities are present. In situations of this nature, ethical decisions depend on both the decision-making process and on the decision makers—their experience, their intelligence, and their integrity.

Responsibilities of Individual Practitioners

The authors Kenneth F. Goodpaster and John B. Matthews, Jr., stress that the desire for ethical behavior has its roots in the actions of individual people and the assumption that they wish to act responsibly.[4] Although this chapter strongly endorses this notion and suggests that some individual public relations people might elect to be ethical while others might not,[5] there is also merit with those, like the ethics scholar Louis A. Day, who say it would be inviting ethical anarchy to let individuals establish their own standards of conduct.[6] Other scholars maintain that the occupational and professional ethics of an individual cannot be separated from personal ethics.[7]

Most people understand the clear-cut differences between good and evil, right and wrong, and similar dichotomies. Ethics represent our ability to distinguish between what is right and what is wrong. When ethical decision making comes down to the bottom line, the final arbiter in separating right from wrong or good from evil is the free will of the decision maker. The authenticity of any ethical decision depends on a universal form of morality. The higher good is purity of motive rather than the good or harm of outcome. The central ethical value in the unwritten contract each of us has with society is fairness of decision making guided by principles upon which anyone and everyone would agree.

Previous research involving communications ethics has covered a number of different contexts—including corporate communications, public relations, broadcasting, and journalism—and the dominant finding has been that ethics is an individual issue. That is, individual practitioners essentially decide whether or not to be ethical regardless of professional ethical codes.[8] Even though it does not directly deal with all the occupational duties of public relations practitioners—e.g., the four models of practice developed by James Grunig and the practitioner role assessments proposed by Glen Broom and David Dozier—this doctrine of the individual suggests press agents could be as ethical as two-way symmetrical communicators, providing the desire to be ethical was present.[9]

Given all the foregoing, this chapter contends that the decision of whether or not to be ethical while practicing public relations remains very much an individual decision even though it obviously can be impacted and influenced by other practitioners, societal mores, and the like.

The Importance of Culture

As studies by Byoungkwon Lee, Ni Chen and Hugh M. Culbertson, and Gabriel M. Vasquez and Maureen Taylor indicate, a variety of cultural influences play intangible roles in and have some impact on international public relations.[10] Despite the fact that cultural factors often have a major influence on ethical decision making, the bulk of the scholarly literature on public relations ethics does not do an adequate job of elaborating on this reality. For many years, most of the research about public relations ethics was concentrated on North America. Even today, most of the literature about international public relations that is published outside North America and Western Europe focuses on the practical rather than the scholarly or the theoretical. A recent exception is the work of public relations scholar Stephen P. Banks, who addresses the multicultural and social interpretations at play when cultural considerations impact ethical decision making.[11]

What kinds of cultural considerations are we talking about? Essentially, ethical decisions frequently are based on deciding what is best for society, and cultural factors have a strong influence on societal needs. In some societies these might involve the individual-collectivist dichotomy, in others a masculine-feminine dichotomy, in others a religious-nonreligious dichotomy, and in others some combination of these and other dichotomies. Vasquez and Taylor provide a fairly thorough overview of how public relations effectiveness is impacted by cultural norms.[12]

Table 10.1   Dimensions of Culture and the Public Relations Professional: Communicating Responsibly across Cultures

From 1967 to 1973, the Dutch intercultural scholar Geert Hofstede conducted a comprehensive study of how values in the workplace are influenced by culture. During these years, he collected and analyzed data from surveys completed by more than 100,000 IBM employees representing 40 countries.[1] Based on the survey data, Hofstede developed a model that identified four primary dimensions that differentiate cultures: power distance, individualism, masculinity, and uncertainty avoidance. After conducting an additional international study with a survey instrument developed with Chinese employees and managers, Hofstede added a fifth dimension: long-term orientation.[2]

Many public relations scholars and practitioners recognize the usefulness of Hofstede's dimensions; those who appreciate these intercultural differences are better able to tailor their messages for international publics and build strong and trustworthy global relationships.[3] In individualistic cultures, for example, which value individual rights and goals more highly than collective rights and goals, the preferred communication style is open and direct. Members of individualistic cultures tend to be verbally straightforward, and they prefer "straight talk"—messages that are clear and to the point. In collectivist cultures, where group harmony is valued over the rights of the individual, the preferred communication style is indirect. Effective communication avoids placing blame for negative situations on discrete individuals and does not include competitive language. A public relations practitioner who wishes to communicate responsibly and ethically with international audiences must be aware of the extent to which the cultural styles of nations—and their citizens—differ.

Hofstede's five dimensions of culture include the following:

Power Distance. This dimension represents the extent to which people in a particular culture tolerate unequal distributions of power in society and within organizations. Cultures that rank high in power distance on Hofstede's global scales tend to embrace

(Continued)

Table 10.1   (Continued)

hierarchical social relationships and autocratic leadership. Sharp distinctions in educational and economic status separate social groups, and the exercise of authority in the workplace and at home is considered normal and appropriate. Individuals are likely to obey such authority figures as parents and employers. A culture that ranks low in power distance emphasizes equality and opportunity for all.

Individualism. This dimension represents the degree to which the society prizes individual or group achievement, and the degree to which the society values interpersonal relationships. A culture that ranks high in individualism on Hofstede's global scales privileges individuality and individual rights. Persons living in individualistic societies may tend to form a larger number of loose interpersonal relationships. A culture that ranks low in individualism is a collectivist society. Collectivist societies prioritize the welfare of the group over the welfare of the individual, and social ties within groups, such as families and coworkers, are very tight.

Masculinity. This dimension describes the degree to which a society emphasizes stereotypical masculine traits such as dominance, success, aggression, competition, and achievement. A culture that ranks high in masculinity on Hofstede's global scales will have significant gender role differentiation, with men typically assigned the outgoing and public roles and women the nurturing and private roles. In these cultures, males dominate a significant portion of the society and power structure, and women are often subject to male domination. A low masculinity ranking indicates that the country has a low level of differentiation between men and women, and all members participate in the public and private spheres. In these cultures, women are equal to men in all aspects of society.

Uncertainty Avoidance. This dimension captures the level of tolerance that people in a particular culture have for uncertainty and ambiguity. People living in a culture that ranks high in uncertainty avoidance on Hofstede's global scales will have little tolerance for the unexpected, will not accept change readily, and will avoid risk whenever possible. Cultures that rank high in this dimension create rules, laws, and regulations to try to reduce uncertainty and ambiguity. A culture that ranks low in uncertainty avoidance will tend to harbor less concern about the unknown, and its citizens will be more amenable to risk and change. Fewer rules and regulations structure the society.

Long-term Orientation. This dimension indicates whether members of the culture value tradition and history, and look to the past for guidance and inspiration. A culture that ranks high in long-term orientation will take pride in its long-term commitments and respect for traditional ways of doing business and living one's life. Individuals in these cultures expect that long-term rewards will be reaped as a result of today's hard work. A culture that ranks low in long-term orientation is said to embrace the idea of living for today and investing in tomorrow. Members of such cultures are said to have a short-term orientation, and they adopt innovations rapidly because traditional ways of doing things are not experienced as barriers to change.

Cultural Landscapes: A Global Snapshot[4]

Country	Power Distance	Individualism	Masculinity	Uncertainty Avoidance	Long-term Orientation
Australia	Low	Very High	Average	Low	Very Low
Brazil	High	Low	Average	High	High
Canada	Low	Very High	Average	Low	Very Low
China	High Average	Very Low	High	Low	Very High
Denmark	Very Low	High	Very Low	Very Low	Low
Germany	Low	High	High Average	High Average	Low
Hungary	Low	High	High	High	Average
India	High	Average	Average	Low	High
Japan	Low Average	Average	Very High	Very High	Very High
Thailand	High	Very Low	Very Low	Average	Average
United States	Low	Very High	High	Low	Very Low

1. Geert Hofstede, *Culture's Consequences: International Differences in Work-Related Values* (Beverly Hills, CA: Sage, 1980).

2. Geert Hofstede and Michael H. Bond, "The Confucius Connection: From Cultural Roots to Economic Growth," *Organizational Dynamics* 16 (1988): 5–21.

3. See, for example, Jamie Feehery-Simmons, "Exploring the Dimensions of Culture: Global Negotiation and Public Relations in Mexico," *Journal of Promotion Management* 8, 2 (2002): 97–122; Stephen P. Banks, *Multicultural Public Relations: A Social-Interpretive Approach* (Thousand Oaks, CA: Sage, 1995); and Nancy J. Adler, John L. Graham, and Thomas Gehrke, "Business Negotiations in Canada, Mexico and the United States," *Journal of Business Research* 15 (1987): 411–29.

4. Countries are ranked as compared with a global average. For the full breakout of scores for each country, see "Geert Hofstede: Cultural Dimensions," http://geert-hofstede.com (accessed September 25, 2005).

—Carolyn Bronstein

Ethics and the Global Society

As Day has pointed out, ethics deal with moral components of human life and reflect "a society's notions about the rightness or wrongness of an act and the distinctions between virtue and vice."[13] Scholars James A. Anderson and Elaine Englehardt claim that ethics concerns the rights and responsibilities of conduct and is closely related between individuals and society.[14] Societies frequently change in terms of what they consider right and wrong as they move from one region of the world to another. The same often holds true as we move from country to country. Any examination of international ethics—whether in public relations or not—must encompass these realities. Because ethics are based on the values and norms of individual societies, it is essential that those who study international ethics understand and accept societal differences.

Although most of the published scholarship about public relations ethics has focused on the United States, the study of ethics has deep global roots. Ethics study began with Socrates (c. 470–399 BC) in ancient Greece, where he claimed virtue could be practiced and identified. His student Plato (c. 428–348 BC) encouraged moral conduct even if it might go against societal norms. Aristotle (348–322 BC), a disciple of Plato, pointed out that moral virtue frequently required difficult choices. Development of the Judeo-Christian ethic brought forward the concept of loving "thy neighbor as thy self," and, in the eighteenth century, the German philosopher Immanuel Kant introduced the "categorical imperative," which was a duty-based moral philosophy. Kant believed in the duty to tell the truth even if it resulted in harming others. The progressive relativism school of thought believes what is right or good for one is not necessarily right or good for another, even under similar circumstances, developed in part as a response to Kant's work.

Moral rules represent the fuel that drives the ethical system. They give us guideposts for resolving ethical dilemmas. They also pose moral duties on us as individuals—something very important in public relations, because public relations practitioners have fewer rules to specifically guide their ethical practice than is the case in most other occupations.

Much of the ethics research literature we get from sociology, psychology, organizational behavior, and business centers on the role of the decision maker in ethical behavior. And, although public relations people do not always make decisions in an organizational context, their counsel quite frequently enters that decision-making process.

Even though ethics always has played a significant and important role in the proper practice of public relations, the importance of ethics in any sort of organizational communication has taken on new meaning as the result of the development of the global business society and the unprecedented number of corporate scandals—e.g., Enron, WorldCom, Tyco, and Global Crossing—that have affected the business world in recent years. Although many of these events took place in the United States, they had great international implications and created considerable upheaval in the world's financial markets. The common denominator underlying each of these scandals was the failure of companies to be honest and ethical in their dealings with the public. Although some blamed failed corporate governance, accounting abuses and outright greed for the problems, one must wonder what role, if any, public relations played in these major business disasters.

All of these cases involved corporate fraud, and situations where share-holders were not provided with the proper information and access required to effectively watch management. In a recent book detailing the Enron bank-ruptcy scandal, author Loren Fox presents a vivid portrait of what happens when a company lives far beyond its means.[15] In another account of the Enron collapse, authors Mimi Swartz and Sherron Watkins blame Ken Lay, former CEO of Enron, and other company executives for privileging greed and arrogance over ethical business decisions.[16] Bernie Ebbers, the former CEO of WorldCom, the telecommunications giant that filed for bankruptcy in the face of a fraudulent accounting scandal, at one point argued that he did not understand why his company was collapsing around him.

Essentially, the predicament for the public relations profession focuses on what sort of role public relations played in these organizational nightmares. Were these companies operating, as most of the world's most successful organizations do, with a chief public relations officer reporting directly to the CEO? Did public relations play a management-influencing, decision-making role in these companies? Or, were the public relations people—like so many other employees—kept totally in the dark until the arrogance and the deceit caught up with senior-level management, bringing forth an embar-rassing unraveling leading to organizational demise?

Perhaps the governance of these companies was such that they did not care about their publics, and did not want the advice of senior-level public relations professionals who advocate two-way symmetrical communication practices. It is interesting to note that none of the companies mentioned above appear to have had a senior-level corporate public relations officer playing an active or dominant role in organizational decision making. One company, Enron, did have a vice president of corporate communications, but he certainly was not as well known in professional circles as his peers holding similar titles in companies of similar size. Because so much of what happened at Enron now is being held up in potential legal lawsuits, it is likely that many years will pass before we will really know what role this public relations officer might have played. Another of these companies, Arthur Andersen, had a very highly noted public relations officer reporting to the CEO until about two years before the Enron crisis. Ironically, Arthur Andersen downgraded the public relations function in 2000, which led to this highly regarded professional leaving that company for a senior-level public relations position elsewhere. By all accounts, it appears that he was not replaced at Arthur Andersen—certainly not at the senior level.

As these U.S-based scandals reverberated throughout the world and caused a tremendous loss of faith in American business practices, they also raised global questions concerning responsible advocacy. Some would argue that duplicity and deception, in public and private life, are substantially greater today than they have been in the past. Dishonesty is blamed on a wide variety of factors, such as disillusionment with government and other traditional forms of authority. As people have relaxed their standards on values, virtues, and so forth, is it any wonder communication difficulties have presented themselves for those who work in public relations?

Ethics and Trust

What all this really boils down to is the matter of trust. It is impossible for a company to be perceived as being ethical unless it develops a sense of trust, and many of the world's companies most certainly have broken any hope of trust they had with their important strategic publics—employees, investors, communities, and many more.

The noted international economics scholar Francis Fukuyama has found that the level of trust inherent in a country is the single most persuasive factor in determining a nation's economic well-being. Fukuyama maintains that societies that permit and support high levels of trust usually prosper with strong economic results.[17] He also points out that low levels of trust, in turn, have a highly negative impact on a society's economic activity. The research of the sociologist Amitai Etzioni strongly supports the Fukuyama thesis.[18]

Regardless of what part of the world they reside and work in, most people understand some of the most basic and straightforward principles of ethics and the central role that trust plays. Around the world, ethics and strust form the cornerstones of effective public relations practice. In China, for example, high levels of trust built and maintained through personal relationships drive public relations practice. The Chinese term *guanxi* signifies the overriding power of personal relationships in this culture, and the extent of an individual's *guanxi* is regarded as the most definitive measure of success in business.[19] Public relations professionals working in China highlight relationship building as the most significant aspect of their day-to-day practice.

Patrick Wang, the head of government relations for Nike, Inc., in China, relied on the power of *guanxi* when Chinese customs officers seized thirty shipments of alleged fake Nike goods in 1999. Chinese trade regulations stipulated that Nike, the brand owner, would have to post a bond in the same amount as the potential value of the shipments, which totaled several million dollars. This bond would be used as liability insurance by the

Chinese government to cover damages owed if the Nike products were found to be legitimate. Although Nike supported the government's effort to prevent the shipment of fraudulent goods, the company was loath to commit millions of dollars to the bond, which in turn would have crippled the company's China operations.[20]

Faced with a serious threat to Nike's well-being, Wang leveraged the power of *guanxi* to aid the company. He used the strong relationships and trust that he had developed with Chinese government officials in the International Property Rights division to arrange an alternative to the bond. After hearing Nike's concerns, the director of the division suggested that Nike and the Chinese customs office sign a memorandum of understanding, which obligated Nike to pay all monetary damages to involved parties if the seized goods turned out to be legitimate, but did not require that the company post the bond. The government officials allowed Nike to issue a bank guarantee in its place, which enabled the company to protect its cash flow. In an account of these events, Wang told a reporter for *China Brief,* a publication of the American Chamber of Commerce for the People's Republic of China, that the key to Nike's success was "the company's relationship with the government built on trust." He added that a "trust relationship" with government counterparts also helped Nike have a voice in the formation of any new government regulations. "If you keep to your business ethic and are open and honest about issues," Wang said, "they will return the same actions."[21]

Need for Increased Scholarship

Unfortunately, scholarly studies on cases such as the Nike incident are scarce in the public relations literature. The international body of knowledge on public relations ethics is particularly underdeveloped. Whatever the reasons may be for this specific lack, a related problem is that general support for public relations education and research is woefully bad. Some might even say that it is deplorable. In the United States, many of the largest research-oriented universities do not offer course work in public relations, much less conduct research in this area. Many schools that do teach public relations give students only meager instruction, and rely on faculty members who are not qualified to conduct cutting-edge research in the field.

Sometimes research about public relations ethics is viewed less than enthusiastically by colleagues in other areas of communication. Those who teach public relations ethics within journalism schools frequently have faculty colleagues who scoff at the suggestion that public relations could be practiced ethically. For this and a number of other reasons, public relations education lacks the depth and maturity of many other academic disciplines. And, because of that, research in the field is less developed.

Some of the most compelling work on trust in public relations has been conducted in the United States by the Arthur W. Page Society, a professional association of senior-level corporate and agency public relations professionals. Arthur W. Page served as vice president of AT&T in the United States from 1927 to 1946. He was the first person in a public relations position to serve as an officer and member of the board of directors of a major public corporation. Page practiced six important principles of public relations management as a means of implementing his philosophy.

The first of these was to "tell the truth." Let the public know what is happening and provide an accurate picture of the organization's character, ideals, and practices. Few could argue this principle would be a great place to start if public relations practitioners really were serious about improving their ethics, and, indeed, their image.

The second principle of Arthur Page was "prove it with action." Public perception of any organization is determined 90% by what it does and 10% by talking about what it does. If the companies involved in the business crises just discussed would have told the truth, and then proved it by their actions, we might not be facing the ethical crises currently plaguing much of the business world.

The recently established Arthur W. Page Center in the College of Communication at Pennsylvania State University works closely with the Arthur Page Society to improve ethical practices in public relations. The center, which is dedicated to the study and advancement of ethics and responsibility in corporate communication and other forms of public communication, provides annual awards to support scholars and professionals who are making important contributions to knowledge, practice, or public understanding of public relations ethics.

Other national and international professional associations also have addressed issues related to public relations ethics and advocacy. The Public Relations Coalition, a partnership of major organizations representing corporate public relations, investor relations, public affairs, and related communications disciplines, has developed practical action models on a number of issues relevant to public relations. For example, the coalition selected three concepts that it argues are essential for restoring trust in corporations. These concepts call upon organizational leaders to adopt ethical principles, pursue transparency and disclosure in everything they do, and make trust a fundamental precept of corporate governance. The coalition has also proposed "Principles for Conducting Public Relations on the Internet," designed to promote the highest possible professional standards and ethical practices in the digital world and to ensure that the information posted on the Internet is accurate and truthful and that the sources for that information are always identified.

In other efforts, IPRA and the Institute for Public Relations, based at the University of Florida, have partnered in an attempt to develop a set of principles designed to foster greater transparency in the dealings between public relations professionals and the media, and to end bribery for media coverage throughout the world. In 2004, IPRA and the Institute for Public Relations were joined on this project by other noted organizations: the International Press Institute, the International Federation of Journalists, Transparency International, and the Global Alliance for Public Relations and Communications Management.

The principles embodied in this initiative are the following:

- News material should appear as a result of the news judgment of journalists and editors, and not as a result of any payment in cash or in kind, or any other inducements.
- Material involving payment should be clearly identified as advertising, sponsorship, or promotion.
- No journalist or media representative should ever suggest that news coverage will appear for any reason other than its merit.
- When samples or loans of products or services are necessary for a journalist to render an objective opinion, the length of time should be agreed on in advance and loaned products should be returned afterward.
- The media should institute written policies regarding the receipt of gifts or discounted products and services, and journalists should be required to sign the policy.

Codes of Ethics

Beginning in the mid-1900s, professional associations in public relations responded to ethical concerns with formalized codes of ethics. The Public Relations Society of America (PRSA) code of ethics is the best known among U.S. practitioners and arguably has the greatest impact. While such codes can be useful, however, their voluntary nature—that is, their inability to be enforced—breeds inherent problems, especially the reality that compliance for all codes is voluntary. As Wright noted,

> Most codes of ethics for communication-related associations are filled with meaningless rhetoric, do not accomplish much, and are not taken seriously by most of the people who work in (public relations). These codes might be able

to make ethical behavior less likely because of awareness. With or without professional codes of conduct, most who practice communication will choose to be ethical because they want to be, not because they have to be.[22]

Furthermore, as the public relations scholars Scott Cutlip, Allen Center, and Glen Broom point out, the enforcement of these codes often is uneven and infrequent.[23] Also, as James Grunig and Todd Hunt explain, many public relations people do not belong to professional associations and have no membership obligation to uphold codes of ethics.[24] While this particular problem certainly prevails in the United States, it is even more pronounced in other nations.

Differences related to culture and values also add to the difficulties of developing and enforcing international codes of conduct. For example, throughout the global society, there are laws some people might not consider right or proper. These include, but are not limited to, many rules and regulations that some might say discriminate against individuals based on their sex, race, sexual orientation, or other personal attributes. The societal values held toward these attributes tend to differ from one society to another. The same holds true for rules and regulations concerning topics such as abortion, pollution, and the death penalty. It is sometimes difficult for citizens of one country to understand the cultural differences they might have from people who live in another country. This problem frequently becomes pronounced when it comes to interpreting and understanding legal and ethical matters.

Despite such concerns, the public relations educator Dean Kruckeberg has argued for the development of an international code of ethics in public relations. He envisions the "development of a universal, multilaterally honored code of ethics endorsed and subscribed to by professional communicators in all transnational corporations worldwide."[25] Although acknowledging that many overseas public relations practitioners are bound by other operational codes dictating the international behavior of international companies, Kruckeberg argues that the development of an international code of ethics for public relations would make international commerce more ethical and trustworthy. He also says such a code would be welcomed by multinationals.

In fact, some progress has been made toward establishing universal standards for global public relations practitioners. The IPRA, which has become a relevant, resourceful, and influential professional association for senior-level, international public relations practitioners, developed codes more than forty years ago that continue to guide the work of contemporary practitioners. With members in more than one hundred different countries, IPRA provides intellectual leadership to international public relations practice through conferences, seminars, various special events, and its Web site.

The International Public
Relations Association Code (IPRA)

The IPRA has a Code of Conduct and a Code of Ethics, both of which have attempted to provide a global approach to ethical standards in public relations. Although these codes come with the same limitations and obstacles mentioned previously, they are worth examining here. The Code of Conduct of IPRA was adopted in Venice in 1961. Although critics of this code question how it can be valuable since it is more than forty years old, the fact that it has survived the test of time might be one of its strengths. It has been adopted by IPRA members in more than one hundred different countries.

International Public Relations Association Code of Conduct (adopted in Venice–May 1961)

A. Personal and Professional Integrity

1. It is understood that by personal integrity is meant the maintenance of both high moral standards and a sound reputation. By professional integrity is meant observance of the Constitution rules and, particularly, the Code as adopted by IPRA.

B. Conduct towards Clients and Employers

1. A member has a general duty of fair dealing towards his/her clients or employers, past and present.
2. A member shall not represent conflicting or competing interests without the express consent of those concerned.
3. A member shall safeguard the confidences of both present and former clients or employers.
4. A member shall not employ methods tending to be derogatory of another member's client or employer.
5. In performing services for a client or employer a member shall not accept fees, commission or any other valuable consideration in connection with those services from anyone other than his/her client or employer without the express consent of his/her client or employer, given after a full disclosure of the facts.
6. A member shall not propose to a prospective client that his/her fees or other compensation be contingent on the achievement of certain results; nor shall he/she enter into any fee agreement to the same effect.

(Continued)

(Continued)

C. Conduct towards the Public and the Media

1. A member shall conduct his/her professional activities with respect to the public interest and for the dignity of the individual.
2. A member shall not engage in practice which tends to corrupt the integrity of channels of public communication.
3. A member shall not intentionally disseminate false or misleading information.
4. A member shall at all times seek to give a faithful representation of the organization which he/she serves.
5. A member shall not create any organization to serve some announced cause but actually to serve an undisclosed special or private interest of a member of his/her client or employer, nor shall he/she make use of it or any such existing organization.

D. Conduct towards Colleagues

1. A member shall not intentionally injure the professional reputation or practice of another member. However, if a member has evidence that another member has been guilty of unethical, illegal or unfair practices, including practices in violation of this Code, he/she should present the information to the Council of IPRA.
2. A member shall not seek to supplant another member with his employer or client.
3. A member shall co-operate with fellow members in upholding and enforcing this Code.

SOURCE: Reprinted with permission of International Public Relations Association.

This code addresses issues related to responsible advocacy primarily in the section on "Conduct towards the Public and the Media," in which it states that IPRA members "shall not engage in practice which tends to corrupt the integrity of channels of public communication." Additionally, the code requires members to "not intentionally disseminate false or misleading information" and that members "shall at all times seek to give a faithful representation of the organization which he/she serves." These provisions mirror closely the PRSA code, which promotes the free flow of accurate and truthful information—including source disclosure—that contributes to informed decision making.

The Code of Athens

The Code of Athens was adopted as the official code of ethics of IPRA at Athens in May 1965 and was modified slightly during a meeting in Teheran in April 1968. This code was authored by Lucien Matrat of France. Over the years, it has been translated into twenty languages, and copies of this code have been presented to numerous heads of state and to the Pope.

The Code of Athens

The International Code of Ethics of the International Public Relation Association

The Code of Athens, which is the international Code of Ethics of PR practitioners was adopted by the International Public Relations Association General Assembly, which was held in Athens on May 12, 1965 and modified at Teheran on April 17, 1968.

CONSIDERING that all Member countries of the United Nations Organization have agreed to abide by its Charter which affirms "its faith in fundamental human rights, in the dignity and worth of the human person" and that having regard to the very nature of the profession, public relations practitioners in these countries should undertake to ascertain and observe the principles set out in this Charter;

CONSIDERING that, apart from "rights," human beings have not only physical or material needs but also intellectual, moral and social needs, and that their rights are of real benefit to them only insofar as these needs are essentially met;

CONSIDERING that, in the course of their professional duties and depending on how these duties are performed, public relations practitioners can substantially help to meet these intellectual, moral and social needs;

And lastly, CONSIDERING that the use of techniques enabling them to come simultaneously into contact with millions of people gives public relations practitioners a power that has to be restrained by the observance of a strict moral code.

On all these grounds, all members of the International Public Relations Association agree to abide by this International Code of Ethics, and that if, in the light of evidence submitted to the Council, a member should be found to have infringed this Code in the course of

---

(Continued)

(Continued)

his/her professional duties, he/she will be deemed to be guilty of serious misconduct calling for an appropriate penalty.

Accordingly, each member:

SHALL ENDEAVOR

1. To contribute to the achievement of the moral and cultural conditions enabling human beings to reach their full stature and enjoy the indefeasible rights to which they are entitled under the "Universal Declaration of Human Rights;"
2. To establish communications patterns and channels which, by fostering the free flow of essential information, will make each member of the group feel that he/she is being kept informed, and also give him/her an awareness of his/her own personal involvement and responsibility, and of his/her solidarity with other members;
3. To conduct himself/herself always and in all circumstances in such a manner as to deserve and secure the confidence of those with whom he/she comes into contact;
4. To bear in mind that, because of the relationship between his/her profession and the public, his/her conduct—even in private—will have an impact on the way in which the profession as a whole is appraised;

SHALL UNDERTAKE

5. To observe in his/her professional duties, the moral principles and rules of the "Universal Declaration of Human Rights;"
6. To pay due regard to, and uphold human dignity and to recognize the right of each individual to judge for himself/herself;
7. To establish the moral, psychological and intellectual conditions for dialogue in its true sense, and to recognize the rights of these parties involved to state in their case and express their views;
8. To act, in all circumstances, in such a manner as to take account of the respective interests of the parties involved; both the interests of the organization which he/she serves and the interests of the publics concerned;
9. To carry out his/her undertakings and commitments which shall always be so worded as to avoid any misunderstanding, and to show loyalty and integrity in all circumstances so as to keep the confidence of his/her clients or employers, past or present, and all of the publics that are affected by his/her actions;

SHALL REFRAIN FROM

10. Subordinating the truth to other requirements;
11. Circulating information which is not based on established and ascertainable facts;
12. Taking part in any venture or undertaking which is unethical or dishonest or capable of impairing human dignity or integrity;
13. Using any manipulative methods or techniques designed to create subconscious motivations which the individual cannot control of his/her own free will and so cannot be held accountable for the action taken on them.

SOURCE: Reprinted with permission of International Public Relations Association.

The Code of Athens focuses significant attention on the obligation to respect human rights, including those related to "intellectual, moral and social needs." The code recognizes the power of public relations in the global society, noting the need for ethical conduct by public relations professionals who have the ability to reach and potentially influence millions of people. Such power must be restrained, according to the code, "by the observance of a strict moral code."

The Code of Athens also addresses the importance of informed decision making. Under this code, public relations professionals should "recognize the right of each individual to judge for himself/herself." The code states that practitioners should establish "conditions for dialogue" that recognize the rights of parties involved to express their views. As such, this model seems to reflect the democratic ideals of marketplace models adopted in the United States and elsewhere.

Two additional code provisions should be noted in a discussion of responsible advocacy in public relations. In the section that outlines prohibited behaviors, the Code of Athens requires that "the truth" should not be subordinated to other requirements and information "not based on established and ascertainable facts" should not be circulated. This last provision seems to suggest that truth be defined on a more objective standard—i.e., that truth be judged by whether information is provably true or false—than do many codes, including the PRSA code, which requires members to "adhere to the highest standards of accuracy and truth."

Finally, the IPRA code of ethics reminds public relations professionals that their individual conduct has an "impact on the way in which the profession as a whole is appraised." Much like its PRSA counterpart, which adopted "enhancing the professional" as a fundamental value of U.S. public relations practitioners, IPRA makes the point that public trust in and respect for public relations begins and ends with individual practitioners throughout the world who ultimately must decide for themselves the definition of "responsible advocacy."

Chapter Notes

Introduction

1. Fritz Cropp and J. David Pincus, "The Mystery of Public Relations: Unraveling Its Past, Unmasking Its Future," in *Handbook of Public Relations*, ed. Robert L. Heath (Thousand Oaks, CA: Sage, 2001), 189.

2. See Jodi Katzman, "What's the Role of Public Relations?" *Public Relations Journal* 49, 4 (April 1993): 11–16; and Ruth Edgett, "Toward an Ethical Framework for Advocacy in Public Relations," *Journal of Public Relations Research,* 14, 1 (2002): 1–26.

3. Dean Kruckeberg and Kenneth Starck, *Public Relations and Community: A Reconstructed Theory* (New York: Praeger, 1988).

4. Quoted in Katzman, "What's the Role?" 12.

5. See Kathy Fitzpatrick, "From Enforcement to Education: The Development of PRSA's Member Code of Ethics 2000," *Journal of Mass Media Ethics,* 17, 2:111–35.

Chapter 1

1. *Abrams v. United States,* 250 U.S. 616 (1919), 630.

2. See Philip Seib and Kathy Fitzpatrick, *Public Relations Ethics* (Fort Worth: Harcourt Brace, 1995).

3. D. Don Welch, ed., *Law and Morality* (Philadelphia: Fortress Press, 1987), 13–14.

4. Peter Cane, *Responsibility in Law and Morality* (Oxford: Hart, 2002), 12.

5. Cane, *Responsibility in Law and Morality,* 14.

6. Scott Cutlip, *The Unseen Power: Public Relations; A History* (Hillsdale, NJ: Lawrence Erlbaum, 1994), xii.

7. Robert L. Heath, "The Wrangle in the Marketplace: A Rhetorical Perspective on Public Relations," in *Rhetorical and Critical Approaches to Public Relations,* ed. Elizabeth L. Toth and Robert L. Heath (Hillsdale, NJ: Lawrence Erlbaum, 1992), 17–36.

8. *Abrams v. United States,* 250 U.S. 616 (1919), 630 (Holmes, J., dissenting).

9. See Christopher T. Wonnell, "Truth and the Marketplace of Ideas," *University of California at Davis Law Review,* 19 (Spring 1986): 669–76, for a review of criticism of marketplace of ideas philosophy.

10. W. Wat Hopkins, "The Supreme Court Defines the Marketplace of Ideas," *Journalism & Mass Communication Quarterly* 73, 1 (Spring 1996): 40.

11. Hopkins, "Supreme Court Defines Marketplace," 40.

12. *Virginia State Bd. of Pharmacy v. Virginia Citizens Consumer Council,* 425 U.S. 748 (1976), 780.

13. *Connick v. Myers,* 461 U.S. 138 (1983), 145.

14. *Red Lion Broadcasting Co. v. FCC,* 395 U.S. 367 (1969), 389.

15. *Lamont v. Postmaster General,* 381 U.S. 301 (1965), 308, (Brennan, J., concurring).

16. *Virginia State Board of Pharmacy,* 862–63.

17. *First National Bank of Boston v. Bellotti,* 435 U.S. 765 (1978), 777.

18. *First National Bank of Boston,* 777.

19. *First National Bank of Boston,* 789.

20. *Federal Election Commission v. Massachusetts Citizens for Life,* 479 U.S. 238 (1966).

21. See, e.g., *Austin v. Michigan State Chamber of Commerce,* 494 U.S. 652, 1990.

22. *New York Times v. Sullivan,* 376 U.S. 254 (1964), 272–73.

23. *Hustler Magazine v. Falwell,* 485 U.S. 46 (1988), 52.

24. *New York Times v. Sullivan,* 272–73.

25. See *Near v. Minnesota,* 283 U.S. 697 (1931).

26. *Consolidated Edison Co. v. Public Service Commission,* 447 U.S. 530 (1980), 537, quoting *Police Department of Chicago v. Mosley,* 408 U.S. 92 (1972), 96.

27. See *McConnell v. FEC,* 540 U.S. 93 (2003).

28. B. K. Petersen and A. R. Lang, "A 200-Year Analysis of U.S. Supreme Court Interpretations of Public Relations" (paper presented at the meeting of the Association for Education in Journalism and Mass Communications Southeast Colloquium, Chapel Hill, NC), 35.

29. *Virginia State Board of Pharmacy v. Virginia Citizens Consumer Council,* 425 U.S. 748 (1976), 761, quoting *Bigelow v. Virginia,* 421 U.S. 809 (1975).

30. *Virginia State Board of Pharmacy,* 825–26.

31. *Central Hudson Gas & Electric Corp. v. Public Service Commission,* 447 U.S. 557 (1980), 564.

32. *Virginia State Board of Pharmacy,* 772, n. 24.

33. See *Zauderer v. Office of Disciplinary Counsel,* 471 U.S. 626 (1985), 638.

34. *Virginia State Board of Pharmacy,* 772.

35. See FTC, "Policy Statement on Deception," 103 F.T.C. 110, 165 (1984).

36. See Kathy Fitzpatrick, "The Legal Challenge of Integrated Marketing Communication (IMC): Combining Commercial and Political Speech," *Journal of Advertising,* 34, 4 (Winter 2005): 93–102.

37. See Consumer Protection from Deceptive Acts and Practices (2004), *New York General Business Law,* sec. 350-a, Article 22-A.

38. See Fitzpatrick, "Legal Challenge."

39. See *Kasky v. Nike, Inc.,* 27 Cal. 4th 939 (2002).

40. See Hopkins, "Supreme Court Defines Marketplace."

41. David Martinson, "Is It Ethical for Practitioners to Represent 'Bad' Clients?" *Public Relations Quarterly,* 44, 4 (Winter, 1999): 22–25.

42. Martinson, "Is It Ethical?" 23.

43. Martinson, "Is It Ethical?" 25.

44. Martinson, "Is It Ethical?" 25.

45. John Warburton, "Corruption, Power and the Public Interest," *Business & Professional Ethics Journal,* 17, 4 (1998): 85.

46. Warburton, "Corruption, Power and the Public Interest," 85.

47. Memorandum from the PRSA Board of Directors and PRSA Board of Ethics and Professional Standards, April 27, 2005, 2.

48. Philip Seib and Kathy Fitzpatrick, *Public Relations Ethics* (Fort Worth: Harcourt Brace, 1995).

49. Ralph Barney and Jay Black, "Ethics and Professional Persuasive Communications," *Journal of Mass Media Ethics,* 20, 3 (1994): 233–48.

50. Barney and Black, "Ethics and Professional Persuasive Communications," 233.

51. Barney and Black, "Ethics and Professional Persuasive Communications," 247.

52. David L. Martinson, "'Truthfulness' in Communication is Both a Reasonable and Achievable Goal for Public Relations Practitioners," *Public Relations Quarterly,* 31, 4 (Winter 1996): 45.

53. Seib and Fitzpatrick, *Public Relations Ethics,* 101.

54. See, e.g., Carol A. Bodensteiner, "Special Interest Group Coalitions: Ethical Standards for Broad-Based Support Efforts," *Public Relations Review,* 23, 1 (Spring 1997): 31–46.

55. See Kathy Fitzpatrick and Michael Palenchar, "Disclosing Special Interests: Constitutional Restrictions on Front Groups," *Journal of Public Relations Research* (forthcoming).

56. *McConnell v. FEC.*

57. *McConnell v. FEC,* 121.

58. *McConnell v. FEC,* 197.

59. *McConnell v. FEC,* 197.

60. See *McIntyre, J., Executor of Estate of Margaret McIntyre, Deceased, Petitioner v. Ohio Elections Commission,* 514 U.S. 334 (1995).

61. Laurence B. Alexander, "Ethical Choices that Become Legal Problems for Media," *Newspaper Research Journal* 17, 1–2 (Winter–Spring 1996): 61.

62. Paul S. Voakes, "Rights, Wrongs and Responsibilities: Law and Ethics in the Newsroom," *Journal of Mass Media Ethics* 15, 1 (2000): 32.

63. Voakes, "Rights, Wrongs and Responsibilities," 32.

64. Voakes, "Rights, Wrongs and Responsibilities," 41.

65. Greg Toppo, "White House Paid Journalist to Promote Law," *USA Today,* January 7, 2005, A1.

66. Robert Pear, "White House's Medicare Videos Are Ruled Illegal," *New York Times,* May 20, 2004, A24.

67. Stuart Elliott, "Strong Stands Taken as the Public Relations Industry Debates Payments Made to a Commentator," *New York Times,* January 19, 2005, C5.

Chapter 2

1. Vincent E. Barry, *Moral Issues in Business* (Belmont, CA: Wadsworth, 1979).

2. Will Barrett, "Responsibility, Accountability and Corporate Activity," *Online Opinion: Australia's E-journal of Social and Political Debate*, August 25, 2004, http://www.onlineopinion.com.au/print.asp?article=2480#.

3. Bernard Gert, *Morality: A New Justification of the Moral Rules* (New York: Oxford University Press, 1988), 214–15. Gert prefers to use *credit* instead of *praise*, as some others hold, since it is the proper opposite of *blame* as a "responsibility standard"; whereas *praise* and its opposite, *condemnation*, are considered to be moral standards.

4. Geoff Hunt, "Accountability," http://www.freedomtocare.org/.

5. John Christman, "Autonomy in Moral and Political Philosophy," in *The Stanford Encyclopedia of Philosophy*, ed. Edward N. Zalta (Fall 2003), http://plato.stanford.edu/entries/autonomy-moral/.

6. Mitchell R. Haney, "Corporate Loss of Innocence for the Sake of Accountability," *Journal of Social Philosophy*, 35, 3 (Fall 2004): 406.

7. Haney, "Corporate Loss of Innoncence," 407.

8. Christman, *Autonomy.*

9. Norman Bowie, *Business Ethics* (Englewood Cliffs: Prentice Hall, 1982), 95–96.

10. Bowie, *Business Ethics.*

11. Gary Watson, "Two Faces of Responsibility," *Philosophical Topics*, 24 (1996): 227–48.

12. Kevin Gibson, "Excuses, Excuses: Moral Slippage in the Workplace," *Business Horizons*, 43, 6 (2000): 65–72.

13. Much of this part of the discussion is based on Thomas H. Bivins, "Ethical Implications of the Relationship of Purpose to Role and Function in Public Relations," *Journal of Business Ethics*, 8, 1 (Spring 1989); and "Professional Advocacy in Public Relations: Ethical Considerations," *Business and Professional Ethics Journal*, 6, 1 (Summer 1989): 82–91.

14. Hunt, "Accountability."

15. Michael D. Bayles, *Professional Ethics*, 2nd ed. (Belmont, CA: Wadsworth, 1989).

16. William H. Simon, "The Ideology of Advocacy: Procedural Justice and Professional Ethics," *Wisconsin Law Review* (1978): 29–144. For a discussion of Simon's argument, see Bayles, *Professional Ethics*, 62–63.

17. Simon, "Ideology of Advocacy," 131.

18. Bayles, *Professional Ethics*, 72.

19. Dorothy Emmet, *Rules, Roles, and Relations* (Boston: Beacon Press, 1996), 15.

20. Bivins, "Professional Advocacy."

21. Bayles, *Professional Ethics*, 68–70.

22. Bayles, *Professional Ethics*, 69.

23. Barrett, "Responsibility, Accountability and Corporate Activity."

24. Marvin Brown, "Ethics in Organizations," *Issues in Ethics*, 2, 1 (1989), http://www.scu.edu/ethics/publications/iie/v2n1/homepage.html.

25. James E. Grunig and Todd Hunt, *Managing Public Relations* (New York: Holt, Rinehart & Winston, 1984), 100.

26. For a look at these effects on other media professions, see Thomas H. Bivins, *Mixed Media: Moral Distinctions in Advertising, Public Relations, and Journalism* (Mahwah, NJ: Lawrence Erlbaum, 2004).

27. Opinion Research Corporation, *Avoiding Failures in Management Communications: Research Report of the Public Opinion Index for Industry* (Princeton, NJ: Opinion Research Corporation, January 1963).

28. Paul R. Timm and Kristen Bell DeTienne, *Managerial Communication*, 3rd ed. (Englewood Cliffs, NJ: Prentice Hall, 1995), 100–105.

29. Gabriel Moran, *A Grammar of Responsibility* (New York: Crossroads, 1996), 137.

30. Bruce Klatt and Shaun Murphy, *Accountability: Getting a Grip on Results*, http://www.refresher.com/!accountabilitykb.html.

31. Dianne Schilling, "The Power of Accountability," WomensMedia.com, http://www.womensmedia.com/seminar-accountability.html.

32. Bivins, *Mixed Media*, 112–14.

33. Laurence Stern, "Deserved Punishment, Deserved Harm, Deserved Blame," Royal Institute of Philosophy, http://www.royalinstitutephilosophy.org/articles/article.php?id=25.

34. Stern, "Deserved Punishment."

35. Gibson, "Excuses, Excuses."

36. This discussion is taken in part from Gibson, "Excuses, Excuses," and Deni Elliott and Paul Martin Lester, "Excuses and Other Moral Mistakes: Taking Responsibility for Your Actions," in "Ethics Matters," a monthly column in *News Photographer* magazine (March 2002), http://commfaculty.fullerton.edu/lester/writings/ethicsmatters032002.html.

37. Rod Powers, "To Obey or Not to Obey," http://usmilitary.about.com/cs/militarylaw1/a/obeyingorders.htm.

38. Elliot and Lester, "Excuses and Other Moral Mistakes."

39. Arthur I. Applbaum, *Ethics for Adversaries: The Morality of Roles in Public and Professional Life* (Princeton, NJ: Princeton University Press, 2000).

40. Gibson, "Excuses, Excuses."

41. Anders Kaye, "Resurrecting the Causal Theory of Excuses," *Nebraska Law Review*, 83, 1116 (2005).

42. Alan Strudler and Danielle Warren, "Authority and Excuses," Maryland School of Public Affairs, http://www.puaf.umd.edu/IPPP/Winter-Spring00/authority_and_excuses.htm.

43. David W. Guth and Charles Marsh, *Public Relations: A Values-Driven Approach* (Boston: Pearson, 2005), 452.

44. Gibson, "Excuses, Excuses."

Chapter 3

1. Kathleen B. Jones and Anna G. Jonasdottir, "Introduction: Gender as an Analytic Category in Political Theory," in *The Political Interests of Gender,* ed. Kathleen B. Jones and Anna G. Jonasdottir (London: Sage, 1988).

2. Kathy E. Ferguson, "Subject-Centeredness in Feminist Discourse," in *The Political Interests of Gender,* ed. Kathleen B. Jones and Anna G. Jonasdottir (London: Sage, 1988).

3. Larissa A. Grunig, "Toward the Philosophy of Public Relations," in *Rhetorical and Critical Approaches to Public Relations,* ed. Elizabeth L. Toth and Robert L. Heath (Hillsdale, NJ: Lawrence Erlbaum, 1992).

4. Morris L. Bigge, *Positive Relativism: An Emerging Educational Philosophy* (New York: Harper & Row, 1971).

5. Bigge, *Positive Relativism.*

6. Larissa A. Grunig, Elizabeth L. Toth, and Linda Hon, "Feminist Values in Public Relations," *Journal of Public Relations Research,* 12, 1 (2000): 49–68.

7. Grunig et al., "Feminist Values," 50.

8. James E. Grunig, "Two-Way Symmetrical Public Relations: Past, Present, Future,"in *The Handbook of Public Relations,* ed. Robert L. Heath (Thousand Oaks, CA: Sage, 2000).

9. Grunig, "Two-Way Symmetrical Public Relations," 28.

10. Larissa A. Grunig, ed., "Women in Public Relations," special issue, *Public Relations Review,* 14 (1988).

11. Carolyn G. Cline et al., *The Velvet Ghetto: The Impact of the Increasing Percentage of Women in Public Relations and Business Communication* (San Francisco: IABC Foundation, 1986); and Elizabeth L. Toth and Carolyn G. Cline, *Beyond the Velvet Ghetto* (San Francisco: IABC Research Foundation, 1989).

12. Marilyn Kern-Foxworth, "Minorities 2000: The Shape of Things to Come," *Public Relations Journal* (August 1989): 14–18, 21–22.

13. Patrizia Zanoni and Maddy Janssens, "Deconstructing Difference: The Rhetoric of Human Resource Managers' Diversity Discourses," *Organization Studies,* 25 (2003): 55.

14. Katie Sweeney, "Managing Diversity in 2014, America's Population Will Be Older and More Ethnically Diverse Than Ever Before: Will We All Get Along? Plus: Corporate Diversity—The View From 2014." Public Relations Tactics, Public Relations Society of America, http://www.prsa.org/_Publications/magazines/0804spot1.asp (accessed June 8, 2005).

15. Linda Aldoory and Elizabeth L. Toth, "Gender Discrepancies in a Gendered Profession: A Developing Theory for Public Relations," *Journal of Public Relations Research,* 14, 2 (2002): 110.

16. Julie L. Andsager and Stacey J. T. Hust, "Differential Gender Orientation in Public Relations: Implications for Career Choices," *Public Relations Review,* 31 (2005): 85–91.

17. U.S. Bureau of Labor Statistics, "Women in the Labor Force: A Databook," http://www.bls.gov/cps/wlf-databook.pdf (accessed January 25, 2005).

18. Donnalyn Pompper, "Linking Ethnic Diversity and Two-Way Symmetry: Modeling Female African American Practitioners' Roles," *Journal of Public Relations Research,* 16, 3 (2004): 271.

19. U.S. Bureau of Labor Statistics, "Women in the Labor Force: A Databook Updated and Available on the Internet," http://www.bls.gov/cps/wlf-databook2005 .htm (accessed June 9, 2005).

20. U.S. Bureau of Labor Statistics, "Women in the Labor Force."

21. L. A. Grunig, Elizabeth L. Toth, and Linda C. Hon, *Women in Public Relations: How Gender Influences Practice* (New York: Guilford Press, 2001), 313.

22. R. Roosevelt Thomas, Jr., *Beyond Race and Gender: Unleashing the Power of Your Total Work Force by Managing Diversity* (New York: Amacom, 1991).

23. Zanoni and Janssens, "Deconstructing Difference."

24. Zanoni and Janssens, "Deconstruction Difference," 66.

25. Lana Rakow, "From the Feminization of Public Relations to the Promise of Feminism," in *Beyond the Velvet Ghetto,* ed. Elizabeth L. Toth and Carolyn G. Cline (San Francisco: IABC Foundation, 1989), 287–98.

26. L. Grunig, Toth, and Hon, "Feminist Values in Public Relations," 58.

27. L. Grunig, Toth, and Hon, "Feminist Values in Public Relations," 54.

28. Linda Aldoory and Elizabeth Toth (unpublished data, 2004).

29. Julie O'Neil, "An Analysis of the Relationships among Structure Influence and Gender: Helping to Build a Feminist Theory of Public Relations," *Journal of Public Relations Research,* 15, 2 (2003): 171.

30. O'Neil, "An Analysis," 172.

31. Youjin Choi and Linda Hon, "The Influence of Gender Composition in Powerful Positions on Public Relations Practitioners' Gender-Related Perceptions," *Journal of Public Relations Research,* 14, 3 (2002): 258.

32. Quoted in Elizabeth L. Toth and Larissa A. Grunig, "Addressing Work-Life Balance," *Tactics,* October 4, 2003.

33. Toth and Grunig, "Addressing Work-Life Balance."

34. Toth and Grunig, "Addressing Work-Life Balance."

35. Toni Muzi Falconi, "On Diversity and Political Correctness," December 13, 2004, http://www.worldprfestival.org/eng/blog.php?id=28 (accessed February 10, 2005).

36. Falconi, "On Diversity."

37. Falconi, "On Diversity."

38. LaForce, quoted in L. Silver, "White Males Still Dominate Top-Level Jobs," *Portland Oregonian,* August 1990, D1.

39. Michael Morley, *How to Manage Your Global Reputation: A Guide to the Dynamics of International Public Relations* (London: Macmillan, 1988).

40. Scott M. Cutlip, Allen H. Center, and Glen M. Broom, *Effective Public Relations,* 8th ed. (Upper Saddle River, NJ: Prentice Hall, 2000), 51.

41. IABC International Association of Business Communicators, "International Association of Business Communicators Code of Ethics for Professional Communicators," http://www.iabc.com/members/joining/code.htm (accessed June 10, 2005).

42. International Public Relations Association, "Code of Athens," http://www .ipra.org/aboutipra/athens.html (accessed June 10, 2005).

43. Global Alliance for Public Relations and Communication Management, "Global Ethics Protocol on Public Relations," Summer 2002, http://www.globalpr .org/knowledge/ethics/protocol.asp (accessed June 10, 2005).

44. Public Relations Society of America, "Member Statement of Professional Values, 2005," http://www.prsa.org/_About/ethics/preamble.asp?ident=eth3 (accessed June 9, 2005).

45. Juan-Carlos Molleda, Colleen Connolly-Ahern, and Candace Quinn, "Cross-National Conflict Shifting: Expanding a Theory of Global Public Relations Management through Quantitative Content Analysis," *Journalism Studies* 6 (2005): 99.

46. Choi and Hon, "Influence of Gender Composition," 81.

47. Bey-Ling Sha, "The Feminization of Public Relations: Contributing to a More Ethical Practice," in *The Gender Challenge to Media,* ed. Elizabeth L. Toth and Linda Aldoory (Cresskill, NJ: Hampton Press, 2001), 158.

48. Sha, "The Feminization of Public Relations," 159.

49. Sha, "The Feminization of Public Relations," 158.

50. Sha, "The Feminization of Public Relations," 159.

51. Pompper, "Linking Ethnic Diversity," 287.

52. Thomas, Jr., *Beyond Race and Gender.*

53. Karl E. Weick, *The Social Psychology of Organizing,* 2nd ed. (Reading, MA: Addison-Wesley, 1979).

54. Larissa A. Grunig, James E. Grunig, and David M. Dozier, *Excellent Public Relations and Effective Organizations: A Study of Communication Management in Three Countries* (Mahwah, NJ: Lawrence Erlbaum, 2002), 12.

55. Grunig et al., *Excellent Public Relations.*

56. Grunig et al., *Excellent Public Relations,* 115.

57. Public Relations Society of America, *Multi-Connections* (New York: Public Relations Society of America, Fall 1997).

58. Barbara Diggs-Brown and R. Zaharna, "Ethnic Diversity in the Public Relations Industry," *Howard Journal of Communication,* 6, 1–2 (1995): 114–23.

59. L. Grunig, J. Grunig, and Dozier, *Excellent Public Relations.*

60. Zanoni and Janssens, "Deconstructing Difference."

61. For more on roles and gender, see David M. Dozier, Larissa A. Grunig, and James E. Grunig, *Manager's Guide to Excellence in Public Relations and Communication Management* (Mahwah, NJ: Lawrence Erlbaum, 1995); Elizabeth L. Toth and Larissa A. Grunig, "The Missing Story of Women in Public Relations," *Journal of Public Relations Research,* 5 (1993): 153–75; Larissa A. Grunig, Elizabeth L. Toth, and Linda C. Hon, "Feminist Values in Public Relations," *Journal of Public Relations Research,* 12, 1 (2000): 23–48; and Linda C. Hon, Larissa A. Grunig, and David M. Dozier, "Women in Public Relations: Problems and Opportunities," in *Excellence in Public Relations and Communication Management,* ed. James E. Grunig (Hillsdale, NJ: Lawrence Erlbaum, 1992).

62. James E. Grunig and Todd Hunt, *Managing Public Relations* (New York: Holt, Rinehart & Winston, 1984).

63. Grunig and Hunt, *Managing Public Relations,* 144.

64. Roger J. Sullivan, *Immanuel Kant's Moral Theory* (Cambridge: Cambridge University Press, 1989).

65. William D. Ross, *The Right and the Good* (Oxford: Clarendon Press, 1930).

66. Ron A. Pearson, "A Theory of Public Relations Ethics" (doctoral dissertation, Ohio University, Athens, 1989); and James E. Grunig and Larissa A. Grunig, "Implications of Symmetry for a Theory of Ethics and Social Responsibility in Public Relations" (paper presented to the Public Relations Interest Group, International Communication Association, Chicago, May 1996).

67. J. Grunig and Hunt, *Managing Public Relations.*

68. L. Grunig, J. Grunig, and Dozier, *Excellent Public Relations,* 11.

69. J. Grunig and L. Grunig, "Implications of Symmetry."

70. Shannon A. Bowen, "A Theory of Ethical Issues Management: Contributions of Kantian Deontology to Public Relations' Ethics and Decision Making" (doctoral dissertation, University of Maryland, College Park, 2000).

71. L. Marcil-Lacoste, "The Trivialization of the Notion of Equality," in *Discovering Reality: Feminist Perspectives on Epistemology, Metaphysics, Methodology, and Philosophy of Science,* ed. Sandra Harding and Merrill B. Hintikka (Dordrecht, Holland: D. Reidel, 1983); and L. Grunig, "Toward the Philosophy of Public Relations."

72. L. Grunig, "Toward the Philosophy of Public Relations."

73. Muzi Falconi, "On Diversity and Political Correctness."

Chapter 4

1. Anthony Effinger, "Low Wage Battle Emerges as Grocery Store's Weakest Link: As Wal-Mart Pushes for Greater Expansion, Union Clashes Over Cost-cutting Are Set to Increase," *Sunday Tribune,* October 7, 2004, https://web.lexis-nexis.com/universe.

2. Charles Fishman, "The Wal-Mart You Don't Know," 2003, http://www.fastcompany.com/magazine/77/walmart.html.

3. Victorino Matus, "Dollar-Menu Death Wish," *Daily Standard,* 2002 (accessed October 7, 2004).

4. Abercrombie and Fitch Protest, http://www.tow.com/photogallery/2002/20020418_abercrombie_protest/ (accessed October 15, 2004).

5. Elizabeth Dougall, "Revelations of an Ecological Perspective: Issues, Inertia, and the Public Opinion Environment of Organizational Populations," *Public Relations Review,* forthcoming.

6. Michael Karlberg, "Remembering the Public in Public Relations Research: From Theoretical to Operational Symmetry," *Journal of Public Relations Research* 8, 4 (1996): 263–78; and David M. Dozier and Martha Lauzen, "Liberating the Intellectual Domain from the Practice: Public Relations, Activism and the Role of the Scholar," *Journal of Public Relations Research* 12, 1 (2000): 3–22.

7. James E. Grunig and Todd Hunt, *Managing Public Relations* (New York: Holt, Rinehart & Winston, 1984).

8. Larissa A. Grunig, James E. Grunig, and David M. Dozier, *Excellent Public Relations and Effective Organizations* (Mahwah, NJ: Lawrence Erlbaum, 2002).

9. James E. Grunig, "A Roadmap for Using Research and Measurement to Design and Evaluate an Excellence Public Relations Function," *Brazilian Journal of Organizational Communication and Public Relations*, forthcoming.

10. Shannon A. Bowen, "Expansion of Ethics as the Tenth Generic Principle of Excellence: A Kantian Theory and Model for Managing Ethical Issues," *Journal of Public Relations Research* 16, 1 (2004): 65–92.

11. Ron Pearson, "Beyond Ethical Relativism in Public Relations: Coorientation, Rules, and the Idea of Communication Symmetry," in *Public Relations Research Annual*, ed. James E. Grunig and Larissa A. Grunig (Hillsdale, NJ: Lawrence Erlbaum, 1989), 67–86; and Ron Pearson, *A Theory of Public Relations Ethics* (doctoral dissertation, Ohio University).

12. James E. Grunig and Larissa A. Grunig, "Implications of Symmetry for a Theory of Ethics and Social Responsibility in Public Relations" (paper presented at the annual meeting of the International Communication Association, Chicago, 1996).

13. Shannon A. Bowen, "Expansion of Ethics as the Tenth Generic Principle of Excellence: A Kantian Theory and Model for Managing Ethical Issues," *Journal of Public Relations Research* 16, 1 (2004): 65–92.

14. Juliet Roper, "Symmetrical Communication: Excellent Public Relations or a Strategy for Hegemony?" *Journal of Public Relations Research* 17, 1 (2005): 69–86.

15. Scott Smallwood, "Speaking for the Animals of the Terrorists?" *Chronicle of Higher Education*, 48, August 5, 2005, L1.

16. Shankar Gupta, "Dell Computer to Respond to Bloggers' Complaints," http://publications.mediapost.com/ (accessed September 12, 2005).

17. Grunig and Hunt, *Managing Public Relations*.

18. Grunig, "Roadmap for Using Research."

19. Grunig, "Roadmap for Using Research."

20. Douglas Quenqua, "Advocacy Groups—the Proactive Approach to Averting Protests," *PR Week*, January 6, 2003, https://web.lexis-nexis.com/universe/ (accessed October 7, 2004).

21. Mary Ann Pires, "Working With Activist Groups," *Public Relations Journal* 45, 4 (1989): 30–32.

22. Larissa A. Grunig, "Activism: How it Limits the Effectiveness of Organizations and How Excellent Public Relations Departments Respond," in *Excellence in Public Relations and Communication Management*, ed. James E. Grunig (Hillsdale, NJ: Lawrence Erlbaum, 1992), 503–30.

23. Grunig and Hunt, *Managing Public Relations*.

24. Grunig and Hunt, *Managing Public Relations*.

25. Circle of Life, "Luna and the Tree Sit," http://www.circleoflife.org/inspiration/luna/index.htm (accessed September 12, 2005).

26. Sustainability.com, "The 21st Century NGO: Roles, Rules, and Risks," http://www.sustainability.com/ (accessed November 11, 2004).

27. James E. Grunig, ed., *Excellence in Public Relations and Communication Management* (Hillsdale, NJ: Lawrence Erlbaum, 1992).

28. Quenqua, "Advocacy Groups."

29. James E. Grunig and Yi-Hui Huang, "From Organizational Effectiveness to Relationship Indicators: Antecedents of Relationships, Public Relations Strategies, and Relationship Outcomes," in *Public Relations as Relationship Management,* ed. John A. Ledingham and Stephen D. Bruning (Mahwah, NJ: Lawrence Erlbaum, 2000), 23–54.

30. Glen M. Broom and David M. Dozier, *Using Research in Public Relations: Applications to Program Management* (Englewood Cliffs, NJ: Prentice Hall, 1990).

31. Grunig and Hunt, *Managing Public Relations.*

32. Grunig and Hunt, *Managing Public Relations.*

33. Grunig and Huang, "From Organizational Effectiveness."

34. James E. Grunig, "Two-Way Symmetrical Public Relations: Past, Present, and Future," in *Handbook of Public Relations,* ed. Robert L. Heath (Thousand Oaks, CA: Sage, 2001), 11–30.

35. Yi-Hui Huang, "Public Relations Strategies, Relational Outcomes, and Conflict Management Strategies" (doctoral dissertation, College Park, MD, 1994); and Ken D. Plowman, "Congruence Between Public Relations and Conflict Resolution" (doctoral dissertation, University of Maryland, College Park, MD, 1995).

36. Linda C. Hon and James E. Grunig, *Guidelines for Measuring Relationships in Public Relations* (Gainesville, FL: Institute for Public Relations, 1999), http://www.instituteforpr.org.

37. Texaco Corporation, "Texaco Announces Comprehensive Plan to Ensure Fairness and Economic Opportunity for Employees and Business Partners," 1996, http://www.texaco.com/sitelets/diversity/press/pr12_18.html (accessed November 29, 2004).

38. Hon and Grunig, *Guidelines for Measuring Relationships.*

39. Quenqua, "Advocacy Groups."

40. Hon and Grunig, *Guidelines for Measuring Relationships.*

41. Quenqua, "Advocacy Groups."

42. Quenqua, "Advocacy Groups."

43. Hon and Grunig, *Guidelines for Measuring Relationships.*

44. Monsanto, "The Monsanto Pledge," 2004, http://www.monsanto.com/monsanto/layout/our_pledge/default.asp (accessed November 22, 2004).

45. Monsanto, "The Monsanto Pledge."

46. Greenpeace, "Victory: Monsanto Drops GE Wheat," 2004, http://www.greepeace.org/international_en/news/details?campaign%5fid=3942&item% (accessed November 22, 2004).

47. Organic Consumers Association, "Monsanto's Ties to Government," 2004, http://www.organicconsumers.org/monlink.html (accessed December 17, 2004).

48. Hon and Grunig, *Guidelines for Measuring Relationships.*

49. Peter Ford, "NGOs: More than Flower Power," *Christian Science Monitor,* July 11, 2003, http://web.lexis-nexis.com/universe/ (accessed October 7, 2004).

50. Ford, "NGOs: More than Flower Power."

51. Ford, "NGOs: More than Flower Power."

52. Ford, "NGOs: More than Flower Power."

53. Ford, "NGOs: More than Flower Power."

54. Ford, "NGOs: More than Flower Power."

55. Hon and Grunig, *Guidelines for Measuring Relationships.*

56. Hon and Grunig, *Guidelines for Measuring Relationships.*

57. Hon and Grunig, *Guidelines for Measuring Relationships.*

58. Target Corporation, "Together, We're Here for Good: National Giving Partnerships at Target," 2004, http://target.com/target_group/community_giving/partnerships.jhtml;jsessionid=WQU4X (accessed November 22, 2004).

59. Grunig and Huang, "From Organizational Effectiveness."

60. Grunig and Huang, "From Organizational Effectiveness."

61. Grunig and Huang, "From Organizational Effectiveness."

62. Public Relations Society of America, "PRSA Member Code of Ethics," 2000, http://www.prsa.org/_About/ethics/values.asp?ident=eth4 (accessed December 17, 2004).

63. Public Relations Society of America, "PRSA Member Code of Ethics."

64. Quenqua, "Advocacy Groups."

65. Grunig and Huang, "From Organizational Effectiveness."

66. Grunig and Huang, "From Organizational Effectiveness."

67. Grunig and Huang, "From Organizational Effectiveness."

68. Grunig and Huang, "From Organizational Effectiveness."

69. World Wildlife Fund, "South Florida Conservation Results," 2004 http://worldwildlife.org/wildplaces/sfla/results.cfm (accessed November 11, 2004).

70. World Wildlife Fund, "South Florida Conservation Results."

71. World Wildlife Fund, "South Florida Conservation Results."

72. World Wildlife Fund, "South Florida Conservation Results."

73. Ken Plowman, "Power in Conflict for Public Relations," *Journal of Public Relations Research* 10, 4 (1998): 237–62.

74. Program on Negotiation at Harvard Law School, "From Conflict to Cooperation: Opening Lines of Communication in an Idaho/Nez Perce Jurisdictional Dispute," 2004, http://www.pon.harvard.edu/news/2003/event_nez_perce.php3 (accessed November 11, 2004).

75. Program on Negotiation at Harvard Law School, "From Conflict to Cooperation."

76. Program on Negotiation at Harvard Law School, "From Conflict to Cooperation."

77. Alvin Powell, "KSG Professors Mediate Dispute: Questions Over Sovereignty Spark Clash between Idaho Tribe, Nearby Towns," *Harvard University Gazette,* http://www.hno.harvard.edu/gazette/2003/01.30/11-nezperce.html (accessed December 14, 2004).

78. Powell, "KSG Professors Mediate Dispute."

79. Program on Negotiation at Harvard Law School, "From Conflict to Cooperation."

80. Grunig, "A Roadmap for Using Research."

81. Grunig, "A Roadmap for Using Research."

Chapter 5

1. Kathleen S. Kelly, "The Top Five Myths Regarding Nonprofits," *Public Relations Tactics*, August 2000, 29–31.

2. Sam Dyer, Teri Buell, Mashere Harrison, and Sarah Weber, "Managing Public Relations in Nonprofit Organizations," *Public Relations Quarterly*, 47, 4 (Winter 2002): 13–17.

3. Kelly, "Top Five Myths," 29.

4. For previous research on the relationship between economic resources and the efficacy of public relations efforts, see Oscar Gandy, *Beyond Agenda Setting: Information Subsidies and Public Policy* (Norwood, NJ: Ablex, 1982); Edward Herman and Noam Chomsky, *Manufacturing Consent* (New York: Pantheon Books, 1988); and David Croteau and William Hoynes, *The Business of Media: Corporate Media and the Public Interest* (Thousand Oaks, CA: Pine Forge Press, 2001).

5. George Pitcher, *The Death of Spin* (West Sussex, UK: John Wiley & Sons, 2003), 233, 35. See also W. Timothy Coombs, "The Internet as Potential Equalizer: New Leverage for Confronting Social Responsibility," *Public Relations Review*, 24, 3 (1998): 289–303.

6. Pitcher, *Death of Spin*, 233–34.

7. *Business Wire*, "Tenth Annual RSCH Magnet Survey Finds Corporate Credibility Crisis Is Having Dramatic Effects on Business Coverage," April 12, 2004, http://www.businesswire.com.

8. On journalists' views on the impact of the Internet on reporting, see Pew Research Center for the People and the Press, "How Journalists See Journalists in 2004: Views on Profits, Performance and Politics," May 23, 2004, http://www .people-press.org/reports/pdf/214.pdf.

9. Pew Research Center, "How Journalists See Journalists in 2004," sec. 3, Today's Changing Newsroom, http://www.stateofthenewsmedia.org/journalist_survey_prc3.asp.

10. See Gary Wolf, "How the Internet Invented Howard Dean," *Wired*, January 2004, 17–21.

11. The Oceana blog is available at http://community.oceana.org/.

12. *Business Wire*, "Eleventh Annual Euro RSCG Magnet and Columbia University Survey of Media Finds More than Half of Journalists Use Blogs Despite Being Unconvinced of Their Credibility," June 20, 2005, http://www.businesswire .com.

13. *Business Wire*, "Eleventh Annual Survey."

14. See Penn Kimball, *Downsizing the News: Network Cutbacks in the Nation's Capital* (Washington, DC: Woodrow Wilson Center Press, 1994); Benjamin M.

Compaine and Douglas Gomery, *Who Owns the Media? Competition and Concentration in the Mass Media Industry*, 3rd ed. (Thousand Oaks, CA: Pine Forge Press, 2001); Kathryn S. Wenner, "Lesson in Hard Knocks," *American Journalism Review*, 24, 3 (April 2002): 12–14; and Kelly Heyboer and Jill Rosen, "Taking a Walk on Space," *American Journalism Review* 25, 2 (March 2003): 10–12.

15. Marion Just and Tom Rosenstiel, Project for Excellence in Journalism, "All the News That's Fed," *New York Times*, March 26, 2005, A26.

16. See Bureau of Labor Statistics, U.S. Department of Labor, *Occupational Outlook Handbook*, 2004–05 Edition, Public Relations Specialists, http://www.bls.gov/oco/ocos086.htm (accessed August 1, 2005); and Bureau of Labor Statistics, U.S. Department of Labor, *Occupational Outlook Handbook*, 2004–05 Edition, News Analysts, Reporters, and Correspondents, http://www.bls.gov/oco/ocos088.htm (accessed August 1, 2005).

17. Bureau of Labor Statistics, *Occupational Outlook Handbook*.

18. Bureau of Labor Statistics, *Occupational Outlook Handbook*, News Analysts, Reporters, and Correspondents.

19. David P. Demers, *The Menace of the Corporate Newspaper: Fact or Fiction?* (Ames: Iowa State University Press, 1996); and Leonard Downie, Jr., and Robert G. Kaiser, *The News about the News: American Journalism in Peril* (New York: Knopf, 2002).

20. Bureau of Labor Statistics, *Occupational Outlook Handbook*, Public Relations Specialists.

21. Council of Public Relations Firms, "Labor Statistics," http://www.prfirms.org/career/labor_stats.asp (accessed December 20, 2004).

22. Based on research conducted by WorkinPR.com, Futureworkplace, Inc., estimated the number of public relations practitioners in the U.S. to be close to one million. See Council of Public Relations Firms, "Labor Statistics."

23. On the decline of journalism resources and the push for profits, see Jay G. Blumler and Michael Gurevitch, *The Crisis of Public Communication* (London: Routledge, 1995); Edward Herman and Robert McChesney, *The Global Media: The New Missionaries of Global Capitalism* (London: Cassell, 1997); and Robert G. Picard, *The Economics and Financing of Media Companies* (New York: Fordham University Press, 2002).

24. American Society of Newspaper Editors. "Newsroom Employment Survey 2003, Table A," http://www.asne.org/index.cfm?id=1138 (accessed 28 December 2004). On the Knight Ridder cuts, see "Knight Ridder Workers Protest Cuts," http://www.knightridderwatch.org/actions1.htm. This is the Web site of the Knight Ridder Council, a hub for union locals representing employees of Knight Ridder newspapers.

25. Pew Research Center, "How Journalists See Journalists," sec. 3.

26. Pew Research Center, "How Journalists See Journalists," sec. 3.

27. For additional description of the preparation and use of VNRs, see Glen T. Cameron and David Blount, "VNRs and Air Checks: A Content Analysis of the Use of Video News Releases in Television Newscasts," *Journalism and Mass Communication Quarterly*, 73, 4 (Winter 1996): 890–904.

28. Key findings of the survey are discussed in Just and Rosenstiel, "All the News That's Fed," http://www.journalism.org/.

29. Public relations practitioners are one of the major suppliers of news and entertainment content to the media, with some estimates suggesting that unedited public relations materials make up at least 40% of what appears in our daily newspapers. See Mark Dowie, "Torches of Liberty," in John Stuber and Sheldon Rampton, *Toxic Sludge is Good for You* (Monroe, ME: Common Courage Press, 1995), 1–4; and Kevin Moloney notes that among British journalists and public relations professionals, the former believe that a quarter of all media coverage is based on public relations–sourced material, whereas the latter believe that the total is closer to 40%. See Kevin Moloney, *Rethinking Public Relations: The Spin and the Substance* (London: Routledge, 2000), 29.

30. For information on the league and its VNR, visit the League Against Cruel Sports Web site at http://www.league.uk.com//news/media_briefings.

31. *Business Wire*, "Eleventh Annual Survey." See also *Business Wire*, "Tenth Annual Survey."

32. A VNR kit is generally sent by a public relations practitioner to a television news station. The kit usually contains a prepackaged, ready-to-air news story, accompanied by an anchor lead-in script and video footage known as "B-roll."

33. Robert Pear, "White House's Medicare Videos Are Ruled Illegal," *New York Times*, May 20, 2004, http://nytimes.com/ (accessed December 10, 2004).

34. Ray Richmond, "Passing It Off as News Makes for Some Bad PR," *HollywoodReporter.com*, March 23, 2004, http://www.hollywoodreporter.com/ (accessed December 20, 2004).

35. Many citizen action groups, such as the Center for American Progress, and other senior citizen coalition groups opposed the Medicare prescription drug act on the basis that financial incentives for private insurance companies could lead to serious caps on drug spending. Lower caps set on Medicare reimbursement for higher-cost prescription drugs would arguably lead private insurance companies to develop restrictive lists of "covered" drugs, and to deny seniors needed access to specialty medications, such as latest-generation mental health or cancer drugs.

36. General Accountability Office, "Department of Health and Human Services, Centers for Medicare & Medicaid Services—Video News Releases, B-302710," May 19, 2004, http://www.gao.gov/decisions/appro/302710.htm (accessed December 28, 2004).

37. General Accountability Office, "Video News Releases," 8.

38. Pear, "White House's Medicare Videos."

39. Howard Kurtz, "Administration Paid Commentator: Education Department Used Williams to Promote 'No Child' Law," *Washington Post*, January 8, 2005, A1.

40. Andrew Martin and Jeff Zeleny, "USDA Plants its Own News," *Chicago Tribune*, June 16, 2005, A1.

41. See David Barstow and Robin Stein, "Under Bush, A New Age of Prepackaged TV News," *New York Times*, March 13, 2005, A3.

42. "KFC Supplier Fires 11 After Video of Chicken Abuse," *USAToday.com*, July 20, 2004, http://www.usatoday.com/ (accessed 18 December 2004).

43. See Donald G. McNeil, Jr., "KFC Supplier Accused of Animal Cruelty," *New York Times*, July 20, 2004, 2C; People for the Ethical Treatment of Animals, "Exposé in the KFC Slaughterhouse," http://www.peta.org/feat/moorefield/ (accessed December 27, 2004); "KFC Supplier Fires 11," *USAToday.com*; and Brian Bohannon, "PETA Video Shows Chicken Abuse at KFC Supplier," *USAToday.com*, July 21, 2004, http://www.usatoday.com/ (accessed December 18, 2004).

44. Kant's law of justice obligates people to respect themselves, as well as all other human beings. For a discussion of his theory of ethical decision making, see R. J. Sullivan, *Immanuel Kant's Moral Theory* (Cambridge: Cambridge University Press, 1989). For an extended discussion of Kantian theory as applied to public relations practice, see Shannon A. Bowen, "Expansion of Ethics as the Tenth Generic Principle of Public Relations Excellence: A Kantian Theory and Model for Managing Ethical Issues," *Journal of Public Relations Research* 16, 1 (2004): 65–92.

45. John A. Ledingham and Stephen D. Bruning, "Relationship Management in Public Relations: Dimensions of an Organization-Public Relationship," *Public Relations Review* 24, 1 (Spring 1998): 55–65.

46. Aeron Davis, *Public Relations Democracy: Politics, Public Relations, and the Mass Media in Britain* (Manchester: Manchester University Press, 2002).

47. Davis, *Public Relations Democracy*, 148.

48. On news coverage of the UPS strike, including public relations efforts by the Teamsters Union, see Christopher Martin, *Framed! Labor and the Corporate Media* (Ithaca, NY: Cornell University Press, 2004). See also Christopher Martin, "The 1997 UPS Strike: Framing the Story for Popular Consumption," *Journal of Communication Inquiry* 27, 2 (2003): 190–210.

49. For general information on the IPA, see the organization's Web site at www.ipapilot.org/. The union maintains an up-to-date set of press releases and a media information center on this Web site.

50. The IPA campaign and the efforts of Manning, Selvage, & Lee are described in Brian K Gaudet, "Strategies for Landing a Silver Anvil," *Public Relations Strategist*, Fall 1999, http://www.prsa.org/ (accessed December 15, 2004).

51. The Silver Anvil Award is given to practitioners who address a contemporary issue with exemplary professional skill, creativity, and resourcefulness. The PRSA describes the Silver Anvil as "the pre-eminent achievement of public relations—the highest watermark of success for any practitioner." See the award description on the PRSA Web site, http://www.prsa.org/_Awards/silver/ (accessed January 10, 2005).

52. On the tendency for nonprofits and advocacy groups to share resources, see Jason Salzman, *Making the News: A Guide for Activists and Nonprofits*, rev. ed. (Boulder, CO: Westview Press, 2003).

53. The majority of studies have found that nonprofit groups are seriously disadvantaged by comparative resource disadvantage. Newer studies that take the power of electronic communication into account are more optimistic about the ability of smaller groups to level the playing field using public relations techniques. Earlier studies include Edie N. Goldenberg, *Making the Papers: The Access of Resource-Poor Groups to the Metropolitan Press* (Lexington, MA: D.C. Heath, 1975); Todd Gitlin, *The Whole World Is Watching: Mass Media in the Making and*

Unmaking of the New Left (Berkeley: University of California Press, 1980); Mark Fishman, *Manufacturing the News* (Austin: University of Texas Press, 1980); and David Miller, *Don't Mention the War: Northern Ireland, Propaganda and the Media* (London: Pluto Press, 1994). A more recent study that takes the latter view is Davis, *Public Relations Democracy*.

54. Davis, *Public Relations Democracy*, 121.

55. *Business Wire*, "Eleventh Annual Survey."

56. The organization's blog can be viewed online at http://www.esw.org/earth-page/.

57. Peter Panepento, "Advocacy Groups Discover the Power of Blogs to Spread Their Messages," *Chronicle of Philanthropy*, August 5, 2004, 1–4.

58. Panepento, "Power of Blogs," 3.

59. James Grunig has made this argument for dialogic communication. See James E. Grunig, "Symmetrical Presuppositions as a Framework for Public Relations Theory," in *Public Relations Theory*, ed. C. H. Botan and V. T. Hazelton, Jr. (Hillsdale, NJ: Lawrence Erlbaum, 1989), 17–44.

60. The philosopher Jürgen Habermas has outlined these and other related conditions for ethical dialogue. For a summary of Habermas' position, see Brant R. Burleson and Susan L. Kline, "Habermas' Theory of Communication: A Critical Explication," *Quarterly Journal of Speech* 65 (1979): 412–28.

61. See Robert L. Heath, "New Communication Technologies: An Issues Management Point of View," *Public Relations Review* 24, 3 (1998): 273–88; and Ron Pearson, "Business Ethics as Communication Ethics: Public Relations Practice and the Idea of Dialogue," in *Public Relations Theory*, ed. C. H. Botan and V. T. Hazelton, Jr. (Hillsdale, NJ: Lawrence Erlbaum, 1989), 111–31.

62. Kenneth D. Day, Qingwen Dong, and Clark Robins, "Public Relations Ethics: An Overview and Discussion of Issues for the 21st Century," in *Handbook of Public Relations*, ed. R. L. Heath (Thousand Oaks, CA: Sage, 2001), 408.

63. Some corporations maintain that annual meetings, where corporate officers and stockholders meet, can provide the conditions necessary for dialogic communication. This assumes, however, that all stakeholder publics are stockholders, which is not necessarily true. Employees of Delta Airlines, Condé Nast Publications, Google, Microsoft, Apple, and other large corporations have been fired for blogging.

Chapter 6

1. John A. Byrne, "After Enron: The Ideal Corporation," *Business Week*, 19–26, August 2002, 68; and Klaus Kleinfeld, "Restoring Public Trust," in *Building Trust*, ed. Arthur W. Page Society (New York: Arthur W. Page Society, 2004), 200–212.

2. Kleinfeld, "Restoring Public Trust," 202.

3. Edelman, "Fifth Annual Edelman Trust Barometer," http://www.edelman.com/image/insights/content/Edelman%202004%20Trust%20Barometer%20Findings.doc (accessed September 14, 2005).

4. Robert L. Dilenschneider, "The Transparency Paradox," *Vital Speeches of the Day* 70, 9 (2004), 280.

5. PR Coalition, "Restoring Trust in Business: Models for Action," September 2003, 6, http://www.instituteforpr.com/reputation.phtml?article_id=2003_restoring (accessed September 14, 2005).

6. Associated Press, "Status of High-Profile Corporate Scandals," *Associated Press Financial Wire*, July 13, 2005, http://web.lexis-nexis.com/.

7. Associated Press, "High-Profile Corporate Scandals."

8. Liz Willen, "What to Do with Halls of Shame?" *Montreal Gazette*, July 21, 2005, B7.

9. Niko Corley, "Saved by Scrutiny," *College News*, Spring–Summer 2005, 9.

10. Corley, "Saved by Scrutiny."

11. *Webster's New World College Dictionary*, 4th ed., s.v. "transparent."

12. PR Coalition, "Restoring Trust in Business," 6.

13. PR Coalition, "Restoring Trust in Business," 6.

14. Al Golin, "Q&A with Al Golin," *Public Relations Strategist*, Fall 2003, 28.

15. *Communication World*, "More than a Social Virtue: Public Trust Among Organizations' Most Valuable Assets," April–May 2003, 11.

16. Kevin Lane Keller and David A. Aaker, "The Impact of Corporate Marketing on a Company's Brand Extensions," in *Revealing the Corporation*, ed. John M. T. Balmer and Stephen A. Greyser (London: Routledge, 2003), 276.

17. Golin, "Q&A with Al Golin," 28.

18. John W. Thibaut and Harold H. Kelley, *The Social Psychology of Groups* (New York: Wiley, 1959).

19. Roger Cotterrell, "Transparency, Mass Media, Ideology and Community," *Cultural Values* 3 (1999): 424.

20. Cotterrell, "Transparency," 423.

21. Bojinka Bishop, "When the Truth Isn't Enough: Authenticity in Public Relations," *Public Relations Strategist*, 9, 4 (Fall 2003), 22.

22. Bryan H. Reber and Karla K. Gower, "Avow or Avoid? The Public Communication Strategies of Enron and WorldCom." *Journal of Promotion Management: Special Edition on Crisis Communications* 12, 3 (2006).

23. Steven D. Jamar, "The Human Right of Access to Legal Information: Using Technology to Advance Transparency and the Rule of Law," *Global Jurist Topics*, 27 September 2001, 1.1, 2; and William Mock, "On the Centrality of Information Law: A Rational Choice Discussion of Information Law and Transparency," *John Marshall Journal of Computer & Information Law* 17 (1999): 1069, 1082.

24. Eric Armstrong, "Transparency Keeps Tech-Product Flaws from Being Fatal," *PR Week*, June 20, 2005, 6.

25. Jack M. Balkin, "How Mass Media Simulate Political Transparency," *Cultural Values* 3 (1999): 393–413; and Michele Sutton, "Between a Rock and a Judicial Hard Place: Corporate Social Responsibility Reporting and Potential Legal Liability Under Kasky v. Nike," *University of Missouri at Kansas City Law Review* 72 (2004): 1159–85.

26. Cotterrell, "Transparency," 419.

27. *Communication World,* "More than a Social Virtue," 11.

28. Robert L. Dilenschneider, "The Transparency Paradox," *Vital Speeches of the Day* 70, 9 (2004): 280.

29. Cotterrell, "Transparency," 419.

30. Reber and Gower, "Avow or Avoid?"

31. *Economist,* "Bankrupt," November 29, 2001, para. 8, http://web.lexis-nexis .com/.

32. Lars Thùger Christensen and George Cheney, "Self-Absorption and Self-Seduction in the Corporate Identity Game," in *The Expressive Organization,* ed. Majken Schultz, Mary Jo Hatch, and Mogens Larsen (Oxford: Oxford University Press, 2000), 246–70.

33. Sutton, "Between a Rock," 1159–85.

34. Douglas Quenqua, "The Trust Timeline," *PR Week,* June 13, 2005, 11.

35. Lars Thùger Christensen, "Corporate Communication: The Challenge of Transparency," *Corporate Communications: An International Journal* 7 (2003): 162–68.

36. Balkin, "How Mass Media Simulate," 394.

37. Dilenschneider, "Transparency Paradox"; and PR Coalition, "Restoring Trust in Business," 8.

38. Dilenschneider, "Transparency Paradox."

39. Dilenschneider, "Transparency Paradox."

40. Robert Galford and Anne Seibold Drapeau, "The Enemies of Trust," *Harvard Business Review,* 81, 2 (February 1, 2003): 88–95, 126.

41. Institute for Crisis Management, "Crisis Definitions," http://www.crisis experts.com/crisisdefinitions.htm (accessed September 2, 2005).

42. Robert L. Heath and Dan P. Millar, "A Rhetorical Approach to Crisis Communication: Management, Communication Processes, and Strategic Responses," in *Responding to Crisis: A Rhetorical Approach to Crisis Communications,* ed. Dan P. Millar and Robert L. Heath (Mahwah, NJ: Lawrence Erlbaum, 2004), 6.

43. Heath and Millar, "Rhetorical Approach," 15.

44. Øyvind Ihlen, "Defending the Mercedes A-Class: Combining and Changing Crisis-Response Strategies," *Journal of Public Relations Research* 14 (2002): 185–206.

45. W. Timothy Coombs, "An Analytic Framework for Crisis Situations: Better Responses from Better Understanding of the Situation," *Journal of Public Relations Research* 10, 3 (1998): 186; and W. Timothy Coombs, "Deep and Surface Threats: Conceptual and Practical Implications for 'Crisis' vs. 'Problem,'" *Public Relations Review* 28, 4 (2002): 339–45.

46. Susan L. Brinson and William L. Benoit, "The Tarnished Star: Restoring Texaco's Damaged Public Image, *Management Communication Quarterly* 12 (1999): 483–510.

47. W. Timothy Coombs and Lainen Schmidt, "An Empirical Analysis of Image Restoration: Texaco's Racism Crisis," *Journal of Public Relations Research* 12, 2 (2000): 163–78.

48. ICM 2004 Crisis Report, "News Coverage of Business Crises," http://www .crisisexperts.com/04report.htm.

49. Jon Bernstein, "Why Should Lawyers Care about PR?" *Crisis Manager*, October 1, 2002, http://www.bernsteincrisismanagement.com/nl/crisismgr021001 .html.

50. Timothy L. Sellnow and Jeffrey D. Brand, "Establishing the Structure of Reality for an Industry: Model and Anti-Model Arguments as Advocacy in Nike's Crisis Communication," *Journal of Applied Communication Research* 29, 3 (2001): 278–95.

51. Steven Fink, "Where Wendy's Went Wrong: Critical Lessons in Crisis Management," *Crisis Manager*, June 15, 2005, http://www.bernsteincrisismanagement .com/nl/crisismgr050615.html.

52. James F. Haggerty, *In the Court of Public Opinion: Winning Your Case with Public Relations* (Hoboken, NJ: John Wiley & Sons, 2003); and Deborah A. Lilienthal, "Legal Meaning in an Age of Images: Litigation Public Relations; The Provisional Remedy of the Communication World," *New York Law School Law Review* 43 (1999–2000): 895.

53. Haggerty, *In the Court*, 2.

54. Haggerty, *In the Court*, 2; Mark Butler, "PR Takes Cases to the Court of Public Opinion," *Corporate Legal Times*, 1996, 40; and Kathy Fitzpatrick, "Practice Management: The Court of Public Opinion," *Texas Lawyer*, September 30, 1996, 30.

55. Fitzpatrick, "Practice Management."

56. Butler, "PR Takes Cases"; and Mawiyah Hooker and Elizabeth Lange, "Limiting Extrajudicial Speech in High-Profile Cases: The Duty of the Prosecutor and Defense Attorney in their Pre-trial Communications with the Media," *Georgetown Journal of Legal Ethics* 16 (2003): 655.

57. Dirk C. Gibson and Mariposa E. Padilla, "Litigation Public Relations Problems and Limits," *Public Relations Review* 25, 2 (1999): 215–33; and Carole E. Gorney, "The New Rules of Litigation Public Relations," *Public Relations Strategist* 1 (Spring 1995): 23.

58. Haggerty, *In the Court*; Clark S. Judge, "Expanded Legal Privilege Needed for Litigation Public Relations," *Tobacco Industry Litigation Reporter*, November 14, 2003, 14; and Fitzpatrick, "Practice Management."

59. Curt Bechler, "Reframing the Organizational Exigency: Taking a New Approach in Crisis Research," in *Responding to Crisis: A Rhetorical Approach to Crisis Communication*, ed. Dan P. Millar and Robert L. Heath (Mahwah, NJ: Lawrence Erlbaum, 2004), 67.

60. Mark McElreath, *Managing Systematic and Ethical Public Relations* (Madison, WI: Brown & Benchmark, 1993).

61. PR Coalition, "Restoring Trust in Business," 9.

62. *Communication World*, "More than a Social Virtue," 10.

63. PR Coalition, "Restoring Trust in Business," 8.

64. Bryan H. Reber, Fritz Cropp, and Glen T. Cameron, "Mythic Battles: Examining the Lawyer-Public Relations Counselor Dynamic," *Journal of Public Relations Research* 13, 3 (2001): 208.

65. Kleinfeld, "Restoring Public Trust," 203.

66. Gerald A. Baron, *Now Is Too Late* (Upper Saddle River, NJ: Financial Times Prentice Hall, 2003), 228–29.

67. Kathy Fitzpatrick and Candace Gauthier, "Toward a Professional Responsibility Theory of Public Relations Ethics," *Journal of Mass Media Ethics* 16, 2 & 3 (2001): 193–212.

68. Albert S. Atkinson, "Ethics in Financial Reporting and the Corporate Communication Professional," *Corporate Communications: An International Journal* 7, 4 (2002): 218.

69. Claire Moore Dickerson, "Ozymandias as Community Project: Managerial/ Corporate Social Responsibility and the Failure of Transparency," *Connecticut Law Review* 35 (2003): 1035–72.

Chapter 7

Web resources were all accessed in December 2004 or January 2005.

1. Christina Cooper, "Rumors of Draft Are Hard to Kill Despite Denials," *Wall Street Journal,* September 27, 2004, sec. B, 1, 3; and Snopes.com, "Claim: The U.S. Military Will Be Reinstating the Draft by Spring 2005," October 6, 2004, http:// www.snopes.com/politics/military/draft.asp. See also MoveOn.org Student Action Web site, http://www.moveonstudentaction.org.

2. Kirk Hallahan, "Online Public Relations," in *The Internet Encyclopedia,* eds. Hussein Bidgoli (Hoboken, NJ: Wiley, 2004), 2: 769–83; Kirk Hallahan, "Online Public Relations," in *Encyclopedia of Public Relations,* ed. Robert L. Heath (Thousand Oaks, CA: Sage, 2005), 2: 587–92; Kirk Hallahan, "Building Organizational-Public Relationships in Cyberspace," in *Public Relations Theory,* eds. Tricia Hansen-Horn and Bonita Dostal Neff (Boston: Allyn & Bacon, forthcoming); and Kirk Hallahan, "Strategic Public Relations Media Planning," in *Handbook of Public Relations,* ed. Robert L. Heath (Thousand Oaks, CA: Sage, 2001), 461–70.

3. Online communications have been a part of the media mix used by public relations practitioners for a little more than a decade. When the commercialization of the Internet began in 1994, practitioners were relatively slow and cautious in adopting the new technology. Today, online communications are being used across specialties to promote new ideas, products, and services; to build relationships; to manage issues; and to respond to crises.

4. Clare Hoertz Badaracco, "The Transparent Corporation and Organized Community," *Public Relations Review* 23, 3 (1998): 265–72; Robert L. Heath, "New Communications Technologies: An Issues Management Point of View," *Public Relations Review* 23, 3 (1998): 273–88; and W. Timothy Coombs, "The Internet as Potential Equalizer: New Leverage for Confronting Social Responsibility," *Public Relations Review* 23, 3 (1998): 289–305.

5. Jerden van den Hoven provides an insightful model that expands on this point. Internet-*related* issues are ethical problems that can occur online or offline, such as false claims or fraud. Internet-*dependent* issues are problems where network technology is required for moral problems to arise, such as illegal hacking or the introduction of viruses or worms. Internet-*determined* problems are concerns that are bound to occur when a technology is introduced, such as poor quality content

and inequality of access. Internet-*specific* issues can exist only on the Internet and not occur elsewhere, such as the misuse of cookies, robots, and avatars. Jerden van den Hoven, "The Internet and Varieties of Moral Wrongdoing," in *Internet Ethics,* ed. Langford Duncan (New York: St. Martin's Press, 2000), 127–57.

6. Public Relations Society of America, "Member Code of Ethics 2000," http://www.prsa.org/_About/ethics; International Association of Business Communicators, "Code of Ethics for Professional Communicators," http://www.iabc.com/members/joining/code.htm; International Public Relations Association, "Code of Athens and Code of Venice," http://www.ipra.org/; and National Investor Relations Institute, "Code of Ethics Revised Spring 2002," http://www.niri.org/about/codeof_ethics.cfm.

7. Personal communications to author from Todd T. Hattori (IABC), December 15, 2004; Donald K. Wright (IPRA), January 3, 2005; Angela Mumeka (NIRI), January 3, 2005; and Judy Voss (PRSA), January 4, 2005.

8. Arthur W. Page Society, "Page Society Takes First Step to Establish Internet Codes of Ethics," news release, April 13, 2001; "Applying the Page Principles to the Internet," news release, April 4, 2004; and "PR Coalition Endorses Internet Ethics Code," news release, December 2001, http://www.awpagesociety.com/newsroom/more_news/.

9. Arthur W. Page Society, "Establishing Principles for Public Relations on the Internet," December 2001, http://www.awpagesociety.com/newsroom/more_news/InternetPR.asp.

10. PRSA Technology Section, http://www.prsa.org/_Networking/Technology; and ISOC, http://www.onlinecommunicators.org/.

11. Pontifical Council for Social Communications, "Ethics In Internet," February 22, 2002, www.vatican.va/roman_curia/pontifical_councils/pccs/documents/rc_pc_pccs_doc_20020228_ethics-internet_en.html; and John Norton, "Vatican Encourages Church to Embrace Internet," *Catholic Herald,* February 2002, http://www.catholicherald.com/cns/internet.htm.

12. Association of Online Appraisers, "Code of Ethics," http://www.aoaonline.org/aoacode.htm; American Medical Association, "AMA Code of Medical Ethics," http://www.ama-assn.org (see sections E-5.026, December 2002, on the use of electronic mail, and E-5.027, June 2003, on the use of health-related Web sites); and American Psychological Association, "APA Ethics Code," June 1, 2003, http://www.apa.org/ethics/.

13. American Marketing Association, "AMA Code of Ethics," 2003, http://www.marketingpower.com; Interactive Advertising Bureau, "Standards and Guidelines," http://www.iab.com; and International Chamber of Commerce, "ICC Guidelines on Marketing and Advertising Using Electronic Media," October 2004, http://iccwbo.org.

14. Direct Marketing Association, *Do the Right Thing* (New York: DMA, 2004); and Direct Marketing Association, *Guidelines for Ethical Business Practice* (New York: DMA, February 2004). Also see the DMA's Web site: http://www.the-dma.com/.

15. Electronic Frontiers Foundation Web site, http://www.eff.org; and Electronic Privacy Information Center Web site, http://www.epic.org/.

16. WiredSafety.org includes WiredKids.org, WiredPatrol.org, and Cyberlawen forcement.org, http://www.wiresafety.org/.

17. Email Service Provider Coalition, "Fighting Spam While Protecting E-Mail as a Legitimate Communication Tool, http://www.espcoalition.org/index.php. For details on International Council on Internet Communications, see Institute for Spam and Public Policy, "International Spam Council Announced by Internet Policy Institute," news release by private consulting firm, August 24, 2004, http://www .isipp.com/icic-news.php.

18. ePhilanthropy Foundation, "Code of Ethical Online Philanthropic Practices," 2002, http://www.ephilanthropy.org/; Network for Online Commerce, "Code of Ethics," http://www.noconline.org/.

19. John Mack, "History of the [Internet Health] Coalition," 2000; "eHealth Code of Ethics," 2000; and Bette-Jane Criger, "Foundations of the 'eHealth Code of Ethics,'" 2002, all available at http://www.ihealthcoalition.org/ethics/. Health Internet Ethics, "Welcome to Hi-Ethics," 2001, http://www.hiethics.com/.

20. Truste, "Truste's Mission," http://www.truste.com/; and International Council of Online Professionals, "Guidelines for Using the iCop Seal," http://www .i-cop.org/guidelines.htm.

21. URAC, "About URAC," http://www.urac.org/; and Health on the Net Foundation Web site, http://www.hon.ch/Global. For a discussion of the use of information technology in health care, see James G. Anderson and Kenneth W. Goodman, eds., *Ethics and Information Technology: A Case-Based Approach to a Health Care System in Transition* (New York: Springer, 2002). Also see Arhmad Risk and Joan Dzenowagis, "Review of Internet Health Information Quality Initiatives," *Journal of Medical Internet Research* 3, 4 (2001), Article e28, http:// www.jmir.org/2001/4/e28.

22. International Association of Privacy Professionals Web site, http://www .privacyassociation.org/html/certification.html; Organization of Search Engine Optimization Professionals Web site, http://www.seopros.org/; and Bruce Clay, "SEO Code of Ethics," http://www.bruceclay.com/.

23. Search the United States Code on the Web site of the Legal Information Institute, http://www.law.cornell.edu/uscode/. Thomas, the Library of Congress's online service, is an online depository of laws, regulations, and pending legislation, http://thomas.loc.gov/. Federal regulations and a wide range of materials are available on the Government Printing Office's electronic access site, http://www.gpoaccess .gov/. A growing number of books address Internet law in the United States. A useful primer is Doug Isenberg, *Gigalaw Guide to Internet Law* (New York: Random House, 2002). Doug Isenberg's Web site is available at http://www.gigalaw.com. See also Richard A. Spinello, *Regulating Cyberspace: The Policies and Technologies of Control* (Westport, CT: Quorum Books, 2002).

24. Federal Trade Commission, "Advertising and Marketing on the Internet: Rules of the Road," Facts for Business Series Publications Series,

http://www.ftc.gov/bcp/conline/pubs/buspubs/rulesroad.htm; and Federal Trade Commission, "Dot Com Disclosures," Facts for Business Publications Series, http://www.ftc.gov/bcp/ conline/pubs/buspubs/dotcom/index.html.

25. Food and Drug Administration, "Buying Medicines and Medical Products Online," http://www.fda.gov/buyonline; Linda Bren, *FDA Consumer Magazine,* September–October 2001, http://www.fda.gov/fdac/features/2001/501_war.html; and U.S. Food and Drug Administration, "FDA Public Service Messages: Online Sales of Prescription Drugs," http://www.fda.gov/oc/buyonline/buyonline_ads/fdabannerads.html.

26. Securities and Exchange Commission, "Regulation S-T—General Rules and Regulations for Electronic Filings," 17 USC 232, http://www.access.gpo.gov/nara/cfr/waisidx_02/17cfr232_02.html; Raymond Hennessey and Phyllis Plitch, "SEC's New Rules on 'Quiet Period' Create Debate," *Wall Street Journal,* December 27, 2004, sec. C, 3; and Raymond Hennessey and Phyllis Plitch, "SEC Proposes Increasing Role of Web in IPOs," *Wall Street Journal,* January 3, 2005, sec. C, 4.

27. Tom Forester and Perry Morrison, *Computer Ethics: Cautionary Tales and Ethical Dilemmas in Computing* (Cambridge, MA: MIT Press, 1990); Roy DeJoie, George Fowler, and David Paradice, *Ethical Issues in Information Systems* (Boston: Boyd & Fraser, 1991); Stacey L. Edgar, *Morality and Machines: Perspectives on Computer Ethics* (Boston: Jones & Bartlett, 1997); Kevin W. Bowyer, ed., *Ethics and Computing: Living Responsibly in a Computerized World,* 2nd ed. (New York: IEEE Press, 2001); D. Micah Hester and Paul Ford, eds., *Computers and Ethics in the Cyberage* (Upper Saddle River, NJ: Prentice Hall, 2001); and Stephen Northcutt, *IT Ethics Handbook: Right and Wrong for IT Professionals* (Rockland, MA: Syngress, 2004).

28. John Weickert and Douglas Adeney, *Computer and Information Ethics* (Westport, CT: Greenwood Press, 1997), 17–26. For links to major codes, go to the Web site of the Online Ethics Center for Engineering and Science at Case Western Reserve University, "Codes of Ethics and Conduct," http://www.onlineethics .org/codes/index.html. ACM/IEEE-CS Joint Task Force on Software Engineering Ethics and Professional Practices, "Software Engineering Code of Ethics and Professional Practice," Version 5.2, 1999, http://www.acm.org/serving/se/code.htm; Donald Gotterbarn, "Virtual Information and the Software Engineering Code of Ethics," in *Internet Ethics,* ed. Duncan Langford (New York: St. Martin's Press, 2000), 200–219; and R. Anderson, "The ACM Code of Ethics: History, Process and Implications," in *Social Issues in Computing: Putting Computing in Its Place,* ed. Chuck Huff and Thomas Finholt (New York: McGraw-Hill, 1994), 48–71.

29. Originally published as Ramon C. Barquin, "In Pursuit of a 'Ten Commandments' for Computer Ethics," Computer Ethics Institute, May 7, 1992, request for paper available at http://www.brook.edu/its/cei/papers/Barquin_Pursuit_1992.htm.

30. Computer Ethics Institute, "Ten Commandments of Computer Ethics," 1992, http://www.brook.edu/its/cei/overview/Ten_Commanments_of_Computer_Ethics.htm.

31. Richard T. De George, *The Ethics of Information Technology and Business* (Malden, MA: Blackwell, 2003), http://www.loc.gov/catdir/toc/fy036/2002005756.html.

32. Jacques Ellul, *The Technological Society,* trans. John Wilkinson (New York: Vintage Books, 1964); Jacques Ellul, *Propaganda: The Formation of Men's Attitudes,* trans. Konrad Kellen and Jean Lerner (New York: Knopf, 1965); and Neil Postman, *Technopoly: The Surrender of Culture to Technology* (New York: Knopf, 1992).

33. Richard O. Mason, Florence M. Mason, and Mary Culnan, *Ethics of Information Management* (Thousand Oaks, CA: Sage, 1995), 20–22.

34. John Weckert, "What is New or Unique About Internet Activities?" in *Internet Ethics,* ed. Duncan Langford (New York: St. Martin's Press, 2000), 47–64.

35. van den Hoven, "Moral Wrongdoing."

36. Lawrence Lessig, *Code and Other Laws of Cyberspace* (New York: Basic Books, 2000); and Richard A. Spinello, *Case Studies in Information Technology Ethics* (Upper Saddle River, NJ: Prentice Hall, 2003), 1–25.

37. Richard A. Spinello, *Cyberethics: Morality and Law in Cyberspace* (Boston: Jones & Bartlett, 2000), 3–6, 17. Spinello uses "Consequentialism/Utilitarianism" for the category labeled here as "Consequences-Based Morality."

38. David L. Martinson, "Enlightened Self-Interest Fails as an Ethical Baseline in Public Relations," *Journal of Media Ethics* 9, 2 (1994): 100–108.

39. John Stuart Mill, "Utilitarianism," in *Moral Philosophy: An Introduction,* ed., Jack Glickman (New York, St. Martin's Press, 1976), 540; and Jeremy Bentham, *An Introduction to the Principles of Morals and Legislation,* ed. J. H. Burns and H. L. A. Hart (New York: Oxford University Press, 1996).

40. Immanuel Kant, *Foundation of the Metaphysics of Morals* (Indianapolis, IN: Bobbs-Merrill, 1959).

41. William D. Ross, *The Right and the Good* (New York: Oxford University Press, 2002; originally published by Clarendon Press, 1930); Tom L. Beauchamp and Thomas F. Childress, *Principles of Biomedical Ethics,* 5th ed. (New York: Oxford University Press, 2001); and Michael Josephson, "Teaching Ethical Decision Making and Principled Reasoning," in *Business Ethics,* Annual Editions 1993–1994 (Guilford, CT: Duskin, 1993), 15.

42. Joseph Fletcher, *Situation Ethics: The New Morality* (Philadelphia: Westminster, 1966); and Cornelius Pratt, "Critique of the Classical Theory of Situational Ethics in U.S. Public Relations," *Public Relations Review* 19, 3 (1993): 219–34.

43. Roy Leeper, "In Search of a Metatheory for Public Relations: An Argument for Communitarianism," in *Handbook of Public Relations,* ed. Robert L. Heath (Thousand Oaks, CA: Sage, 2001), 93–104.

44. John Rawls, *A Theory of Justice* (New Haven, CT: Yale University Press, 1971).

45. Patrick F. Sullivan, *Cyberspace and Moral Community* (Washington, DC: Computer Ethics Institute, April 27, 1993), http://www.brook.edu/its/cei/papers/Sullivan_Cyberspace_1993.htm (abstract). See also Howard Rheingold, *The*

Virtual Community: Homesteading on the Electronic Frontier (New York: Addison-Wesley, 1993).

46. Mason, Mason, and Culnan, *Ethics of Information Management.*

47. Mason, Mason, and Culnan, *Ethics of Information Management,* 28–30.

48. Mark McElreath, *Managing Systematic and Ethical Public Relations* (Dubuque, IA: Brown & Benchmark, 1993), 320; Karla A. Gower, *Legal and Ethical Restraints on Public Relations* (Prospect Heights, IL: Waveland Press, 2003); Philip Seib and Kathy Fitzpatrick, *Public Relations Ethics* (Fort Worth, TX: Harcourt Brace College, 1995), 29–34; and Patricia Parsons, *Ethics in Public Relations: A Guide to Best Practice* (Sterling, VA: Kogan Page, 2004).

49. Aristotle, *The Basic Works,* ed. Richard McKeon (New York: Random House, 1941). See the Nichomachean Ethics. Stanley B. Cunningham, "Getting It Right: Aristotle's 'Golden Mean' as Theory Deterioration," *Journal of Mass Media Ethics* 14, 1 (1999): 5–15.

50. An informative discussion of commitment is found in Francis Dummer Fisher, "But Will the New Health Media Be Forthcoming?" in *Health and the New Media: Technologies Transforming Personal and Public Health,* ed. Linda M. Harris (Mahwah, NJ: Lawrence Erlbaum, 1995), 209–27.

51. Katie Hafner, "The Camera Never Lies, but the Software Can," *New York Times,* March 11, 2004.

52. Zealous Web site designers wanting to funnel all activity through online communications often forget that other communications might be appropriate or preferable, and ignore the fact the mere availability of alternatives can enhance an organization's credibility among doubtful users.

53. Users obviously have an ethical obligation to use online information responsibly and to become informed and astute users of Internet tools. A key question involves what is reasonable for the typical users to understand about the veracity of online information. A large number of Web sites and other resources are available to educate users on how to evaluate online information. Most users are unaware that they can conduct a "/whois" search through one of the various site registration services to locate the name and address of domain name registrants.

54. Not surprisingly, deceptive participation or lurking outrages some chat room participants. Violators of user covenants are sometimes barred or attacked (*flamed*) by others in the group.

55. Kirk Hallahan, "Protecting an Organization's Digital Public Relations Assets," *Public Relations Review* 30 (2004): 255–68.

56. Spyware can be maliciously used in the same way as hacking or the purposeful distribution of software viruses or e-mail worms. See Hallahan, "Protecting Assets."

57. Association for Interactive Marketing, "Technical White Paper for Search Engine Marketing," July 14, 2004, http://www.kingproc.com/examples/imarketing .html; and C. J. Newton, "Guide to Search Engine Optimization," 2002, American Marketing Association, http://www.marketingpower.com/content14922.php.

58. 24k Web Internet Marketing Services, "Search Engine Ethics," 2004, http://24kweb.com/search_engine_ethics.htm; and Clay, "SEO Code of Ethics."

59. Hall Dicker Kent Goldstein and Wood LLC, "Product Placement Spreads Online," July 29, 2004, http://www.adlaw.com or http://www.marketingpower.com/content20797.php.

60. American Society of Magazine Editors, "Guidelines for Editors and Publishers: Best Practices for Digital Media," 11th ed., January 2002, http://www.magazine.org/content/Files/digitalmediaguidelines.pdf. See also Robert L. Berkman and Chritopher A. Shumway, *Digital Dilemmas: Ethical Issues for Online Media Professionals* (Ames: Iowa State Press, 2003).

61. A useful discussion is found in Gerald R. Baron, *Now is Too Late: Survival in the Era of Instant News* (Upper Saddle River, NJ: Prentice Hall Financial Times, 2003).

62. James E. Grunig, "Two-Way Symmetrical Public Relations. Past, Present and Future," in *Handbook of Public Relations,* ed. Robert L. Heath (Thousand Oaks, CA: Sage, 2001), 11–30.

63. Ron Pearson, "Business Ethics as Communication Ethics: Public Relations Practice and the Idea of Dialogue," in *Rhetorical and Critical Approaches to Public Relations,* ed. Elizabeth L. Toth and Robert L. Heath (Hillsboro, NJ: Lawrence Erlbaum, 1992), 111–131; and Michael L. Kent, Maureen Taylor, and William J. White, "The Relationship between Website Design and Organizational Responsiveness to Stakeholders," *Public Relations Review* 29 (2003): 63–78.

64. For useful discussions of the importance of interactivity in public communications, see Debra A. Lieberman, "Using Interactive Media in Communication Campaigns for Children and Adolescents," in *Public Communication Campaigns,* 3rd ed., ed. Ronald E. Rice and Charles K. Atkins (Thousand Oaks, CA: Sage, 2001), 373–89; and Thomas R. Eng and David H. Gustafson, eds., *Wired for Health and Well-Being* (Washington, DC: U.S. Department of Health and Human Services, U.S. Government Printing Office, 1999).

65. Kirk Hallahan, "Community as the Framework for Public Relations Theory and Research," *Communication Yearbook 28* (2004): 233–79.

66. Stanton McCandish, "EFF's Top 12 Ways to Protect Your Online Privacy," April 10, 2002, http://www.eff.org/Privacy/eff_privacy_top_12.html.

67. A breach of privacy or security that becomes widely known can become an explosive situation that generates negative publicity, a loss of reputation, and direct costs and legal liabilities for an organization.

68. Kirk Hallahan, "Improving Public Relations Websites Through Usability Research," *Public Relations Review* 27 (2001): 223–39.

69. Specifications for users with disabilities have been created by the World Wide Web Consortium, an international group that establishes Web technical standards, as part of its Web Accessibility Initiative, www.W3.org/WAI. The General Services Administration operates a special Web site to facilitate compliance with Section 508

of the Workforce Investment Act of 1998 (also known as the U.S. Rehabilitation Act), www.usability.gov/. A leading HTML validator is Watchfire's Bobby software, www.watchfire.com/.

70. For society in general, the Internet poses a wide range of ethical issues that reach far beyond the PR practice. Examples include pornography, online gambling, the sale of illegal products or services, cyberstalking of adults and children, trafficking in student term papers, and downloading of pirated music files—just to a name a few.

71. Hallahan, "Protecting Assets," 261–62.

72. van den Hoven, "Moral Wrongdoing"; Weckert, "What Is New?"; and Lessig, *Code and Other Laws.*

73. James E. Grunig and Yi-Hui Huang, "From Organizational Effectiveness to Relationship Indicators: Antecedents of Relationships, Public Relations Strategies and Relationship Outcomes," in *Public Relations as Relationship Management: A Relational Approach to the Study and Practice of Public Relations,* ed. John A. Ledingham and Stephen D. Bruning (Mahwah, NJ: Lawrence Erlbaum, 2000), 23–53; and Linda Hon and James E. Grunig, *Guidelines for Measuring Relationships in Public Relations* (Gainesville, FL: Institute for Public Relations, 1999).

74. Hallahan, "Building in Cyberspace."

Chapter 8

1. Ulrich Beck, *Risk Society toward a New Modernity* (London: Sage, 1992).

2. Mary Douglas, *Risk and Blame: Essays in Cultural Theory* (London: Routledge, 1992).

3. Richard Jones, "Challenges to the Notion of Publics in Public Relations: Implications of the Risk Society for the Discipline," *Public Relations Review* 28, 1 (2002): 49.

4. Eleanor Singer and Phyllis M. Endreny, "Reporting Hazards: Their Benefits and Costs," *Journal of Communication* 37, 3 (1987): 10–25.

5. National Research Council, *Improving Risk Communication* (Washington, DC: National Academy Press, 1989).

6. Alonzo Plough and Sheldon Krimsky, "The Emergence of Risk Communication Studies: Social and Political Context," *Science, Technology & Human Values* 12, 3–4 (1987): 4–10.

7. Vincent T. Covello and Jerry Mumpower, "Risk Analysis and Risk Management: An Historical Perspective," *Risk Analysis,* 5 (1985): 103–19.

8. Roger E. Kasperson and Pieter Jan M. Stallen, "Risk Communication: The Evolution of Attempts," in *Communicating Risks to the Public,* ed. Roger E. Kasperson and Pieter Jan M. Stallen (Boston: Kluwer, 1991), 1–14.

9. William Leiss, "Three Phases in the Evolution of Risk Communication Practice," *American Academy of Political and Social Sciences* 545 (1996): 85–94.

10. National Research Council, *Improving Risk Communication,* 21.

11. Vincent T. Covello, "Risk Communication: An Emerging Area of Health Communication Research," in *Communication Yearbook 15*, ed. Stanley A. Deetz (Newbury Park, CA: Sage, 1992): 359.

12. Leiss, "Three Phases."

13. Leiss, "Three Phases," 87.

14. Leiss, "Three Phases"; and Michael J. Palenchar and Robert L. Heath, "Another Part of the Risk Communication Model: Analysis of Communication Processes and Message Content," *Journal of Public Relations Research* 13, 2 (2002): 127–158.

15. Palenchar and Heath, "Another Part."

16. Palenchar and Heath, "Another Part," 89.

17. Palenchar and Heath, "Another Part."

18. Sheldon Krimsky and Alonzo Plough, *Plant Closure: The ASARCO/Tacoma Copper Smelter; Environmental Hazards; Communicating Risks as a Social Process* (Dover, MA: Auburn House, 1988).

19. Harry Otway, "Public Wisdom, Expert Fallibility: Toward a Contextual Theory of Risk," in *Social Theories of Risk,* ed. Sheldon Krimsky and Dominic Golding (Westport, CT: Praeger, 1992), 227.

20. Hippocrates G. Apostle, *Aristotle's Nichomachean Ethics* (Grinnell, IA: Peripatetic Press, 1984).

21. Henry R. West, *An Introduction to Mill's Utilitarian Ethics* (Cambridge: Cambridge University Press, 2004).

22. Thomas H. Bivins, "Ethical Implications of the Relationship of Purpose to Role and Function in Public Relations," *Journal of Business Ethics* 8 (1980): 65–73; and Ron Pearson, "Beyond Ethical Relativism in Public Relations: Coorientation, Rules, and the Idea of Communication Symmetry," in *Public Relations Research Annual,* ed. James E. Grunig and Larissa A. Grunig (Hillsdale, NJ: Lawrence Erlbaum, 1989) 1: 67–86.

23. Kathy Fitzpatrick and Candace Gauthier, "Toward a Professional Responsibility Theory of Public Relations Ethics," *Journal of Mass Media Ethics* 16, 2–3 (2001): 193–212.

24. James E. Grunig and Jon White, "The Effect of Worldviews on Public Relations Theory and Practice," in *Excellence in Public Relations and Communication,* ed. James E. Grunig (Hillsdale, NJ: Lawrence Erlbaum, 1992), 57.

25. James E. Grunig and Todd Hunt, *Managing Public Relations* (New York: Holt, Rinehart & Winston, 1984), 59.

26. Robert L. Heath and Michael Ryan, "Public Relations' Role in Defining Corporate Social Responsibility," *Journal of Mass Media Ethics* 4, 1 (1989): 21–38.

27. Robert L. Heath, "A Rhetorical Perspective on the Values of Public Relations: Crossroads and Pathways toward Concurrence," *Journal of Public Relations Research* 12, 1 (2000): 69.

28. Nicholas Freudenberg, *Not in Our Backyards! Community Action for Health and the Environment* (New York: Monthly Review Press, 1984).

29. Robert L. Heath, "A Rhetorical Enactment Rationale for Public Relations: The Good Organization Communicating Well," in *Handbook of Public Relations,* ed. Robert L. Heath (Thousand Oaks, CA: Sage, 2001), 46.

30. J. Graham Spickett-Jones, Philip. J. Kitchen, and Jon D. Reast, "Social Facts and Ethical Hardware: Ethics in the Value Proposition," *Journal of Communication Management* 8, 1 (2003): 69.

31. Pearson, "Beyond Ethical Relativism."

32. Apostle, *Aristotle's Nichomachean Ethics.*

33. Baruch Fischhoff, "Risk Issues in the News: Why Experts and Laymen Disagree," *News Backgrounders* (Washington, DC: Foundation for American Communities, 1990), 84.

34. Baruch Fischhoff, "Managing Risk Perceptions," *Issues in Science and Technology* 2, 1 (1985): 83–96.

35. Robert L. Heath and Michael J. Palenchar, "Community Relations and Risk Communication: A Longitudinal Study of the Impact of Emergency Response Messages," *Journal of Public Relations Research* 12, 2 (2000): 131–62.

36. Napoleon K. Juanillo, Jr., and Clifford W. Scherer, "Attaining a State of Informed Judgments: Toward a Dialectical Discourse on Risk," in *Communication Yearbook, 18,* ed. Brant R. Burleson (Thousand Oaks, CA: Sage, 1995), 278–299.

37. Juanillo and Scherer, "Informed Judgments," 292.

38. Palenchar and Heath, "Another Part."

39. Caron Chess, "Organizational Theory and the Stages of Risk Communication," *Risk Analysis* 21, 1 (2001): 178–88.

40. American Chemistry Council, *ACC Media Kit on Security,* 2004, http://www.americanchemistry.com (accessed January 2004).

41. Robert L. Heath, Julie Bradshaw, and Jaesub Lee, "Community Relationship Building: Local Leadership in the Risk Communication Infrastructure," *Journal of Public Relations Research* 14, 4 (2002): 317.

42. Susan Hadden, *A Citizen's Right to Know: Risk Communication and Policy* (Boulder, CO: Westview, 1989).

43. Robert L. Heath and Douglas D. Abel, "Proactive Responses to Citizen Risk Concerns: Increasing Citizen's Knowledge of Emergency Response Practices," *Journal of Public Relations Research* 8, 3 (1996): 151–71; Heath and Palenchar, "Community Relations and Risk Communication"; and Palenchar and Heath, "Another Part."

44. Kim Witte, "Generating Effective Risk Messages: How Scary Should Your Risk Communication Be?" in *Communication Yearbook 18,* ed. Brant R. Burleson (Thousand Oaks, CA: Sage, 1995), 229–54.

45. Heath and Abel, "Proactive Responses."

46. Vincent T. Covello and Brandon B. Johnson, "The Social and Cultural Construction of Risk: Issues, Methods and Case Studies," in *The Social Construction of Risk: Essays on Risk Selection and Perception,* ed. Brandon B. Johnson and Vincent T. Covello (Dordecht, Holland: D. Reidel, 1987), vii–xiii; Heath and Palenchar, "Community Relations and Risk Communication"; and John H. Sims and Duane D. Baumann, "Educational Programs and Human Response to Natural Hazards," *Environment and Behavior* 15, 2 (1983): 438–57.

47. Suzanne C. Thompson, "Will It Hurt Less If I Can Control It? A Complex Answer to a Simple Question," *Psychological Bulletin* 90, 1 (1981): 89–101.

48. Covello, "Risk Communication"; and Richard J. Bord and Robert E. O'Connor, "Risk Communication, Knowledge and Attitudes: Explaining Reactions to a Technology Perceived as Risky" *Risk Analysis* 10, 4 (1990): 499–506.

49. Harold I. Sharlin, "EDB: A Case Study in Communicating Risk," *Risk Analysis* 6, 1 (1986): 61–68; and Rob A. Weterings and Josee Van Eijndhoven, "Informing the Public about Uncertain Risks," *Risk Analysis* 9, 4 (1989): 473–82.

50. Roger E. Kasperson, "Six Propositions on Public Participation and Their Relevance for Risk," *Risk Analysis* 6, 3 (1986): 275–81.

51. Billie J. Hance, Caron Chess, and Peter M. Sandman, "Setting a Context for Explaining Risk," *Risk Analysis* 9, 1 (1989): 113–17; and Barry L. Johnson, "Health Risk Communication and the Agency for Toxic Substances and Disease Registry," *Risk Analysis* 7 (1987): 409–12.

52. Sims and Baumann, "Educational Programs."

53. Robert L. Heath, "Corporate Environment Risk Communication: Cases and Practice Along the Texas Gulf Coast," in *Communication Yearbook 15,* ed. Brant R. Burleson (Thousand Oaks, CA: Sage, 1995): 273.

54. L. P. Driskill and Jone R. Goldstein, "Uncertainty: Theory and Practice in Organizational Communication," *Journal of Business Communication* 23, 3 (1986), 41.

55. Terrance L. Albrecht, "Communication and Personal Control in Empowering Organizations," in *Communication Yearbook 15*, ed. James A. Anderson (Newbury Park, CA: Sage, 1988), 380–404.

56. Aristotle, *Rhetoric,* trans. H. C. Lawson-Tancred (London: Penguin, 1991).

57. Charles Berger and Richard J. Calabrase, "Some Explorations in Initial Interaction and Beyond: Toward a Developmental Theory of Interpersonal Communication," *Human Communication Research* 1, 4 (1975): 99–112.

58. Weterings and Van Eijndhoven, "Informing the Public."

59. Otway, "Public Wisdom, Expert Fallibility."

60. Covello, "Risk Communication"; Fischhoff, "Managing Risk Perceptions"; Kasperson, "Six Propositions"; and Richard Wilson and E. A. C. Crouch, "Risk Assessment and Comparisons: An Introduction," *Science* 236 (1987): 267–70.

61. Bord and O'Connor, "Risk Communication."

62. Heath and Abel, "Proactive Responses"; Kathy Nathan, Robert L. Heath, and William Douglas, "Tolerance for Potential Environmental Health Risks: The Influence of Knowledge, Benefits, Control, Involvement and Uncertainty," *Journal of Public Relations Research* 4 (1992): 235–58.

63. Vincent T. Covello, "Informing People about Risks from Chemicals, Radiation and Other Toxic Substances: A Review of Obstacles to Public Understanding and Effective Risk Communication," in *Prospects and Problems in Risk Communication,* ed. William Leiss, (Ontario, Canada: University of Waterloo Press, 1989), 1–25; Baruch Fischhoff et al., "How Safe Is Safe Enough? A Psychometric Study of Attitudes Toward Technological Risks and Benefits," *Policy Sciences* 9, 2 (1978): 127–52.

64. Covello, "Risk Communication"; and Krimsky and Plough, *Plant Closure.*

65. U.S. Department of Homeland Security, "Threats and Protection: Advisory Section," http://www.dhs.gov/dhspublic/display?theme=29 (accessed February 17, 2005).

66. Hadden, *Citizen's Right to Know.*

67. Heath and Abel, "Proactive Responses"; Heath and Palenchar, "Community Relations"; and Palenchar and Heath, "Another Part."

68. Ortwin Renn and Debra Levine, "Credibility and Trust in Risk Communication," in *Communicating Risks to the Public,* eds. Roger E. Kasperson and Pieter Jan M. Stallen (Boston: Kluwer, 1991), 175–218.

69. David Ropeik and George Gray, *Risk: A Practical Guide for Deciding What's Really Safe and What's Really Dangerous in the World Around You* (New York: Houghton Mifflin, 2002).

70. Brian N. R. Baird, "Tolerance for Environmental Health Risks: The Influence of Knowledge, Benefits, Voluntarism and Environmental Attitudes," *Risk Analysis* 55 (1986): 425–35.

71. Baruch Fischhoff, "Risk Perception and Communication Unplugged: Twenty Years of Process," *Risk Analysis* 15 (1995): 137–45; and Fischhoff et al., "How Safe?"

72. Gerald T. Gardner and Leroy C. Gould, "Public Perceptions of the Risks and Benefits of Technology," *Risk Analysis* 9, 2 (1989): 225–42.

73. Carolyn S. Konheim, "Risk Communication in the Real World," *Risk Analysis* 8, 3 (1988): 367–73.

74. Heath and Abel, "Proactive Responses"; Robert L. Heath, Shu-Heui Liao, and William Douglas, "Effects of Involvement on Reactions to Sources or Messages and to Message Clusters," in *Public Relations Research Annual,* eds. James E. Grunig and Larissa A. Grunig (Hillsdale, NJ: Lawrence Erlbaum, 1993), 3: 179–93.

75. James Flynn et al., "Trust as a Determinant of Opposition to a High-Level Radioactive Waste Repository," *Journal of Mass Media Ethics* 16, 2–3 (1992): 417–29.

76. Flynn et al., "Trust as a Determinant."

77. Heath et al., "Effects of Involvement."

78. Ortwin Renn, "Concepts of Risk: A Classification," in *Social Theories of Risk,* ed. Sheldon Krimsky and Dominic Golding (Westport, CT: Praeger, 1992), 53–79.

79. Fischhoff et al., "How Safe?"

80. Plough and Krimsky, "Emergence," 5.

81. William N. Elwood, "Public Relations Is a Rhetorical Experience: The Integral Principle in Case Study Analysis," in *Public Relations Inquiry as Rhetorical Criticism: Case Studies of Corporate Discourse and Social Influence,* ed. William N. Elwood (Westport, CT: Praeger, 1995), 3–24.

82. Kenneth Burke, *Language as Symbolic Action* (Berkeley: University of California Press, 1966).

83. Heath, "Rhetorical Enactment Rationale," 32.

84. Robert L. Heath, *Management of Corporate Communication: From Interpersonal Contacts to External Affairs* (Hillsdale, NJ: Lawrence Erlbaum, 1994).

85. Walter R. Fisher, "The Narrative Paradigm: An Elaboration," *Communication Monographs* 52 (1985): 347–67; and W. R. Fisher, *Human Communication as Narration: Toward a Philosophy of Reason, Value and Action* (Columbia: University of South Carolina Press, 1987).

86. U.S. Department of Energy, Richland Operations Office, "About Us: Hanford Site Overview," http://www.hanford.gov/rl?page=57&parent=45 (accessed August 29, 2005).

87. U.S. Department of Energy, Richland Operations Office, "Hanford's Long-Term Stewardship Program," http://www.hanford.gov/rl?page=57&parent=45 (accessed August 29, 2005).

88. Hanford Watch, "Hanford Watch Needs Your Help," http://www/hanford-watch.org/archive (accessed August 29, 2005).

89. Hanford Watch, "Hanford Watch."

90. Fisher, "Narrative Paradigm," 347.

91. Fisher, *Human Communication as Narration,* 18, xi.

92. Steve Rayner, "Cultural Theory and Risk Analysis," in *Social Theories of Risk,* ed. S. Krimsky and D. Golding (Westport, CT: Praeger, 1992), 83–115.

93. Jones, "Challenges to the Notion," 54.

Chapter 9

1. Stanley Kelley, Jr., *Professional Public Relations and Political Power* (Baltimore: Johns Hopkins, 1966), 3.

2. Philip Seib and Kathy Fitzpatrick, *Public Relations Ethics* (Fort Worth, TX: Harcourt Brace, 1995), 94.

3. Seib and Fitzpatrick, *Public Relations Ethics,* 1.

4. Ghaith Abdul-Ahad, "Seeking Salvation in City of Insurgents," *Washington Post,* November 11, 2004, A30.

5. Christopher Ross, "Pillars of Public Diplomacy," *Harvard International Review* xxv, 2 (Summer 2003), 22.

6. Stephen Johnson and Helle Dale, "How to Reinvigorate U.S. Public Diplomacy," *Heritage Foundation Backgrounder,* April 23, 2003, www.heritage.org/research/nationalsecurity/bg1645.cfm.

7. Stephen Hess and Marvin Kalb, eds., *The Media and the War on Terrorism* (Washington, DC: Brookings Institution, 2003), 225.

8. Paul Richter, "U.S. Struggles in War of Ideas, Panel Says," *Los Angeles Times,* July 25, 2004.

9. Charles Wolf, Jr., and Brian Rosen, "Public Diplomacy: How to Think About It and Improve It," RAND occasional paper, 2004.

10. Jay Black, "Semantics and Ethics of Propaganda," *Journal of Mass Media Ethics* 16, 2–3 (2001), 121.

11. Black, "Semantics and Ethics of Propaganda," 128.

12. Black, "Semantics and Ethics of Propaganda," 135.

13. Charlotte Beers, Hearing on American Diplomacy and Islam, United States Senate Committee on Foreign Relations, February 27, 2003.

14. Michael Dobbs, "Envoy to 'Arab Street' Stays Hopeful," *Washington Post*, June 10, 2003, A19.

15. Terence Smith, "Public Diplomacy," *NewsHour*, Public Broadcasting System, January 21, 2003.

16. Paul Cochrane, "Is Al-Hurra Doomed?" worldpress.org, June 11, 2004.

17. Ellen McCarthy, "Virginia-Based, U.S.-Financed Arabic Channel Finds Its Voice," *Washington Post*, October 15, 2004, A1.

18. Neil MacFarquhar, "Washington's Arabic TV Effort Gets Mixed Reviews," *New York Times*, February 20, 2004, A3.

19. Cochrane, "Is Al-Hurra Doomed?"

20. Javid Hassan, "Top Judge Blasts Al-Hurra TV's Ideological War," *Arab News*, March 9, 2004.

21. Barbara Slavin, "VOA Changes Prompt Staffer Protests," *USA Today*, July 12, 2004.

22. Arab Advisors Group, "Al-Jazeera Viewers," Arab Advisors Group news release, September 5, 2004.

23. Dana Zureikat Daoud, "Al-Hurra: An Insider's View," *Adham Center News*, Fall 2004, www.adhamonline.com/.

24. Shibley Telhami, "Finding the Right Media for the Message in the Middle East," testimony before the Senate Foreign Relations Committee, April 29, 2004.

25. Glenn Kessler, "The Role of Radio Sawa in Mideast Questioned," *Washington Post*, October 13, 2004, A12.

26. In'am el-Obeidi, "A Palestinian Perspective on Satellite Television Coverage of the Iraq War," *Transnational Broadcasting Studies Journal*, Spring–Summer 2003, http://www.tbsjournal.com/Archives/Spring03/obeidi.html.

27. Todd Hunt and James E. Grunig, *Public Relations Techniques* (Fort Worth, TX: Harcourt Brace, 1994), 77.

28. Joseph S. Nye, Jr., *Soft Power: The Means to Success in World Politics* (New York: PublicAffairs, 2004), x.

29. Nye, *Soft Power*, 89–92.

30. Nye, *Soft Power*, 123.

31. Joseph S. Nye, Jr., "The Decline of America's Soft Power," *Foreign Affairs*, May–June 2004, 17.

32. Mark Helmke, "The Mess of American Public Diplomacy" (remarks presented at the Public Diplomacy Council, School of Media and Public Affairs, George Washington University, June 9, 2003).

33. Hady Amr, *The Need To Communicate: How to Improve U.S. Public Diplomacy with the Islamic World* (Washington, DC: Saban Center for Middle East Policy at the Brookings Institution, 2004), 19.

34. Amr, *Need To Communicate*, 20.

35. Gary R. Bunt, *Islam in the Digital Age* (London: Pluto Press, 2003), 211.

36. http://www.internetworldstats.com/.

37. Wolf and Rosen, "Public Diplomacy."

38. Christopher Ross, "Public Diplomacy Comes of Age," *Washington Quarterly*, Spring 2002, 77.

39. Amr, *Need To Communicate*, 21.

40. Advisory Commission on Public Diplomacy, "New Strategic Direction Urged for Public Diplomacy," press release, U.S. Department of State, October 1, 2003, http://www.state.gov/.

41. Shibley Telhami, "The Need for Public Diplomacy," *Brookings Review*, Summer 2002, 47.

42. Frances Stonor Saunders, *The Cultural Cold War* (New York: New Press, 2000), 1, 85.

43. Anne E. Kornblut, "Problems of Image and Diplomacy Beset U.S.," *Boston Globe*, March 9, 2003, A25.

Chapter 10

1. Krishnamurthy Sriramesh and Jon White, "Societal Culture and Public Relations," in *Excellence in Public Relations and Communication Management*, ed. J. E. Grunig (Hillsdale, NJ: 1992), 597–614.

2. James E. Grunig, ed., *Excellence in Public Relations and Communication Management* (Hillsdale, NJ: Lawrence Erlbaum, 1992).

3. Donald K. Wright, "Communication Ethics," in *An Integrated Approach to Communication Theory and Research*, ed. Michael B. Salwen & Don W. Stacks (Mahwah, NJ: Lawrence Erlbaum, 1996), 519.

4. Kenneth F. Goodpaster and John B. Matthews, Jr., "Can a Corporation Have a Conscience?" in *Ethics in Practice: Managing the Moral Corporation*, ed. K. R. Andrews (Boston: Harvard Business School Press, 1989), 115–67.

5. Donald K. Wright, "Social Responsibility in Public Relations: A Multi-Step Theory," *Public Relations Review* 2, 1 (1976): 24–36.

6. Louis A. Day, *Ethics in Media Communications: Cases and Controversies* (Belmont, CA: Wadsworth, 1976).

7. Phillip V. Lewis and N. L. Reinsch, "Ethical and Unethical Behaviors in Business Communication," in *Business Communication: The Corporate Connection*, ed. Sam J. Bruno (proceedings of the American Business Communication Convention, 1983), 54–63.

8. See Wright, "Multi-Step Theory"; Donald K. Wright, "Professionalism and Social Responsibility in Public Relations," *Public Relations Review* 5, 1 (1979): 24–36; Donald K. Wright, "The Philosophy of Ethical Development in Public Relations," *IPRA Review* 9 (1982): 18–25; and Donald K. Wright, "Individual Ethics Determine Public Relations Practice," *Public Relations Journal* 41 (1985): 38–39.

9. James E. Grunig, "Organizations and Public Relations: Testing a Communication Theory," *Journalism Monographs* 46 (1976); and Glen M. Broom

and David M. Dozier, "Advancement for Public Relations Role Models," *Public Relations Review* 12, 1 (1986): 37–56.

10. Byoungkwon Lee, "Corporate Image Examined in a Chinese-Based Context: A Study of a Young, Educated Public in Hong Kong," *Journal of Public Relations Research* 16 (2004): 1–34; Ni Chen and Hugh M. Culbertson, "Guest Relations: A Demanding but Constrained Role for Lady Public Relations Practitioners in Mainland China," *Public Relations Review* 22, 3 (1996): 279–96; and Gabriel M. Vasquez and Maureen Taylor, "What Cultural Values Influence American Public Relations Practitioners?" *Public Relations Review* 25, 4 (1999): 433–49.

11. Stephen P. Banks, *Multicultural Public Relations: A Social-Interpretive Approach* (Thousand Oaks, CA: Sage, 1995).

12. Vasquez and Taylor, "Cultural Values."

13. Louis A. Day, *Ethics in Media Communications: Cases and Controversies* (Belmont, CA: Wadsworth, 1996), 2.

14. James A. Anderson and Elaine E. Englehardt, *The Organizational Self and Ethical Conduct* (Fort Worth: Harcourt Brace, 2001).

15. Loren Fox, *Enron: The Rise and Fall* (Hoboken, NJ: John Wiley & Sons, 2003).

16. Mimi Swartz and Sherron Watkins, *Power Failure: The Inside Story of the Collapse of Enron* (New York: Doubleday, 2003).

17. Francis Fukuyama, "Social Capital and Development: The Coming Agenda," *SAIS Review* 22, 1 (2002): 23–37; and Frances Fukuyama, *The Great Disruption: Human Nature and the Reconstruction of Social Order* (New York: Free Press, 1999).

18. Amitai Etzioni, *Next: The Road to the Good Society* (New York: Basic Books, 2001); and Conrad C. Fink, *Media Ethics: In the Newsroom and Beyond* (New York: McGraw-Hill, 1988).

19. Sheila Rae, "The Ins and Outs of Chinese Government Relations," *China Brief*, http://www.amcham-china.org.cn (accessed September 20, 2005).

20. Rae, "Ins and Outs."

21. Rae, "Ins and Outs."

22. Donald K. Wright, "Communication Ethics," in *An Integrated Approach to Communication Theory and Research,* ed. Michael B. Salwen and Don W. Stacks (Mahwah, NJ: Lawrence Erlbaum, 1996), 528.

23. Scott M. Cutlip, Allen H. Center, and Glen M. Broom, *Effective Public Relations,* 6th ed. (Englewood Cliffs, NJ: Prentice Hall, 1985).

24. James E. Grunig and Todd Hunt, *Managing Public Relations* (New York: Holt, Rinehart & Winston, 1984).

25. Dean Kruckeberg, "The Need for an International Code of Ethics," *Public Relations Review* 15, 2 (1989): 6.

Index

Abercrombie and Fitch, 53
Access
    disclosure and, 12–13, 61
    marketplace of ideas and, 9–10
    online communications issues, 120–121
    relationship management strategy, 61–62
Accountability, xi
    autonomy and environmental factors,
        23–25, 37–38
    blame, 31–32
    defining, 21
    illegitimate excuses, 31–34
    in-house public relations, 30
    legitimate excuses, 35–37
    military law, 32–33
    moral buck passing, xi, 29, 31
    organizational structure and decision
        making, 29–31
    personal, 37–38
    transparency implications, 95–96
    See also Responsibility
Accountable actors, 22–23
Activist publics, defining, 56–57
Activist publics, organizational relationships
        with, xi, 53–69
    activist tools, 57–58
    autonomy and, 57–58
    distributive strategies, 65
    effective relationship management, 59–64
    environmental scanning, 58
    hidden agendas, 56
    identifying publics, 59
    integrative strategies, 66
    networking, 64
    new media forms, 55, 57, 85–86
    symmetrical conflict resolution, 64–68
    two-way symmetrical model, 54–55
    See also Nonprofit organizations

Addiction excuse, 37
Advertising
    online ethical issues, 124
    veracity, 94
    See also Deceptive or misleading
        communication; Online
        communication ethics issues
Advocacy
    ideology of, 25
    objectivity and subjectivity, 27–28
    public relations role, ix–x
    third-party interests and, 26–27
Adware, 123
African American women in public
        relations, 42, 48
African Institute of Corporate Citizenship, 63
Agency model, 25–26, 27–28
AIDS activism, 61
Alexander, Laurence, 16
Al-Hurra, 160
Al-Jazeera, 160, 162, 169
Al-Khudairi, Sheikh Ibrahim, 160
American Indians, 67–68
American Institute for Managing Diversity, 48
American Marketing Association, 112
American Society of Magazine Editors
        (ASME), 124
Amin, Hussein, 160
Amnesty International, 64
Anderson, James A., 177
Andsager, Julie, 41
Angel, Phil, 63
Animal Liberation Front, 55
Anti-Cybersquatting Consumer Protection
        Act, 114
Applebaum, Arthur, 33
Aristotle, 20, 31, 120, 136, 138,
        144, 150, 178

Armstrong, Eric, 95
Arthur Andersen, 34, 89, 179
Arthur W. Page Society, 109, 110, 182
Association for Computing Machinery, 116
Autonomy
    activist publics and, 57–58
    environment and accountability,
        23–25, 37–38
    fiduciary model of, 28
    professional status and, 26, 27
    responsibility and, 22–23, 38
Aware publics, 59

Balkin, J. M., 97
Banks, Stephen P., 175
Barney, Ralph, 12
Baron, Gerald, 104
Barrett, Will, 20, 27
Barry, Vincent E., 20
Bayles, Michael, 26
Bechler, Curt, 102
Beers, Charlotte, 159
Bentham, Jeremy, 118, 136
Bernstein, Jon, 100
Bhopal, India, 140
Bigge, Morris L., 40
Bivins, Thomas, xi, 19–38, 137
Black, Jay, 12, 158–159
Blame
    crisis public relations, 99
    moral buck passing, 29
    moral excuses, 31–34
Blind obedience, 32–33
Blogs, 55, 73–74, 85–86
Bowen, Shannon, 51, 54
Bowie, Norman, 22
Bradshaw, Julie, 141
Brennan, William, 4–5
Bronstein, Carolyn, xii–xiii, 71–87, 177
Broom, Glen, 174, 184
Brown University, 90–91
Bunt, Gary R., 166
Bureau of Labor Statistics, 42
Burke, Kathy, 45
Burns, William, 148

Cameron, Glen, ix
Cane, Peter, 2
Career opportunities, 75
Categorical imperative, 26, 51, 118, 178
Causal theory, 35

Center, Allen, 184
Central Intelligence Agency (CIA), 169
Chen, Ni, 174
Chevron, 45
Children's Online Protection Act, 114
China, 171–172, 180–181
Choice, 128
Christman, John, 22
Coalition Against Unsolicited Commercial
        Email, 112
Codes of ethics, 183–184
    deontology, 28, 51, 69, 118
    diversity and, 46–47
    international public relations and,
        184–190
    International Public Relations Association,
        46, 185–186, 187–190
    online communications and, 109
    Public Relations Society of America, ix,
        1–2, 10, 13, 28, 109, 122, 183
Cold War foreign policy, 162, 169
Collaborative advocacy, 40
Collectivism, 176
Commercial speech, 7–8
    truth in, 11–12
Communication flow, organizational,
        29–30
Communitarianism, 118
Community
    decision making, risk communication
        and, 143–144, 146
    ethics and, 118
    relativism, 148–150
    right-to-know legislation, 140–141
    virtual, 119, 167
Computer ethics. See Online communication
        ethics issues
Computer Ethics Institute, 116
Computer Fraud and Abuse Act, 113
Computer Software Copyright Act, 113
Confidentiality
    online communications and, 127–128
    transparency and, 97–98
Conflict resolution, symmetrical, 64–68
Connolly-Ahern, Colleen, 47
Consequentialist ethics, 23, 50–51,
        55–56, 69, 117, 118
Control sharing, strategic risk
        communications and, 143–144
Cook, Fred, 97
Cookies, 123, 126

Corporate political speech, 5
Corporate scandals, xiii, 89, 178–180
    consequences of, 89–91
    crisis public relations, 98–102
    defining, 93
    transparency perceptions, 96–97, 105
Corporate transparency. *See* Transparency
Cost-benefit analysis, 28
Covello, Vincent T., 134, 143
Covert propaganda, 16–17, 77–79, 84
Covert video surveillance, 81
Crisis public relations, 13, 98–102
    emergency response systems, 142
    legal considerations, 99–101
    rebuilding trust, 102–103
    strategic risk communication and, 140
    See also Corporate scandals; Risk
        communication
Culbertson, Hugh M., 174
Culnan, Mary, 119
Cultural considerations, international
        public relations and, 174–177, 184
Customization, 126
Cutlip, Scott, 3, 184
Cybersquatting, 114

Dajani, Nabil, 160
Danaher, Kevin, 63
Davis, Aeron, 83, 85
Day, Louis A., 174
Dean, Howard, 74
Deceptive or misleading communication,
        7–8, 11–12
    front groups, 13–15
    online communications and, 122–124
Defamation, 6
DeGeorge, Richard T., 117
Denying facts, 34
Deontological ethics, 28, 51, 69, 118
Digital divide, 120
Digital Millenium Copyright Act, 114
Diplomacy, public. *See* Public diplomacy
Direct Marketing Association (DMA), 112
Disclosure, 6, 12–13
    front groups versus, 14–15
    manipulation of, 97
    media conflicts of interests, 11
    product flaws, 95
    relationship management strategy, 61
Distributive communication strategies, 65
Distributive justice, 118

Diversity issues in public relations, xi, 39–52
    conceptual issues, 42–43
    cultural factors and international public
        relations, 174–177
    devaluation due to feminine beauty,
        42, 47–48
    feminist and organizational values, 43–45
    global business considerations, 47
    legal standard, 46
    lookism, 42
    oppressing women's identities, 48
    oppression and changing demographics,
        40–43
    organizational effectiveness and, 45–50, 52
    philosophical approaches, 50–51
    positive relativism, 39–40, 52
    tolerating versus valuing difference, 48
    White female practitioners, 40, 41
    White male hegemony, 49, 60–61
    See also Activist publics, organizational
        relationships with
Djerejian, Edward, 168
Doorely, John, 61, 65
Dougall, Elizabeth, 54
Douglas, Mary, 132
Dozier, David, 174
Draft rumor, 107–108
Duffey, Joseph, 157
Duke, David, 168
Dunne, John, 35
Duty-based morality, 117, 118, 178. *See also*
    Deontological ethics

Earth Share, 85–86
Ebbers, Bernie, 179
Eddie Bauer, 62
Edelman Barometer of Trust, 90
Educators, oppression of, 40
Egoism, 118
El Obeidi, In'am, 163
Electronic Communications Privacy
    Act, 114
Electronic Frontier Foundation, 112
Electronic Privacy Information Center, 112
Electronic Signatures in Global and National
    Commerce Act, 114
Elliot, Deni, 35
Ellul, Jacques, 117
E-mail. *See* Online communication
    ethics issues
Email Service Provider Coalition, 112

Emergency Planning and Community
    Right-To-Know Act, 140
Emergency response systems, 142
Emmer, Dorothy, 26
Empowering women in public relations.
    See Diversity issues in public relations
Englehardt, Elaine, 177
Enlightened self-interest principle, 118
Enron, 13, 34, 89, 93, 94, 96, 99,
    102, 178, 179
Environmental Protection Agency
    (EPA), 133
Environmental risk communication.
    See Risk communication
Environmental scanning, 58
EPhilanthropy Foundation, 112
Ethical relativism, 33–34
Ethical standards, convergence with legal
    standards, 15–16
Ethics, defining, 120, 136
Ethics, law and, 2–3
Ethics and moral philosophies, 173, 178
    consequentialist perspective, 23, 50–51,
        55–56, 69, 117, 118
    deontology, 28, 51, 69, 118
    metanorms, 117
    rights-based morality, 118–119
    teleology, 28, 50–51, 55–56, 69, 118
    utilitarianism, 36, 50, 118, 136–137
Etzioni, Amitai, 180
Excellence Project, 48
Excuses
    buck passing, 31–34
    legitimate, 35–37
Executioner, 33
Exxon Valdez, 98, 140

Facts, 94
    denying, 34
    ignorance of, 36
Fair Credit Reporting Act, 113
False political speech, 6
False-front organizations, 13–15, 122
Falwell, Jerry, 168
Family Educational Rights and
    Privacy Act, 113
Federal Trade Commission (FTC), 7
Federal Trade Commission (FTC), ethical
    communications guidelines, 115
Federal Trademark Dilution Act, 114
Femininity, 176

Feminist and organizational values, 43–45
    ethic of care, 49, 52
    See also Diversity issues in public relations
Fiduciary model, 25–26, 28
Fink, Steven, 100
First Amendment issues, 1
    commercial advocacy regulation, 7–8
    political advocacy regulation, 4–7
    See also Marketplace of ideas
Fischhoff, Baruch, 139, 147, 149
Fisher, Walter, 151
Fitzpatrick, Kathy, xi, 1–17, 104, 137
Fletcher, Joseph, 118
Flynn, James, 148
Food and Drug Administration (FDA), 115
Foreign policy. *See* Public diplomacy
Fox, Loren, 179
Free speech issues. *See* First Amendment
    issues; Marketplace of ideas
Friedrich, Bruce, 62
Front groups, 13–15, 122
Fukuyama, Francis, 180
Fulton, Barry, 170

Gauthier, Candace, 104, 137
Gender issues
    devaluation due to beauty, 47–48
    feminist and organizational
        values, 43–45
    oppressed public relations
        practitioners, 39–52
    See also Diversity issues in public relations
General Accountability Office (GAO), 78
Genetically engineered foods, 63
Gibson, Kevin, 23, 32, 35
Global Alliance for Public Relations,
    45, 47, 183
Global Crossing, 89, 178
Global Exchange, 63
Global public relations. *See* International
    public relations issues
Golden mean, 120, 136
Golin, Al, 92–93
Goodpaster, Kenneth F., 173
Government regulation, online
    communications and, 113–116
Governmental public relations, 155
    "covert propaganda," 16–17, 77–79, 84
    See also Public diplomacy
Gower, Karla, xiii, 89–105
Greenpeace, 55, 62

Grunig, James, 40, 50, 51, 54, 55, 59, 68–69, 137, 174, 184
Grunig, Larissa, xi, 39–52, 54
Guanxi, 180–181

Habermas, Jürgen, 39
Hadden, Susan, 142
Hallahan, Kirk, xiii, 107–130
Haney, Mitchell, 22
Hanford nuclear site, 151
Harvard University, 90
Health Insurance Portability and Accountability Act, 114
HealthSouth, 89, 101
Heath, Robert, xiii, 3, 94, 131–153
Helmke, Mark, 165
Hill, Julia Butterfly, 56–57
Hill and Knowlton, 33–34
Hofstede, Geert, 175
Holmes, Oliver Wendell, 1–2
Hon, Linda, xi, 40, 53–69
Huang, Yi-Hui, 60
Humane Society, 81
Hunt, Geoff, 21
Hunt, Todd, 137, 184
Hust, Stacey, 41

Independent Pilots Association (IPA), 84
Independent public relations counselors, 24
Individual ethics, public relations practitioners, 173–174
Individualistic approach to moral responsibility, 29
Individualistic cultures, 175, 176
Industrialization, 131
Information sharing, 132, 142
Informed decision making, 4, 189
    access and, 9–10
    deceptive speech and, 11–12
    disclosure and, 12–13
    See also Marketplace of ideas
In-house public relations, accountability and responsibility considerations, 30
Institute for Crisis Management, 99
Institute of Electrical and Electronics Engineers, 116
Integrative conflict resolution strategies, 66
Intel, 95
Interactive Advertising Bureau, 112
International Association of Business Communicators (IABC), 41, 46, 109, 172

International Association of Online Communicators, 111
International Campaign to Ban Land Mines, 164
International Chamber of Commerce, 112
International Council for Internet Communication, 112
International Federation of Journalists, 183
International Press Institute, 183
International Public Relations Association (IPRA), 109, 172, 183, 184
    codes of ethics, 46, 185–190
International public relations issues, xiv, 171–190
    codes of ethics, 184–190
    cultural factors, 174–177, 184
    diversity considerations, 47
    research needs, 181–183
    societal differences, 177–178, 184
    trust, 180–181, 182
    See also Diversity issues in public relations; Public diplomacy
Internet, 107–108
    activist media, 55, 57, 85–86
    corporate transparency and, 92
    Islamic world and, 166–167
    joint statement of principles on public relations and, 109–111
    nonprofit organizations and, 72–74
    organizational Web sites, 64
Internet, ethics issues. See Online communication ethics issues
Intifada, 163
Islamic radicalism, 156–157, 158, 165
Islamic world, U.S. public diplomacy versus, 159–162, 166–168

Jackson, Jesse, 61
Jarvis, Jeff, 55
Job opportunities, 75
Johnson & Johnson, 100
Journalism. See News media
Juanillo, Napoleon K., 139
Judeo-Christian ethic, 178
Just, Marion, 76

Kant, Immanuel, 26, 51, 81, 118, 178
Kasky, Marc, 94
Kelley, Stanley, 155
Ketchum, Inc., 16, 77–79
KFC, 81

Kiam, Victor, 34
Klatt, Bruce, 30
Kleinfeld, Klaus, 90, 104
Kleptomania, 37
Kozlowski, Dennis, 91
Kruckeberg, Dean, 184

Labor movement, 83–84
Latent publics, 59
Law
    causal theory, 35
    converging legal and ethical
        standards, 15–16
    ethics and, 2–3
    military, 32–33
Lay, Ken, 179
League Against Cruel Sports, 76
Lee, Byoungkwon, 174
Lee, Jaesub, 141
Legal counsel collaboration, 100–103
Leiss, William, 134–136
Lessig, Lawrence, 117
Litigation public relations, 100–101
LL Bean, 62
Local emergency planning committees
    (LEPCs), 141
Lookism, 42
Loyalty, 24, 38

Magazine Publishers Association, 124
Marketplace of ideas, xi, 1, 3–16
    access and representation, 9–10
    converging legal and ethical standards,
        15–16
    disclosure, 12–13
    distributive communication strategies, 65
    front groups versus, 13–15
    informed decision making and, 4
    political advocacy regulation, 4–7
    process, 10–11
    propaganda and, 158–159
    sellers and buyers, 5
    truth, 11–12
Masculinity, 176
Mason, Florence, 119
Mason, Richard, 119
Mass media. See News media
Matthews, John B., Jr., 173
McDonald's, 53
Media, news. See News media
Medicare reform program, 17, 77–79

Merck, 61, 65
Mertz, C. K., 148
Metanorms, 117
Middle East Television Network, 160
Military draft rumor, 107–108
Military law, 32–33
Mill, John Stuart, 34, 118, 136
Minority public relations practitioners,
    oppressed status of, 41. See also
    Diversity issues in public relations
Molleda, Juan-Carlos, 47
Monsanto Corporation, 62–63
Moral agents, 22–23
Moral buck passing, xi, 29, 31
    excuses, 31–34
Moral philosophies. See Ethics and moral
    philosophies
Moral responsibility, 20–21
    agency model, 27–28
    individualistic approach, 29
    See also Responsibility
Moran, Gabriel, 30
Moshoeshoe, Macbeth, 63
MoveOn.org, 108
Multiculturalism. See Diversity issues in
    public relations
Murphy, Shaun, 30
Muzi Falconi, Toni, 45, 52

Narrative view of public relations, 150–152
National Association for the Advancement
    of Colored People (NAACP), 57
National Investor Relations Institute, 109
National Research Council, 134
Native Americans, 67–68
Nelson, Richard, 94
Network for Online Commerce, 112
Networking, 64
New social contract, 119
News media, 10–11
    disclosing conflicts of interest, 11
    indigenous Arab media, 162–163, 169
    objectivity, 163–164
    public diplomacy and, 157, 160–162
    U.S.-sponsored Arab media, 160–162
    video news releases, 71, 75–76
    vulnerabilities and PR opportunities, 74–76
Nez Perce, 67
Nike, Inc., 8, 94, 180–181
9/11 Commission, 158
No Child Left Behind policy, 16, 79, 84

Nongovernmental organizations (NGOs), 57, 164
  relationship management strategies, 63–64
  See also Nonprofit organizations
Nonprofit organizations, xii–xiii, 71–87
  dialogic communication, 86
  electronic media, 72–74
  ethical role models, 77
  nonethical methods, 80–82
  relationship management strategy, 82–84
  resource constraints, 71–72
  resource sharing, 84–86
  video news releases, 71, 75–76, 79
  See also Activist publics, organizational relationships with
"Not my problem" excuse, 35
Notice, 128
Nuclear waste, 148, 151
Nye, Joseph, 164–165

Obedience, blind, 32–33
Objectivity, 27, 163–164
Oceana, 74
O'Neil, Julie, 44
Online communication ethics issues, xiii, 55, 107–130
  access and choice, 120–121
  accreditation programs, 112–113
  amoral technology myth, 117
  codes of ethics, 109
  content accuracy and credibility, 121–122
  content source identity, 122–123
  deceptive practices, 122–124
  dependability, 124–125
  educational programs and organizations, 112
  interactivity and involvement, 125–126
  joint statement of principles, 109–111, 182–183
  new social contract, 119
  notice, choice, and redress, 128
  organizational Web sites, 64
  paid product placements, 124
  personalization and customization, 126–127
  privacy and security, 127–128
  private-sector initiatives, 111–113
  public-sector efforts, 113–116
  resources, 130
  rumors and, 107–108
  search engines, 123–124

  standards and guidelines, 112
  Ten Commandments, 116
  tracking technology, 123
  usability, 128–129
  virtual community, 119, 167
  See also Internet
Oppression in public relations. *See* Diversity issues in public relations
Organic Consumers Association (OCA), 63
Organizational communication, ethical framework for, 45–46
Organizational communication flow, 29–30
Organizational effectiveness, diversity and, 45–50, 52
Organizational structure, moral decision making and, 29–31
Organizational transparency. *See* Transparency
Organizational trust. *See* Trust
Organizational values, gender and diversity issues, 43–45. *See also* Diversity issues in public relations
Organizational Web sites, 64
Organizations, activist publics and. *See* Activist publics, organizational relationships with
Organized labor, 83–84

Page Society, 109, 110, 182
Palenchar, Michael, xiii, 131–153
Palestinians, 162–163
Parmenides, 136
Patriot Act, 114
Pearson, Ron, 54, 137, 138
People for the Ethical Treatment of Animals (PETA), 62, 77, 80–82
Pepsi, 100
Personal accountability, 37–38
Personalization, 126
Physical attractiveness, oppression due to, 47–48
Pilgrim's Pride, 81
Pires, Mary Ann, 56
Pitcher, George, 73
Plato, 138, 178
Plowman, Ken D., 60, 67
Political advocacy, regulation of, 4–7
Pompper, Donnalyn, 42, 48
Positive relativism, 39–40, 52
Positivity strategy, 60–61
Postman, Neil, 117

Poultry plant abuses, 81
Power distance, 175–176
Privacy issues, online communications and,
    127–128
Professional-client relations
    agency model of, 25–26
    fiduciary model of, 25–26
Project for Excellence in Journalism, 76
Propaganda, 16–17, 77–79, 158–159, 169
Public diplomacy, xiv, 155–170
    Cold War, 162, 169
    defined, 155
    effective communication, 165
    indigenous access to information
        versus, 166–168
    indigenous media versus, 162–163, 169
    Islamic world and, 159–162
    objectivity, 163–164
    propaganda, 158–159, 169
    public policy versus, 170
    religious/cultural sensitivity, 159
    soft power, 164–165
    traditional diplomacy, 157
    U.S. media and, 157
    U.S. shortcomings and reforms, 168–170
    U.S.-sponsored Arab media, 160–162
Public interest, competing versions of, 10
Public relations
    advocacy role of, ix–x
    job opportunities in, 75
    narrative view of, 150–152
    rhetorical heritage of, 137–138, 150
Public Relations Coalition, 182
Public Relations Society of America
    (PRSA)
    code of ethics, ix, 1–2, 10, 13, 28,
        65, 109, 122, 183
    diversity and, 46–47, 49
    marketplace of ideas and, 65
    Technology Section, 111
    White female majority, 41

Quenqua, Douglas, 58
Quinn, Candace, 47

Radio Sawa, 161–162
Rainbow Coalition, 61
Rakow, Lana, 43
Rawls, John, 118
Redress, 128

Relationship management, xi
    activist public relationship model, 59–64
    nonprofit organizations and, 82–84
    strategies, 60–64
    symmetrical conflict resolution, 64–68
    task sharing, 63
    See also Activist publics, organizational
        relationships with; Two-way
        symmetrical model
Resource sharing, 84–86
Responsibility, xi
    agency model, 25, 27–28
    autonomy and, 22–23, 38
    consequentialist versus merit
        perspectives, 23
    crisis management and accepting, 99
    defined, 20
    fiduciary model of, 28
    individual PR practitioners, 173–174
    in-house public relations, 30
    legal concept, 2
    moral obligations, 20–21
    See also Accountability
Responsible actors, 22–23
Responsible advocacy, 136–139
    international practitioners and, 172
    See also Ethics and moral philosophies;
        Two-way symmetrical model;
        specific issues and models
Responsible advocacy, principles for
    practice of, 104
Responsible Care Program, 140
Rhetorical heritage of public relations,
    137–138, 150
Rice, Condoleezza, 158
Rights-based ethics, 118–119
Riley, John Dillon, 45
Risk assessment, uncertainty in, 140, 145
Risk communication, xiii, 131–153
    community decision making, 146
    community narratives, 150–152
    community relativism, 148–150
    community right-to-know legislation,
        140–141
    definition of, 134
    dialogic advocacy, 133
    emergency response systems, 142
    environmental uncertainty, 140, 144–146
    historical evolution of, 134–136
    individual values and, 147–148

information sharing paradigm, 132, 142
institutional barriers, 142
motivators, 132
public partnership, 140–143
public's right-to-know, xiii, 138
responsible advocacy guidelines, 139–140
shared control, 143–144
terrorism and, 141
trust and collaboration, 147
utilitarianism, 136–137
See also Crisis public relations
Risk-benefit analysis, 147–148
Robertson, Pat, 168
Role models for responsible advocacy, 77
Roper, Juliet, 55
Rosenstiel, Tom, 76
Ross, Christopher, 168
Ross, William, 51
Rumors, 107–108
Ryan, Michael, 137

Sarbanes-Oxley Act, 13, 90, 91
Sawa, 161–162
Scandals. *See* Corporate scandals
Scherer, Clifford W., 139
Scrushy, Richard, 101
Search engines, 123–124
Securities and Exchange Commission (SEC)
    corporate financial scandals, 89, 90,
        93, 94, 96
    online communications and, 115
Seib, Philip, xiv, 155–170
Self-identity, 47
Seton Hall University, 91
Sha, Bey-Ling, 47
Sidgmore, John, 96
Simon, W. H., 25, 28
Situational ethics, 81
Situational theory, 59
Slovik, Paul, 148
Smith, Larry, 56
Social contract, new, 119
Social exchange theory, 93
Socrates, 178
Spam, organizations opposing, 112
Spinello, Richard, 117
Spyware, 123
Sriramesh, Krishnamurthy, 172
Starbucks, 63
Stern, Laurence, 31

Stewart, Martha, 89
Stewart, Potter, 120
Strategic risk communication. *See* Risk
    communication
Students, oppression of, 40
Subjectivity, 27–28
Superfund Amendments and Reauthorization
    Act, 140–141
Swartz, Mimi, 179
Symmetrical communication, online
    public relations, 125–126
Symmetrical conflict resolution strategies,
    64–68
Symmetrical model for public relations
    ethics. *See* Two-way symmetrical model

Target Corporation, 64
Taylor, Maureen, 174, 175
Team player, 24
Teamsters Union, 83–84
Teleological ethics, 28, 50–51, 55–56, 69,
    118. *See also* Consequentialist ethics
Telhami, Shibley, 169
Terrorism, 55, 141
Texaco, 60–61
Texas Gulf Sulphur Company, 93
Thomas, R. Roosevelt, Jr., 42–43
Thompson, Suzanne C., 143
Tortugas Marine Reserve, 66–67
Toth, Elizabeth, xi, 39–52
Transparency, 95
    accountability implications, 95–96
    confidentiality and, 97–98
    corporate scandals and, 96–97, 105
    crisis public relations, 98–102
    defining, 92
    disclosing product flaws, 95
    maintaining trust, 103–104
    manipulation of, 97
    post-crisis trust restoration, 102–103
    process, 96
    professional standard, 183
    regulatory requirements, 91
    relationship management strategy, 61
Transparency International, 183
Truman, Harry S., 19, 38
Trust, 92, 180–181, 182
    corporate scandals and, 89–91
    defining, 92–93
    maintaining, 103–104

post-crisis restoration, 102–103
risk communication and, 147
stakeholder expectations, 93
Truth
    advertising veracity, 94
    defining, 93
    IPRA code of ethics, 189
    marketplace of ideas and, 11–12
Two-way symmetrical model, 40,
    54–55, 60, 137
    conflict resolution strategies, 64–68
    online communications and, 125–126
Tyco, 89, 178
Tylenol tampering incident, 100

Umbro, 36
Uncertainty, 140, 144–146
Uncertainty avoidance, 176
Unions, 83–84
United Parcel Service (UPS), 83–84
University of Missouri, 91
U.S. Department of Agriculture (USDA), 79
U.S. Department of Health and Human
    Service, 128
U.S. Supreme Court, converging ethical and
    legal standards, 15–16
USA Patriot Act, 114
Utilitarianism, 36, 50, 118, 136–137

Values
    gender and organizational, 43–45
    individual, risk communication and,
        147–148
    white male model, 43
Van den Hoven, Jerden, 117
Vasquez, Gabriel M., 174, 175
Video news releases (VNRs), 71, 75–76,
    78–79

Video surveillance, 81
Virtual community, 119, 167
Voakes, Paul, 16

Wal-Mart, 53, 93
Wang, Patrick, 180–181
Warburton, John, 10
Watkins, Sherron, 179
Welch, Don, 2
Wendy's, 100
White, Jon, 137
White female majority in public
    relations, 40, 41
White House Press Office, 155
White male hegemony in public relations,
    41, 49. See also Diversity issues in
    public relations
White male model of organizational
    values, 43
Williams, Armstrong, 16, 79, 84
Win-win or no deal strategy, 67
WiredSafety.org, 112
Witte, Kim, 142
Women public relations practitioners,
    oppressed/disadvantaged status of,
    39–52. See also Diversity issues in
    public relations
Workforce Investment Act, 114
Work-life programs, 45
World Conservation Union, 56–57
World Public Relations Festival, 45
World Wildlife Fund (WWF), 66–67
WorldCom, 89, 96, 178, 179
Wright, Donald, xiv, 171–190

Yucca Mountain, 148

Zyklon, 36

About the Contributors

Kathy Fitzpatrick (Editor) is an Associate Professor of Communication at DePaul University in Chicago, where she directs the master's degree program in public relations and advertising. In 2005, Fitzpatrick was named the Wicklander Fellow in Applied and Professional Ethics. She teaches a range of undergraduate and graduate courses in public relations, public relations ethics, communication law, and crisis management. Her research focuses on issues involving public relations, ethics, and law. Fitzpatrick is the coauthor of *Public Relations Ethics* and *Journalism Ethics* (with Philip Seib) and the author of articles in *Public Relations Review, Journal of Public Relations Research, Journal of Mass Media Ethics, Journal of Advertising, Journalism and Mass Communication Educator, Journal of Communication Management,* and *Corporate Reputation Review.* She is a licensed attorney, an accredited member of the Public Relations Society of America (PRSA), and a past president of the PRSA Dallas Chapter. In 2002, Fitzpatrick was elected to head the PRSA Educators Academy. She served for six years on the PRSA Board of Ethics and was a member of the task force that developed the Member Code of Ethics 2000. She is a member of the Arthur W. Page Society and serves on the editorial review boards of *Journal of Public Relations Research, Public Relations Review,* and *Journal of Mass Media Ethics.*

Carolyn Bronstein (Editor) is an Assistant Professor of Communication at DePaul University in Chicago, where she teaches undergraduate and graduate courses that focus on the cultural impact of public relations and advertising in a global society. Her research examines the role of the mass media in the construction of social issues, with emphasis on mainstream news and advertising. She received the Nafziger-White research award from the Association for Education in Journalism and Mass Communication (AEJMC) for a study of the relationship among advertising trends in the 1970s, gender consciousness, and the development of the American feminist antipornography movement. Her work appears in a variety of mass media journals, including *Journalism and Mass Communication Quarterly*, *Journalism & Communication Monographs*, and *Journalism and Mass Communication Educator*.

Thomas H. Bivins is the John L. Hulteng Chair in Media Ethics in the School of Journalism and Communication at the University of Oregon, where he teaches courses in media ethics and in public relations. He has been a member of the faculty for twenty years. During that time, he has consulted for numerous clients in public relations and, for a while, was a freelance editorial cartoonist. Bivins spent six years as a broadcast specialist in the Armed Forces Radio and Television Service. He also worked in advertising, in corporate public relations, and as a graphic designer and editorial cartoonist. He taught public relations and television production at the University of Delaware. Bivins is the author of books on media ethics, public relations writing, publication design, advertising, and newsletter publication. He is currently working on a new book dealing with persuasion and ethics. He also has published a book of poetry and a children's book.

Karla K. Gower is an Attorney and an Associate Professor in the Advertising and Public Relations Department of the College of Communication and Information Sciences at the University of Alabama. Her research focuses on legal issues affecting public relations and the history of public relations. Her publications include *Liberty and Authority in Free Expression Law: The United States and Canada* and *Legal and Ethical Restraints on Public Relations*. She has also published articles in *Communication Law & Policy*, *Journalism and Mass Communication Quarterly*, *American Journalism*, and *Journalism History*. Gower served as editor of *American Journalism* from 2000 until 2004.

Larissa A. Grunig, Professor Emerita, recently retired from the faculty of the University of Maryland, College Park, where she had taught public relations and communication research since 1978. She has received the Pathfinder Award for excellence in research, sponsored by the Institute for Public Relations; the Jackson, Jackson, and Wagner Behavioral Science Prize; and the Outstanding Educator Award of the Public Relations Society of America. She was cofounder and coeditor of the *Journal of Public Relations Research* and has written more than two hundred articles, book chapters, monographs, reviews, and conference papers on public relations, activism, science writing, feminist theory, communication theory, and research. She was a member of an international grant team, sponsored by the IABC Research Foundation, investigating excellence in public relations and communication management. The newest Excellence book won the 2002 PRIDE award sponsored by the Public Relations Division of the National Communication Association. She coauthored the first book about women in public relations. Grunig serves as a consultant in public relations.

Kirk Hallahan is Associate Professor of Journalism and Technical Communication at Colorado State University, where he is also affiliated with the Center for Research on Communication and Technology. He attended UCLA and completed his master's and doctorate degrees at the University of Wisconsin-Madison. A prior practitioner for nineteen years in California, Hallahan has devoted a major portion of his recent research to the uses of technology in public relations. His related research has appeared in *Public Relations Review, Public Relations Quarterly, Handbook of Public Relations, Encyclopedia of Public Relations,* and *Internet Encyclopedia.* He was the recipient in 2001 of the Jackson, Jackson & Wagner Behavioral Science Prize awarded by the Public Relations Society of America Foundation. He is founder and editor of PR-education.org, a Web portal devoted to public relations education.

Robert L. Heath is a Professor of Communication at the University of Houston. He has published extensively on topics related to risk communication, organizational identity, environmentalism, crisis communication, issues management, and reputation management. Heath is the author of numerous books, including *Strategic Issues Management: How Organizations Meet Public Policy Challenges; Managing Corporate Communication: From Interpersonal Contacts to External Affairs; Issues Management* (coauthored with Richard A. Nelson); *Human Communication Theories and Research: Concepts, Contexts, and Challenges* (coauthored with Jennings Bryant); and *Realism and Relativism: A Perspective on Kenneth Burke.* He is the editor of the *Handbook of Public Relations,* senior editor of the *Encyclopedia of Public Relations,* and coeditor of several books, including *Responding to Crisis: A Rhetorical Approach to Crisis Communication,* and *Rhetorical and Critical Approaches to Public Relations.* Heath has won numerous awards for his scholarly and professional accomplishments, including the Pathfinder Award of the Institute for Public Relations (1992), PRSA Foundation, Jackson, Jackson, and Wagner (1998), as well as two Pride Awards for books (1997, 1992) and one Pride Award for journal articles (2000) from the Public Relations Division of the National Communication Association.

Linda Hon is a Professor in the Department of Public Relations and the Al and Effie Flanagan Professor of Journalism and Communications at the University of Florida. Her research focuses on public relations evaluation, relationship management, and gender and diversity issues in public relations. She is the author (with Larissa Grunig and Elizabeth Toth) of *Women in Public Relations: How Gender Influences Practice.* Hon received the 2001 Pathfinder Award of the Institute for Public Relations. She served as editor of *Journal of Public Relations Research* from 2000–2005.

Michael J. Palenchar is an Assistant Professor of Public Relations at the University of Tennessee. His research interests include risk communication related to energy development and manufacturing, community relations and community awareness of emergency response and manufacturing risks, issues management, and crisis management. He has more than a decade of professional experience working in nonprofit and firm public relations and has served as a risk communication and issues management research consultant for industry associations, corporations, and governmental agencies. Palenchar has published in the *Journal of Public Relations Research* and *Communication Research Reports,* authored several book chapters, and has presented "top papers" at national and international conferences. He is currently a member of the editorial board of *Communication Studies.* Palenchar was the recipient, along with coauthor Robert L. Heath, of the National Communication Association's 2000 Pride Award for top published article in public relations.

Philip Seib is the Lucius W. Nieman Professor of Journalism at Marquette University, where he teaches courses in the ethical problems of mass communication, and news media and foreign policy. His research interests include ethics, effects of news coverage on foreign policy, and political journalism. His books include *Beyond the Front Lines: How the News Media Cover a World Shaped by War, The Global Journalist: News and Conscience in a World of Conflict, Public Relations Ethics* and *Journalism Ethics* (with Kathy Fitzpatrick), and *Campaigns and Conscience.*

Elizabeth L. Toth is Professor of Communication at the University of Maryland. She formerly served as associate dean for academic affairs and professor of public relations at the S. I. Newhouse School of Public Communications at Syracuse University. Toth is the coauthor (with Linda Childers Hon and Larissa Grunig) of *Women and Public Relations: How Gender Influences Practice,* as well as numerous other books and articles on the subject of public relations practice. Her coedited book *Rhetorical and Critical Approaches to Public Relations* won a National Communication Association award. Toth is coeditor of *Journalism Studies,* and served for six years as editor of the *Journal of Public Relations.* She received the Pathfinder Award from the Institute for Public Relations for her research on gender issues and the Outstanding Educator Award from the Public Relations Society of America.

Donald K. Wright is a Professor of Communication at the University of South Alabama. His research focuses on public opinion, employee communications, communication ethics, and corporate public relations, and he has worked as a consultant to numerous Fortune 500 corporations. He has received both the Pathfinder Award of the Institute for Public Relations and the Public Relations Society of America's Outstanding Educator Award. Wright is past president of the International Public Relations Association and a member of the Board of Trustees of both the Arthur W. Page Society and the Institute for Public Relations. *PR Week* named Wright as one of the top ten public relations educators in the United States in the year 2000.